D1447647

GHOSTLY
DESIRES

GHOSTLY
DESIRES

QUEER SEXUALITY AND VERNACULAR BUDDHISM

IN CONTEMPORARY THAI CINEMA

ARNIKA FUHRMANN

Duke University Press   Durham and London   2016

© 2016 Duke University Press
All rights reserved

Typeset in Arno Pro and Avenir by Westchester Publishing Services

Library of Congress Cataloging-in-Publication Data
Names: Fuhrmann, Arnika, [date] author.
Title: Ghostly desires : queer sexuality and vernacular Buddhism
in contemporary Thai cinema / Arnika Fuhrmann.
Description: Durham : Duke University Press, 2016. |
Includes bibliographical references and index.
Identifiers: LCCN 2015047559 (print) | LCCN 2015049477 (ebook)
ISBN 9780822361190 (hardcover : alk. paper)
ISBN 9780822361558 (pbk. : alk. paper)
ISBN 9780822374251 (e-book)
Subjects: LCSH: Motion pictures—Thailand. | Buddhism in motion pictures. |
Ghosts in motion pictures. | Sexual minorities in motion pictures.
Classification: LCC PN1993.5.T5 F847 2016 (print) | LCC PN1993.5.T5 (ebook) |
DDC 791.4309593—dc23
LC record available at http://lccn.loc.gov/2015047559

COVER ART: Still from *Morakot* (Emerald), Apichatpong Weerasethakul, 2007.
Courtesy of the artist.

Duke University Press gratefully acknowledges the support of the Hull Memorial Fund
of Cornell University, which provided funds toward the publication of this book.

UNIVERSITY
OF SHEFFIELD
LIBRARY

ACKNOWLEDGMENTS

In the long course of writing this book I have accumulated incalculable debt to artists and scholars, teachers and activists, family and friends, and cultural and intellectual communities in Asia, Europe, and North America. In striving to acknowledge these contributions I begin with those who have helped most in shaping the book's contents.

The art of Araya Rasdjarmrearnsook and the activist vision of Anjana Suvarnananda formed the initial inspiration for this project. Araya and Anjana were then and remain today at the forefront of transformations in aesthetic form and sexual citizenship in Thailand. I thank them for generously sharing their work and insights with me over many years. The work of Pimpaka Towira and Apichatpong Weerasethakul soon came to exert a mesmerizing influence on me as well. Both Pimpaka and Apichatpong showed me exceptional kindness in making their work available to me.

When the time came to put these observations into writing, Yang Hull stood out in the amount of time he invested, and his formative influence remains evident in the text. Hoang Tan Nguyen provided rigorous critiques of successive drafts; only with his generous input was I able to turn my manuscript into a book. My greatest intellectual debt reaches back to my graduate education in Chicago, where Lauren Berlant was most instrumental in helping to shape the contours of this project.

Some of my greatest gratitude is reserved for Tani Barlow. Not only do her profound interventions into Asia critique inspire my work, but I have also been fortunate to receive her feedback as well as her unwavering support for all my scholarly endeavors.

Since I first met her in person in 2008, Bliss Cua Lim has been one of my most profoundly supportive interlocutors. She is one of Duke University Press's readers who has allowed me to thank her by name. I would like to express my gratitude to Bliss for the inordinate amount of intellectual energy that she invested in this project. I would also like to extend heartfelt thanks to the other, anonymous reader, whose succinct reviews likewise helped to improve the book tremendously.

Many others provided valuable feedback on parts of this book at various stages: In Chicago, my project benefited immensely from the intellectual input and resolute support of my committee members Danilyn Rutherford and Wendy Doniger. Jonathan M. Hall, Andy Rotman, Sivan Schneider, Malte Fuhrmann, Julia Eksner, Olivia Pils, Daniel Monterescu, and Wasana Wongsurawat all brought further precious expertise to its improvement. Special thanks to Sudarat Musikawong and Lawrence Chua for their incisive reading of large parts of the manuscript.

In Ken Wissoker I was extremely fortunate to have the best possible editor. Whether we met in North America, Hong Kong, or Bangkok, Ken unstintingly provided astute guidance, gracious encouragement, and wonderful company. I thank Ken for his belief in this project and careful nurture of its development. At Duke University Press I am also very grateful to Elizabeth Ault, Amy Buchanan, and Liz Smith, who lent their valuable expertise to different stages of the publishing process. I am grateful to Daniel McNaughton for lending his sharp eye to the indexing and proofing process.

Many cultural and intellectual communities in Thailand made this book possible. The acumen of Kong Rithdee's film and cultural critique and the crucial insights of Chalida Uabumrungjit, Sanchai Chotirosseranee, and Wimonrat Aroonrojsuriya at the Thai Film Archive were instrumental in propelling this project forward. I thank the filmmakers and artists Thunska Pansitthivorakul, Nonzee Nimibutr, Chaisiri Jiwarangsan, Panu Aree, Anocha Suwichakornpong, and Michael Shaowanasai for significant contributions and engaging conversations.

With regard to my analysis of Thai sexual politics, I found wonderful and resourceful interlocutors in Nantiya Sukontapatipark, Phra Chai Warathammo, Sulaiporn Chonwilai, Matthana Chetamee, Chantalak Raksayu, Suchada Taweesit, Kritaya Archavanitkul, Timo Ojanen, and Paisarn Likhitpreechakul.

I thank a diverse contingent of interlocutors, teachers, and friends that includes Chutima Prakatwutisarn, Trisilpa Boonkhachorn, Thanapol Limapichart, Thosaeng Chaochuti, Nalinee Tanthuwanit, Villa Vilaithong, Gridthiya Gaweewong, Ida Aroonwong, Chusak Pattarakulvanit, Oradol Kaewprasert, Thassanan Trinok, Ranwarat Poonsri, and Phatthanaphol Engsusophon. In the Wongsurawat family I thank Janice, Kovit, Winai, and Pare for warm hospitality, and John, Rosie, and Khun Amh (Nattapong Tiendee) for teaching me so much about media politics.

I am indebted to the patrons of the shrine of Mae Nak at Wat Mahabut and to the practitioners of *asupha-kammathan* in Bang Yi Khan, Bangkok, who generously shared their thoughts and motivations with me, as well as to numerous government officials who made valuable materials and background information available.

At Cornell University I am above all grateful for the faith that my colleagues in the Department of Asian Studies have placed in this project. Chair Keith Taylor enabled my work in every way, Anne Blackburn provided invaluable guidance, and Brett de Bary opened up new opportunities and challenges at every turn. I have also been extremely fortunate to enjoy the collegiality and friendship of Nick Admussen.

Many others across the campus welcomed me into their midst with warmth: Amy Villarejo, Andrea Hammer, Saida Hodžić, Lucinda Ramberg, Eric Cheyfitz, Naminata Diabate, Andrea Bachner, Itziar Rodriguez, Sabine Haenni, Emily Fridlund, Mostafa Minawi, Tim Murray, Kent Kleinman, Lily Chi, Jeremy Foster, Lorenzo Perillo, and Christine Balance. In the Southeast Asia Program I have enjoyed the collegiality of Thamora Fishel, Kaja McGowan, Abby Cohn, Tamara Loos, Eric Tagliacozzo, and Thak Chaloemtiarana.

I will never forget the moment in 2010 when Daniel Chua, then head of the School of Humanities at the University of Hong Kong, invited me to spend two years in the Society of Scholars in the Humanities and the Department of Comparative Literature. I am grateful to have had the opportunity to deepen my understanding of cinematic representation and urban culture across East and Southeast Asia through interactions with a wider Hong Kong academic community: Esther Cheung, Esther Yau, Yau Ching, Lucetta Kam, Rajeev Balasubramanyam, Divya Ghelani, Denise Tang, Vivian Chu, Alma Mikulinsky, Giorgio Biancorosso, and Derek Lam. I am particularly grateful for Gina Marchetti's hospitality and unwavering support.

Having to return to Berlin in late 2008 was one of the best things that could have happened to me. Over the course of 2009–10 I was initiated into the vivid intellectual and cultural Berlin of Sun-ju Choi, Anja Michaelsen, Kimiko Suda, and Feng-Mei Heberer. This was the beginning of enduring friendship and long-term collaboration. Later encounters with Grada Kilomba, Amy Evans, Tobaron Waxman, Michaela Wünsch, and Alana Lentin at the Institute for Cultural Inquiry prompted renewed engagement with questions of performance, race, and embodiment in transnational frameworks. One of the greatest pleasures of living in Berlin came from Olivia Pils's art, thought, and company.

Scattered across the academic diaspora of Asian studies, gender studies, and other scholarly and artistic contexts, many people have made this project possible. Both their work and their friendship reminded me again and again of why it might be worth persevering. I thank Jonathan M. Hall, Gopika Solanki, Riki Rosenfeld, and Suphak Chawla for friendship across continents and decades; Justin McDaniel and Orit Bashkin for their unstinting support, especially during difficult times; and old and new friends Tyrell Haberkorn, Sukit Manthachitra, Martin Platt, Ayu Saraswati, Megan Sinnott, Adele Tan, Cathy Davidson, Dredge Kang, Ara Wilson, Peter Jackson, Jin Haritaworn, Ricco Siasoco, Farid Muttaqin, and Joya Escobar for inspiring conversations and encounters across the globe.

Since the mid-2000s, when I had the good fortune to come into contact with the Southeast Asian Cinemas crowd, I have benefited from the irreplaceable knowledge of Mariam Lam, Lan Duong, May Adadol Ingawanij, Sophia Harvey, Gaik Cheng Khoo, Adam Knee, Tamara Ho, Natalie Böhler, Tilman Baumgärtel, Aryo Danusiri, Brett Farmer, Rachel Harrison, and Fiona Lee.

In Germany I had the good fortune to share intellectual projects with Michael Zimmermann, Benjamin Baumann, Wolfram Schaffar, Christian Bauer, Volker Grabowsky, Barend Terwiel, Vincent Houben, Nadja Schneider, and Monika Arnez.

Looking back to the time of my graduate education, I am incredibly grateful for the enduring connections forged at the University of Chicago: Sean MacDonald, Guy Leavitt, Yang Hull, Smadar Winter, Andy Rotman, Daniel Monterescu, Maria Garrett, Moeen Lashari, Lale Uner, Orit Siman-Tov, Po-Chen Tsai, Siri Jenthanomma, John Emerzian, David Wise, Rebecca Zorach, Julia Cassaniti, Yigal Bronner, Galila Spharim, Sultan Doughan, Jean Ma, Erik Davis, and Manan Ahmed each contributed immeasurably to my well-being and the progress of this project. I could never have done it without Sivan Schneider.

It is a pleasure to be able to acknowledge the considerable institutional and financial support that I received for the revision of this book. At Cornell

University my completion of the manuscript was enabled by research support through the Department of Asian Studies in 2012–13, the College of Arts and Sciences, the President's Council of Cornell Women, and the Society for the Humanities in 2012–13 and 2014. As a faculty member of the Diversity Fellowship Seminar I received valuable feedback on this work from 2013 to 2014. The position of scholar in the Society of the Humanities at the University of Hong Kong from 2010 to 2012, a fellowship at the Institute for Cultural Inquiry in Berlin in 2009–10, and welfare payments through the Agentur für Arbeit Friedrichshain-Kreuzberg, Berlin, in 2009 had previously allowed me to develop the project further.

I am fortunate to have had the chance to present parts of this book at larger professional conferences as well as to more intimate audiences in Riverside, London, Hamburg, Bangkok, Chiang Mai, Istanbul, Berlin, Ann Arbor, Canberra, Houston, Göteborg, Hong Kong, Jerusalem, Berkeley, Yogyakarta, Zürich, Toronto, Singapore, Philadelphia, Chicago, Göttingen, Ithaca, Hamilton, New York City, and Bryn Mawr. I benefited immensely from the generous responses of my hosts and interlocutors at the Center for Southeast Asia Studies in Berkeley; the Beyond "Asian Extremes" workshop at New York University; the SculptureCenter, New York; the Visual Culture Colloquium and the Lesbian, Gay, Bisexual, and Transgender Studies Program at Cornell; the workshop Emotions and Ethical Life, organized by Chulalongkorn University in Bangkok; New Media Configurations at Humboldt University, Berlin; the Center for Visual Culture Colloquium at Bryn Mawr College; The Politics of Criticism in Thailand at Cornell; Ghost Movies in Southeast Asia and Beyond at the University of Göttingen; the Thai Studies conference at Humboldt University, Berlin; the Asian Horror Cinema and Beyond Symposium at Berkeley; Ghosts in Asian Cinemas at the University of Zurich; The Supernatural in Southeast Asian Studies at the University of California, Riverside; the Berlin Institute for Cultural Inquiry; the Society of Scholars in the Humanities Lecture Series at the University of Hong Kong; and the Chao Center for Asian Studies at Rice University. I thank especially Pheng Cheah, Angela Zito, Intan Paramaditha, Zhen Zhang, Ruba Katrib, Kaja McGowan, Anissa Rahadi, Asli Menevse, Lucinda Ramberg, Suwanna Satha-anand, Wasana Wongsurawat, Nadja-Christina Schneider, Marcus Michaelsen, Homay King, Hoang Tan Nguyen, Tamara Loos, Peter Braeunlein, Martin Schalbruch, Dan O'Neill, Andrea Riemenschnitter, Mariam Lam, Lan Duong, Justin McDaniel, Christoph Holzhey, Daniel Chua, and Tani Barlow for providing me with these unique opportunities.

Some sections of chapter 1 were previously published in *Discourse: Journal for Theoretical Studies in Media and Culture* 31, no. 3 (2009): 220–47. A previous version of chapter 4 was published in *positions: asia critique* 21, no. 4 (2013): 769–99.

Finally, it is one of the greatest pleasures to be able to thank the people closest to me. In my new surroundings in Ithaca, Shelley Feldman's friendship has been work- and life-sustaining and made Ithaca into a real home.

Wasana Wongsurawat's (re)entry into my life in 2011 brought with it many good surprises. Her generosity, brilliance, and company across three continents brought *fun* and happiness to the endeavor of completing this book.

My brother, Malte, continues to be a stellar example of how to think, write, and live. His support and hospitality through long years and many global locations has been a vital source of encouragement.

This book is written in memory of my unforgettable aunts Veronika Geyer-Iwand and Anemone Iwand.

It is dedicated to my parents, Malve Iwand and Gunther Fuhrmann. They made this book (and so much more) possible through their adventurous spirit, sagacious humor, and knowledge of what is important.

Apichatpong Weerasethakul's short film *Luminous People* (*Khon Rueang Saeng*, 2007) enacts a funereal ceremony.[1] In this fifteen-minute film a boat moves up the Mekong River, and relatives and friends perform a Buddhist ceremony in which they release a father's ashes into the waters. On the return journey a young man improvises a song about encountering his dead father in a dream. While members of the funeral party relax into sleep, quiet sorrow, and playful teasing, a voice-over relates the story of the encounter again and again:

> Last night I dreamed that my father paid me a visit.
> Last night I dreamed that my father came.
> I was very happy.
> I was overjoyed.
> Father.

Rather than vocalize a leave-taking from the father, the song describes a continued relation with him. According to Theravada Buddhist doctrine, the funereal ceremony performed in *Luminous People* would be intended to initiate the process of detachment from the dead. Rather than engender such a break, however, the ceremony seems to prompt continued attachment to the deceased. The scene thereby elaborates a psychological model in which relations with the love object lost through death may continue indefinitely. Such continued attachment to the dead represents a prominent, nondoctrinal feature of Thai Buddhism.

What also stands out in Apichatpong's film is that it uses the space of continued attachment to the deceased father to frame the genesis of a new relationship.[2] The song about reencountering the father provides the sonic script for the interaction of two young men.[3] The establishing shot of the film introduces the men facing each other, engaged in a conversation that we cannot hear and sharing music through a single set of headphones. At the end of its second half, *Luminous* returns to its focus on the two men. As the voice-over intones "Father" for the last time, the two men leave the others and climb onto the boat's roof for a further private conversation (figs. 1.1 and 1.2).

That the potential lovers' interaction is situated in a context of loss is typical of the films of Apichatpong and represents a prominent phenomenon in contemporary Thai mainstream and independent cinema. I call this eroticization in Thai film of the sphere of loss *Buddhist melancholia*.[4]

Taking different mobilizations of Buddhist melancholia as my point of departure, I investigate a particular, Buddhist-inflected formulation of the negativity of queer personhood and femininity in contemporary Thai film and video culture. By negativity I mean not only the ways that women and queer persons are marginalized socially; negativity also describes an ontology and psychology of personhood in which the notion of existence is marked by impermanence and desire is always already destined to fail. This Buddhist-informed negativity is vitally connected to sexuality, for it is desire and attachment that exemplify primary instances in which the truth of impermanence manifests. Desire (craving) and attachment (clinging) occupy central positions in a Theravadin Buddhist epistemology of suffering and in a soteriology rooted in nonattachment. In this theory it is between desire and attachment that the chain of affective engagement that leads to suffering must be interrupted.

Contemporary Thai cinema, however, avails itself of this context precisely to flesh out various scenarios of desire. Instead of teaching nonattachment, the space of loss comes to serve as a register of the erotic in contemporary cinematic representation. Were it a Buddhist teaching, the loss of the father in *Luminous People* should have highlighted the impossibility and the temporal disjuncture that marks the son's desire and, in a subsequent step,

Damn! Why'd you go and die?

FIGURES 1.1–1.2. Conversation between two young men, who then climb on the boat's roof for a further intimate conversation. Apichatpong Weerasethakul, *Luminous People* (*Khon Rueang Saeng*, 2007).

engendered the visceral realization of the fact of impermanence. The doctrinal notion of ontological and psychological negativity thus possesses a temporal dimension: *I want something. I can no longer have it.* In fact temporal incongruity represents a central element of a Theravadin Buddhist pedagogy that uses the occasion of loss to teach about the truth of impermanence and the futility of attachment. By contrast Buddhist melancholia designates all those instances in which persons defy doctrinal temporal logics and delay, stall, or refuse detachment: *I want something. I can no longer have it. Yet I persist in my desire.*

The effect of Buddhist melancholia's nondoctrinal engagement of negativity is that contemporary sexualities are also centrally structured by temporalities other than those of the nation and of capital or those of the secular everyday. Thus Apichatpong's *Luminous People* brings an otherworldly temporality to bear on an emergent queer relationship in the here and now.

Luminous People is one of many contemporary Thai films that bring Buddhist temporalities, aesthetics, and notions of embodiment to bear on sexuality, desire, and gendered personhood. I suggest that we understand this and other Thai films after 1997 as delineating a *Buddhist sexual contemporaneity*, a conception in which sexuality is not solely a matter of citizenship and rights, freedom and prohibition, or nationally defined social convention, but is vitally informed also by Buddhist-inflected forms of representation, practice, and affect. At the core of this contemporaneity lies the way in which both secular and Buddhist notions of social, psychological, and ontological negativity come to bear on minoritized sexual personhood. By minoritized, or minoritarian, I mean the gendered positions and sexualities of women, *kathoeys*, and gay men that have in the past two decades come under the purview of state disciplinary campaigns in Thailand and that are at the same time still accorded karmic, ontological deficiency.[5] In the latter, Buddhist-informed interpretation, homosexuality and the state of being kathoey result from misconduct in a previous life.[6] As karmic outcomes of a past life, they are involuntary, and a strain of modern Thai Buddhist thought stresses that these states of being are to be accorded compassion rather than censure.[7] On the other hand, however, the enduring validity of vernacular notions of karmic causality is also responsible for the stigmatization of homosexuality and trans personhood as diminished. The persistence of this notion in public discourse continues to mark queer and trans persons as characterized by existential damage.

While Thai sexualities have been studied as effects of geopolitics, traced back to pre-heteronormative models, and scrutinized for their potentially transformative alterity, the fundamental ways in which Theravadin and other Buddhist concepts, stories, and imagery inform contemporary understandings of sexuality have not been investigated.[8] If, however, as Tamara Loos argues, Thai modernity was never conceptualized solely as a secular modernity but always remained also a Buddhist modernity, what does this imply for Thai sexualities and notions of personhood in the present?[9]

While much energy has been invested in asserting the global or local provenance of contemporary Thai sexualities, I concentrate on how both the globally circulating Thai cinema of the 1990s and 2000s as well as recent Thai state and activist sexual politics conceptualized sexual personhood as much in nonorthodox and nondoctrinal Buddhist frames of thought as in the domains of law, policy, and nation. What happens when desire and sexual personhood are rendered neither exclusively in terms of liberalism nor entirely in local idioms purported to be antithetical to liberalism?

In *Ghostly Desires* I investigate how the pervasive engagement with Buddhist-inflected conceptions allows contemporary cinema not only to parse problematics of desire but also to probe the possibilities of agency of women and queer persons as well as to arbitrate the grievances of minoritized persons. This is a deeply historical undertaking, for I examine a turning point in political ideology and cultural production in contemporary Thailand. My analysis focuses on the concurrence of cinema and sexuality during a period marked by the "transvaluation of erotic and aesthetic values" in Thailand after the 1997 Asian financial crisis.[10] What stands out during these nearly two decades is that transnational and local, legal and vernacular Buddhist rhetorics of negativity collude to forge problematic new forms of sexual regulation in the official public sphere as well as novel frames of thinking about minoritarian injury in cinematic representation.

At the turn of the twenty-first century new modes of social and cultural policy that were developed in the context of a postcrisis, refurbished Thai nationalism attempted to regulate the sexualities of urban populations. The 1997 regional financial crisis had prompted renewed engagement with notions of Thai culture and heritage and its profitable integration into political and Buddhist-coded economic programs such as the sufficiency policy. *Sufficiency* (*khwam pho phieng*) designates a Buddhist-coded notion of economic, political, and affective moderation, or a localized notion of austerity.[11] Invoked in a royal speech in 1998, sufficiency was broadly adapted into post–financial crisis policy. As royally initiated policy, the ongoing, constantly diversifying sufficiency projects are not subject to criticism and receive significant funding. They are promoted by a variety of ministries, government units, and NGOs. Sufficiency finds a parallel in the ongoing attempts in social and cultural policy to achieve moderation in the way that sexuality appears in the public domain. The policies, rhetorics, and campaigns initiated at this time became foundational for all subsequent modes of regulating sexuality.

After 1997 new cultural and social policy took recourse to bodies and sexualities, and national cultural identity and citizenship came to be closely articulated with normative prescriptions for sexuality.[12] Rhetorics of the deficiency of sexual minorities and women derived from psychology, religion, and policy combined in a detrimental fashion. The existing social censure of gender "deviance" in Thailand was thus compounded by the almost unprecedented state condemnation of sexual deviance. In this context homosexuality, the public performance of femininity, and transidentitarian positions fell under the scrutiny of the state in unprecedented ways but also came to stand at the center of new discourses about sexual rights, public personhood, and democracy.

The mainstream and independent cinema and contemporary digital avant-garde that originate in Thailand after 1997 represent powerful imaginaries regarding both sexual cultures and national futures. Occupying a fraught nexus of visual representation, law, and nation, this cinema's and art's aesthetics and politics are in part strongly aligned with post-1997 nationalist revitalization. In this study it is primarily Nonzee Nimibutr's 1999 heritage film *Nang Nak* that appears in such alignment. In contrast the work from the late 1990s and 2000s of the contemporary independent directors Pimpaka Towira, Apichatpong Weerasethakul, and Thunska Pansitthivorakul as well as the video art of Araya Rasdjarmrearnsook constitute strong alternative publics that represent sexual personhood in ways that challenge nationalist prescription. In further contrast the Hong Kong–Thai coproduced horror cinema of Oxide and Danny Pang occupies a position that speaks also to transnational aspects of gendered personhood. Thematically post-1997 Thai cinema and video art centers especially on themes of ghostly return, and a large quantum of films address minoritized sexual personhood. The combined focus on policy and cinema in this study allows me to engage the question of how minoritization comes about in a neoliberal political context that is simultaneously marked by great recourse to tradition and history. Although much of *Ghostly Desires* is devoted also to the study of femininity, in this introduction male homosexuality serves as my example for how notions of gender and sexuality are currently being reformulated.

Ghostly Desires investigates contemporary Thai sexualities through a different conceptual lens than the prevalent modes of analyzing the politics and geopolitics of sexuality and desire in this location. Tracking the motif of the predominantly female ghost through post-1997 Thai cinema and video art, I examine how Buddhist-coded anachronisms of haunting figure struggles over contemporary Thai sexualities, notions of personhood, and collective life.

Rather than as "the claim that something out of kilter with the present really belongs to a superseded past," I use *anachronism* as a comprehensive, nonevaluative term that designates the coexistence of two or more divergent temporal elements in a given moment or period of time.[13] Anachronism comes to bear on this analysis in several foundational and interconnected ways. As I said, it informs the temporal architecture of Buddhist melancholia; here it comes to the fore on a psychological level in scenes that highlight the temporal incongruities of desire. In close connection, anachronisms so pervasively structure contemporary imaginations of sexuality in the Thai context that we cannot think the present without them. In this sense anachronisms also inform Buddhist sexual contemporaneity, a term that designates the multifaceted conceptual makeup of sexual personhood in Thailand in the present. Throughout this study I use the term *Buddhist-informed*, or synonyms thereof, to indicate the mediated nature of the examples under review and the fact that contemporary cinema and video art do not necessarily reproduce doctrinal Buddhist notions. Rather than suggest that Buddhism structures sexuality in a pervasive, transhistorical way, I am concerned with the invocations of Buddhism in cinema and the deployment of Buddhist notions in policy.

I use the term *liberal* as shorthand to describe an Enlightenment-heritage political perspective on sexually minoritarian personhood that conceives of sexuality as a component of citizenship and a question of rights.[14] A liberal activist agenda locates its primary hope for the amelioration of grievances suffered by sexually minoritized persons in law and policy as well as in social reconciliation within a national framework. I examine liberalism in the Thai context against the background of critiques in cultural and political theory that have pointed to the limitations of liberalism's reparative claims. Thus Wendy Brown argues that claims based on the pain, loss, and injury of sexual minorities reinscribe rather than ameliorate the subordinate status of minority subjects, and Lauren Berlant critiques a liberal model of national sentimentality in which a politics of feeling comes to replace political struggle and locks into place social inequalities rather than fostering structural change.[15]

When national-cultural identity became increasingly sexualized and minoritized sexualities attained newly politicized significance in the Thai public sphere of the 1990s and 2000s, artists and filmmakers also devised new approaches to representing sexual minorities. Thus while official politics articulated especially homosexuality with sociocultural decline and with notions of existential damage, mainstream queer-themed films focused on the question of how the social suffering or injuries of sexual minorities could or should be made to "count politically."[16]

When women and sexual minorities emerged into the public sphere as diminished citizens *and* as hypothetical subjects of rights in Thailand, their concerns were thus in part strongly articulated with notions of injury, as well as with its alleviation through legal means, in activist and official politics as well as in cultural production. In the realm of a reviving commercial cinema, Yongyoot Thongkongthun's popular 2000 comedy *The Iron Ladies I* (*Satree Lek I*) was the first to engage the liberal notion that justice for sexual minorities is to be achieved through legal intervention and national reconciliation. *The Iron Ladies'* establishing scene sets up queerness as a question of national import when it presents the rejection of a queer player from selection to a volleyball team slated to enter national competition. The remainder of the film is devoted to rectifying discrimination based on gender and sexual orientation. In this story resolution is achieved over an educational, sportswo/manlike engagement with the transphobia and homophobia of representative persons like referees, teachers, and athletes. The drama finds its culmination in a resolution that highlights a human rights discourse, articulated at the time of a nationally televised showdown in which the queer team triumphs. As an avenue for achieving justice for sexual minorities, however, the model of inclusive national coherence espoused by *The Iron Ladies* is limited, relying as it does on exceptional achievement on the part of the minoritized person and insight and benevolence on the part of the nation.

If, across several global locations, conceptions of justice for minoritized sexual personhood at present remain overwhelmingly defined by notions of injury and redress in this manner, how does this scenario play out differently in a majority-Buddhist society and a modernity that was never defined solely as secular? Even when Thai political and artistic contexts invoke the rectification of injustices suffered by minoritarian persons in seemingly standard liberal formulations, this does not merely parallel mainstream approaches to gender and sexual inclusivity in other countries. Instead such invocations must be situated in an environment in which contemporary state sexual politics are further complicated by the fact that they draw also on Buddhist notions of personhood, sufficiency, and community. Thus when working on feminist, lesbian, gay, and transidentitarian concerns, activists and artists had to contend with a social negativity that was simultaneously undergirded by a new policy rhetoric that devalued queer and female personhood, by the idea of psychological aberrance as well as by enduring notions of the existential, karmic inferiority of sexual minorities. How, then, did progressive queer politics and art use or refuse rhetorics of loss and injury in a public sphere that was replete with narratives of loss concerning not only culture, economy, and sovereignty but also psychology and ontology?

Framing its stories of queerness by using defamiliarized Buddhist motifs, tales, and images, the independent cinema of directors like Apichatpong Weerasethakul makes a departure from the liberal focus on justice achieved through national reconciliation. I argue that this director's work displays the keen recognition that what is at stake for queer politics in the current moment is the narrow choice between illiberal repression and the reduction of a Thai queer imaginary to a standard liberal frame of policy-oriented activism.

Apichatpong's cinema illustrates how, precisely at a time when minoritized sexual personhood becomes a distinctly national issue and a matter of injury and recompense in the Thai public sphere, independent films after 1997 invent a cinematic, affective, and political language that moves the question of nonnormative sexuality beyond the frameworks of national reconciliation, legal emendation, and good citizenship. Borrowing from Theravadin and other Buddhist imaginaries to describe an alternative Thai sexual contemporaneity, independent cinema mobilizes karmic, soteriological, and other Buddhist tropes of negativity. Manipulating Buddhist pedagogy's central focus on impermanence—or on the suffering that ensues from the fact of constantly impending loss—this cinema deploys Buddhist tropes, stories, and images to move queerness beyond binary notions of liberalism and illiberalism.

Apichatpong's short film *Morakot* (Emerald, 2007, Thailand and Japan) offers further insight into the constitution of Buddhist sexual contemporaneity and indicates how the arbitration of the injuries suffered by minoritized sexual and gendered persons might be addressed differently. Based on a Danish Buddhist novel, *The Pilgrim Kamanita*, the film's "protagonists are reborn as two stars and take centuries to recite their stories to each other, until they no longer exist."[17] Three people who remain largely invisible throughout *Morakot* recount memories of desire as the camera slowly surveys the interior of a derelict boom-time hotel, focusing especially on empty beds. Feathers that slowly float through the abandoned rooms lend the film nostalgic contours.

Thematically *Morakot* engages temporal incongruity in the Buddhist-inflected stories of past desires that its protagonists tell. At the same time, the film invokes another kind of temporal disjuncture by embedding these recollections in a contemporary outside, interspersing shots of a busy Bangkok intersection (fig. 1.3). Apichatpong describes the Morakot as "a derelict and defunct hotel in the heart of Bangkok that opened its doors in the 1980s: a time when Thailand shifted gears into accelerated economic industrialization. . . . Later, when the East Asian financial crisis struck in 1997, these reveries collapsed."[18]

Drawing into relation a Buddhist time of desires threading through lives and afterlives and the post-1997 political and economic context in Thailand, *Morakot* presents contemporary sexual personhood as defined by multiple, divergent constituents and elucidates the workings of Buddhist melancholia further. Aiming to instruct us in the basic unavailability of our objects of desire, Buddhist teachings provide fine-honed tools that parse the incongruities of desire: *I want something; I can no longer have it. I have a desire for someone; it is not reciprocated. Even if I do gain access to the object of my desire, it will no longer, not yet, or not for long be what I want it to be.* Buddhist pedagogy thus relies on temporal discrepancy to underwrite the imperative to detach and takes its most extreme form in examples in which the object of desire is already dead. The Buddhist melancholia of contemporary film improvises on these tools; however, it generally does so for purposes other than those of religious instruction.

FIGURE I.3. The view from the window shows a busy Bangkok intersection. Apichatpong Weerasethakul, *Morakot* (Emerald, 2007).

In *Morakot* Buddhist melancholia describes a process in which a chain of events that have to do with desire is arrested in its conventional tracks, as the film zooms in on and draws out a particular moment. Thus the reflections of one of the protagonists on a long-ago desire take up the better part of the narration. Instead of relegating this desire merely to a moment in her life, the duration of desire is expanded exponentially as *Morakot*'s protagonists "take centuries to recite their stories to each other."

As in *Luminous People*, Buddhist melancholia typically catches attachment at the point of its greatest futility—at the point of loss or impossibility— and takes a closer look. In many instances this kind of intervention in contemporary film pushes desire—and narrative—in a different trajectory than it would conventionally take. In this sense Buddhist melancholia infuses the domain of desire with an additional quantum of mobility.

Morakot further intimates that the question of the *arbitration* of minoritarian grievances can be approached differently than in a film like *The Iron Ladies*. This is in part due to the fact that *Morakot* is an experimental film, but I nevertheless want to consider its conceptual potential in comparison. *Morakot* does not directly frame the speakers' queer sexual personhood as a politicized issue. The speakers' desires are, however, presented in the frame of a problematic, appearing as something that awaits resolution.

The shift in scope that Buddhist melancholia effects lends itself to thinking about the arbitration of minoritarian grievances. Its counterfactual perspective allows for thinking about the "what could have been" and "what could still be" of both psychological and social contexts.[19] While *Morakot* does not conclusively settle the problematic of the desires at hand, it tunes us in to the fact that in the cinematic and artistic archive under investigation, the arbitration of the problematics of desire will occur both on a political-economic as well as on a psychological-philosophical level. Rather than provide a patent solution, *Morakot* outlines a number of factors that come to bear on arbitration that include history and the economy but also engages the dimension of Buddhist cosmological time.

What *Morakot* begins to outline is that the deployment of Buddhist elements in contemporary cinema lets arbitration, or the resolution of problematics related to sexuality and desire, proceed differently. A further effect of such Buddhist framing is that *agency*, or the possibility of the minoritarian subject to maneuver within her or his respective positioning, is also conceptualized in unique ways.

Moving from an analysis of commercial films intended to appeal to broad audiences to independent productions that aim for radical intervention into contemporary sexual politics, my analysis focuses on how Buddhist melancholia provides a different switch point of resolution from that of legal emendation or national reconciliation. It is important to emphasize that the Buddhist fantasy that pervades this cinema is by no means depoliticized. On the contrary, in each of the films reviewed, fantasy comes to stand in close connection to trends and events in national politics.

Invocations of Buddhism occupy a broad spectrum in Thai cinema. In *Ghostly Desires* I am concerned especially with the ways in which Buddhism becomes an element of fantasy and an element of argument. In this context Buddhism is at times severed almost entirely from purposes of religious instruction or philosophical speculation. In some cases it may function merely as a special effect. Buddhism's role as an element of fantasy becomes especially clear in *Morakot*. With its disembodied voices, colorful floating feathers, and superimposition of visuals, *Morakot* occupies the register of fantasy. When viewed in conjunction with these sonic and visual features, the film's invocations of Buddhist reincarnation and cosmological time may be understood as constituent elements of fantasy.

Morakot's only visibly queer moment occurs when the heads of two men are briefly superimposed on two adjacent pillows (figs. 1.4 and 1.5). Rather than merely showcase same-sex desire, however, Apichatpong's film presents a more expansive account of queerness. It is an older woman, Jen, who takes the lead in telling the story of her desire, and the conversation oscillates between three persons: Jen and two younger men. Queerness in *Morakot* thus includes same-sex desire but is refracted by a cross-gender sociality and comes to stand more broadly for as yet unrealized or impossible desires. This is also the sense in which this book undertakes the investigation of queerness.

The term *queer* is a cognate in academic Thai; in addition a plethora of slang terms, neologisms, and older Thai designations differentiate desiring positions and kinds of gendered embodiment.[20] However, I pursue a queer analysis that seeks to transcend the concentration on *categories* and the supposed plasticity of genders that has dominated writing on minoritized sexual and gendered personhood in Thailand. Queerness in this study thus stands more broadly for counternormative or as yet impossible desires. As an idiom of counterfactual possibility, the trope of haunting lends itself particularly well to such an analysis.

What is more, rather than take into account only self-evidently gay, trans, or lesbian cases, I investigate the broader contours of foundational new paradigms of sexual normalization and prohibition instated by disciplinary campaigns in the early 2000s that transformed the logics of regulation in the Thai public sphere. Thus while the first chapter does not examine a story of same-sex desire, it vitally details the parameters of the new sexual normativity. Subsequent chapters place homosociality in relation to an issue of historical accountability and investigate a primarily feminist manifesto of desire. While retaining a focus on the critique of gendered embodiment, sexuality, and desire, I thereby open queerness up to wider, urgent political concerns.

Against the background of contemporary sexual regulation, *Ghostly Desires* examines the possibilities of agency of women, trans people, and gay men both in the political arena and in the cultural imaginary constituted by contemporary cinema and a digital avant-garde. If Thailand has been characterized both as the site of limitless erotic possibility and as a space of severe restrictiveness for women and queers, how can we conceive of the agency of minoritized sexual and gendered persons in this location?

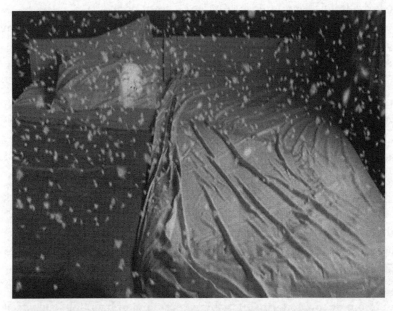

FIGURES 1.4–1.5. The head of the first man is superimposed on a pillow. The head of the second man is superimposed on the pillow to the right. Apichatpong Weerasethakul, *Morakot* (Emerald, 2007).

Rather than derive interpretations of state and societal attitudes from isolated incidents of prohibition, I base this study's conclusions on long-term policy and media analyses as well as ethnographic data. In my film analyses I focus on films that proved formative for Thai cinematic production throughout the 2000s. These films hail from five representative genres, each of which becomes salient for a different aspect of the sexual politics of the present. In the first chapter I investigate the role of femininity under the new parameters of sexual normalization in the heritage genre (Nonzee Nimibutr, *Nang Nak*, 1999). I relate this film's presentation of iconic national femininity to official policies of *social ordering* and *cultural monitoring*. I focus on the film's novel, Buddhist framing of the popular ghost legend and on how the anachronisms of Buddhist haunting may be made available to a feminist analysis. In the second chapter I examine the implications of transnational Chinese femininity and female homosociality in a Hong Kong–Thai coproduced horror genre (Oxide Pang and Danny Pang, *The Eye* [Thai, *Khon Hen Phi*; Cantonese, *Gihn Gwai*], 2002), in which Buddhism functions as a trans-Asian idiom through which we can understand women's historical agency. I then turn to the cultural and political interventions that artists and activists have developed in opposition to nationalist projects of sexual regulation and investigate how the trope of Buddhist melancholia is reconfigured in independent cinema and video art. Thus in chapter 3 I analyze the reimagination of male homosexuality in the independent cinema of Apichatpong Weerasethakul (*Tropical Malady* [*Sat Pralat*], 2004), and in chapter 4 I examine the elaboration of a queer-feminist ideal in the contemporary video art of Araya Rasdjarmrearnsook (1997–2006). In the coda I tweak the investigation of Buddhism vis-à-vis liberal formulations of sexuality in one additional direction by examining the depiction of queer interethnic intimacies in the documentary genre (Thunska Pansitthivorakul, *This Area Is Under Quarantine* [*Boriwen Ni Yu Phai Tai Kan Kak Kan*], 2008).

I place this primary archive of popular, commercial, and independent films and videos in relation with the visual and literary sources that it appropriates as well as with shifts in social and cultural policy, radical political writing, other materials from print and electronic media, and ethnographic materials that relate to the new sexual aesthetic and political spheres. I cull theories of minoritization from the Thai-language materials and bring them into conversation with critical work on haunting, social negativity, temporality, the nation, arbitration, the ordinary, trauma, and assimilation.

Ghostly Desires pursues neither a Buddhist philosophical investigation nor the study of a socially engaged Buddhism. Rather I examine a vernacular, quotidian, and frequently entirely nondoctrinal Buddhism in its role as a framework for fantasy and advocacy in the domain of sexuality.[21] In the films under review Buddhism does not stand in opposition to liberal understandings but rather merges with these to enter different kinds of Buddhist-liberal syntheses.

I consider instances in which both liberalism and Buddhism appear in at times contradictory and highly defamiliarized guises. I use the fact that imaginations of sexuality are concurrently anchored in Buddhist-informed understandings and in frames of thought that conceive of sexuality as a question of rights as an occasion to probe the mobility of the valences of liberal ideologies as well as the variability of meaning of Buddhist-coded representation and political discourse in Thailand. My analysis centers on the problematic effects that the Buddhist-liberal synthesis has engendered for women and for gay, lesbian, and transgender people as well as on the radical possibilities that it opens up. Ultimately I am especially interested in how artists and activists deploy Enlightenment-derived notions of freedom and rights as well as Buddhist images, stories, and concepts to wholly unorthodox, in part radical ends.

While I undertake a critique of liberalism, my perspective and object of research depart from studies such as Saba Mahmood's examination of a religious women's movement that operates outside of the confines of liberalism.[22] Instead I argue for the inseparability of liberal ideology from other Thai conceptions of rights, arbitration, and justice. Rather than make a distinction between the religious and secular-liberal domains, I investigate how Buddhist notions, however mediated, interact with secular, liberal concerns.

Frank Reynolds has outlined the intersections of secular law and Buddhism in his examination of a civic religion in which Buddhist concerns inform the secular domain of politics in contemporary Thailand.[23] Reynolds delineates a public sphere in which Buddhist notions inform ethical discourse and activism. In contrast I am concerned with a different intersection of the secular and religious. Rather than examine Buddhist teachings that are directly applied to social or political concerns, I investigate more mediated and frequently counterdoctrinal forms of Buddhism.

The study of Buddhist melancholia contributes to discussions of sexuality and negativity that have occupied much of queer theorizing in the past two decades. In *Sex, or the Unbearable*, Berlant describes negativity as "the self-cleaving work of the drives, being socially oppressed, and being nonsovereign, affectively undone by being in relation." Together with Lee Edelman, she expands this definition as follows: "Negativity for us refers to the psychic and social incoherences and divisions, conscious and unconscious alike, that trouble any totality or fixity of identity. It denotes, that is, the relentless force that unsettles the fantasy of sovereignty."[24]

My invocation of negativity may seem to parallel this and other studies of negativity in queer theory that draw on psychoanalytic approaches and combine these with biopolitical questions. The notions of negativity mobilized in my analysis of contemporary Thai cinema indeed correspond with some of the elements of negativity outlined by Berlant and Edelman. In particular my study investigates aspects of Buddhist-derived conceptions of negativity that impact the notion of individual sovereignty and agency. In addition I am vitally concerned in *Ghostly Desires* with the social positionality of minoritized persons. However, my analysis is not weighted toward investigating "psychic . . . incoherences," nor do I vitally draw on psychoanalysis. Moreover I primarily focus on the spatially and historically specific domain of Buddhist-inflected formulations of queer personhood and femininity in the contemporary Thai film and video culture of the past two decades. I ask two main questions of this archive: If in such formulations negativity describes an ontology that foregrounds the impermanence of existence, how does this understanding of negativity translate into contemporary logics of minoritization? If negativity includes an understanding in which desire is always already destined to fail, how do artistic materials reinhabit this notion?

My film analyses further focus on a domain of deferral rather than on the radical instantiation of negativity. On one side of the debates over queer negativity stands the radical, affective formalism that Edelman first proposed in *No Future: Queer Theory and the Death Drive*. His work undertakes the thorough dismantling of a future that is always already coded as heterosexual and is iconically embodied in the figure of the child. In rejection of such futurity, he suggests the notion of "a homosexuality distinctively abjected as a figure of the antibiotic, a figure opposed, in dominant fantasy, to life and futurity both."[25] In this context Edelman mobilizes the death drive as an uncompromising instantiation of negativity.

The films under review do not disavow the full obliterating capacity of Buddhist notions of negativity, which could be understood to operate in parallel to a notion like the death drive. However, in contradistinction to Edelman's radical formulation, their emphasis does not lie on negativity's exhaustive instantiation. In a sense these films are more concerned with the cracks in the totalizing force of Buddhist conceptions of negativity and focus on phenomena in the anteroom of impermanence. In this context Buddhist melancholia operates as a trope of mobility. It infuses prescriptive affective trajectories, in which attachment is the mere foil to inevitable expiration, with elasticity. This particular mobilization of Buddhist negativity is situated within a distinct temporal framework.

Detailing the complex notions of time in Theravada Buddhist canonical texts, Steven Collins explains that the ultimate soteriological goal in this tradition is to transcend the status of existence in time and to reach nirvana, a state that is free from time. According to Collins, time represents an essential element of suffering, or of the "unsatisfactoriness" of existence.[26] How closely considerations of time are linked to sexual desire in Theravada Buddhism also becomes clear in Collins's description. To elucidate the different meanings of the Pali word for time, *kāla*, Collins uses the example of a goddess who attempts to induce a young monk to abandon his abstinence. In this example the core ontological quality of time-as-unsatisfactoriness is vitally tied to sexual desire.[27] The young monk refuses to be seduced and thereby signals a path out of the unsatisfactoriness of existence.

By contrast the films and videos discussed in this book do not primarily aim to transcend desire or being-in-time. Rather than focus on a canonical notion of time, I therefore focus on a particular slice of Buddhist time as I concentrate on the proliferation of Buddhist-coded haunting in Thai cultural representation. The films and videos analyzed pause at the very moments that are supposed to point us toward nonattachment. Resisting the imperative to take such moments as occasions for learning about detachment, these visual texts mine moments of Buddhist melancholia for both pleasurable and conceptual possibilities.

In the cinema of Nonzee Nimibutr, Pimpaka Towira, Danny and Oxide Pang, Apichatpong Weerasethakul, and Thunska Pansitthivorakul as well as in the video art of Araya Rasdjarmrearnsook, each case of ghostly return draws on temporal incongruity to negotiate problematics of desire, sexual personhood, history, and the vicissitudes of attachment. This use of Buddhist anachronisms sounds promising, as though the activities of the ghost will, as a matter of course, furnish alternative models of sexuality for the present.[28]

Much contemporary theory uses haunting as a critical trope that allows for the surpassing of conceptual and political impasses. Bliss Lim's study of temporality in film is the most incisive account of the critical potential of ghostly return vis-à-vis historical injustice. *Translating Time: Cinema, the Fantastic, and Temporal Critique* investigates individual historical occurrences, while at the same time focusing on the injustice of a particular temporal regime more broadly. Lim's analysis is particularly trenchant because it brings a "visual-ontological" critique that draws on Henri Bergson's philosophy of time into conversation with a "historical-postcolonial" critique.[29] From this novel theorization of temporality emerges the assertion that the past is never left behind but persists into the present and remains coeval with it. In Lim's theoretical framework this notion enables the survival of temporal alterity, the persistence of demands for historical accountability, and the disruption of the empty, homogeneous time of the nation.

A vital part of Lim's argument centers on the notion of the immiscibility of different temporal registers: "Fantastic narratives, I argue, have a propensity toward temporal critique, a tendency to reveal that homogeneous time translates disparate, noncoinciding temporalities into its own secular code, because the persistence of supernaturalism often insinuates the limits of disenchanted chronology. I refer to traces of untranslatable temporal otherness in the fantastic as immiscible times—multiple times that never quite dissolve into the code of modern time consciousness, discrete temporalities incapable of attaining homogeneity with or full incorporation into a uniform chronological present."[30] The question of multiple temporalities takes on further significance when viewed in the framework of colonial histories. Tracing anachronism's role in colonial rationality, Lim emphasizes that it becomes a tool of the "temporal management" of difference. She explains, "The modern dynamic of contemporaneity and its antinomy, anachronism, is a strategy of temporal containment. It attempts to manage a recalcitrant 'field of differences' by presuming a totalizing historical movement applicable to all peoples and cultures and labeling certain forms of difference as primitive or anachronistic." Engaging with the work of writers such as Dipesh Chakrabarty, Reinhart Koselleck, and Johannes Fabian, she reminds us, "This temporal management of troublesome heterogeneity under the rubric of modern homogeneous time is the imperial move that postcolonial scholars vociferously refute."[31] This is particularly important because the deployment of anachronism, as detailed by Lim, persists into the present.[32] Lim suggests that the "refusal of anachronism, of a past left behind" becomes an imperative in this context.[33] The rectifying intervention Lim makes counters the devaluation of temporal difference by focusing on the alterity of the temporalities of haunting and mobilizing the immiscibility of these temporalities as a historically reparative factor.

A refusal of anachronism in the sense of the devaluation of cultural-temporal difference also motivates my desire to account for the ways that Buddhist elements structure sexual personhood in the present. The notion of resisting anachronism in this sense becomes most explicit in chapter 2, where I investigate a historical case of temporal resilience and critique a transregional politics of temporal difference in the present, and in chapter 3 and the coda, where I consider the imbrication of Thai sexualities with transnational discourses. My study further converges with Lim's account in that it scrutinizes the ghostly as a terrain of critical force. Thus I investigate the impact of defamiliarized Buddhist temporalities on problematics in the domain of sexual personhood. I ask how the temporal incongruity instantiated by Buddhist melancholia provides an expanded framework for thinking about minoritized sexual personhood.

However, Ghostly Desires begins with the analysis of a situation in which the anachronisms of haunting create a more ambiguous terrain. In particular I examine a context in which tropes of haunting are vitally anchored in folkloric and Buddhist figures. These two domains are currently so thoroughly occupied by conservative, nationalist discourses that mobilizing them for political and historical critique is a task fraught with obstacles. I thus include in this discussion an adverse perspective on the critical potential of the comingling of divergent temporalities. Harry Harootunian picks up on the notion of *noncontemporaneous contemporaneity*, a concept with a rich history of analysis, but reviews this trope in the context of "the historical present."[34] What is significant for the purposes of my study is that Harootunian's analysis situates the idea of the comingling of temporalities in the frame of a history that, to an extent, abrogates its critical potential. Investigating global changes in understandings of temporality after the Cold War, Harootunian describes anachronism at this time as a temporal breakdown, a collapse of the tripartite conception of past, present, and future into the time of an enduring present. This account of anachronism high-lights the unprecedented compression of historical time into a "boundless present" after the Cold War: "Severed from its historical past and indefinitely deprived of a future," this present is marked by the coexistence of multiple, differing temporalities, but their critical relationality is largely impaired.[35] The resultant political implications of this "historical present" are dire, since it no longer allows for the possibility of a left, progressive future; that is, resolutions envisioned by socialism, human rights, or even liberalism are largely invalidated. What Harootunian describes, then, is a comingling of times that is devoid of the chafing that would bring a critical effect to bear on the present. I cite this work not to affirm its global applicability but to account for the fact that in certain cases temporalities, such as Buddhist ones, that should to all evidence enter into a critical relation to the present forgo their alterity.

We can see how the critical potential of ghostly return might be under-mined by a present that subsumes all temporal difference into the undif-ferentiated time of an endless now. The image of a ghost straining against the elastic yet unyielding bounds of this endless present may convey better the difficulties of progressive historical and political revision. If this col-lapsing of past, present, and future characterizes the Thai present at least in part, then the historical correction that haunting aims to force into being cannot easily come into evidence as radical temporal difference. My analy-sis of ghostly femininity in the heritage film *Nang Nak* in chapter 1 argues that certain kinds of contemporaneity in Thailand make critical interven-tion into sexual normativity difficult. For one, I refer to the willful temporal recodings, or anachronisms, that contemporary policy brings to bear on bodies and sexualities. Likewise I investigate a case in which the Buddhist-coded time of haunting in part relinquishes its alterity. This initial analy-sis constitutes the background of dominant policy and cultural rhetoric against which other films' treatments of haunting must be calibrated.

Yet the progressively transformative impact of anachronism is by no means foreclosed in the Thai present. Anachronisms provide for critical op-portunity in the majority of the material under review in this book. Valerie Rohy, Elizabeth Freeman, and Carolyn Dinshaw have argued for the critical potential of queer anachronisms, or the strategic affinity with sexual mi-norities across time.[36] In her essay "Ahistorical," Rohy claims the "strategic possibility" of a "critical intimacy with the past." Writing against a domi-nant "historicist" bias in queer literary history, she convincingly details the way that historical work is always already anachronistic.[37] Rohy argues that a pervasive *Nachträglichkeit*, or belatedness, always already informs perception, psychology, and historical inquiry. She urges us to make critical use of this inherent Nachträglichkeit as well as to plumb the temporal alterity that historical texts themselves suggest, for instance, through their narrative structure. Most notably she advocates the use of a critical strategy modeled on "anamorphosis, the optical effect in which a meaningless blot assumes its true form when observed from a certain oblique angle." As she explains, "The anamorphic form appears through a lapse of attention; it is unintelligible when sought directly. Only in hindsight can one recognize [it]." When applied to readings across time, this mode of reading "would make visible a textual shading not available to the direct gaze, an anamorphic afterimage visible to those who turn back in narrative sequence and historical time."[38] Drawing on modes of argumentation rooted in psychoanalysis, theories of literary form, and queer historical analysis, Rohy's work thus usefully makes anachronism available to multiple queer reading strategies. In chapter 1 especially I bring a similar reading across time to bear on the analysis of a hagiographic Buddhist text in conjunction with a contemporary film.

In summary, the critical potential of the anachronisms of Buddhist-coded haunting in the films that *Ghostly Desires* reviews lies in how they determine the duration and pacing of suffering and pleasure, redefine frameworks of resolution for cases of minoritarian injury, and reimagine trajectories of attachment.

Throughout this study *anachronism* figures as a comprehensive term that allows for the study of different psychological and historical aspects of temporal comingling. In the conceptual landscape delineated thus far, anachronisms designate building blocks of contemporaneity rather than marking contemporaneity's opposite. As outlined earlier, anachronism emerges as a highly elastic figure in the temporal order and neoliberal political configuration of the present. Possessed of significant ideological mobility, anachronisms may either signify the temporalities and features of an imagined sexual past forcibly dragged into the present (as in new state sexual politics) or designate the creative irruption of temporal and sexual alterity into the present (that is the hallmark of independent cinema).

I use *anachronism* as nearly synonymous with *temporal incongruity*; both describe the temporal operations of Buddhist melancholia. Buddhist melancholia thus brings about transformations of scale, such as temporal dilation or prolongation. The notion of *contemporaneity* refers to the simultaneous existence of two aspects of sexual personhood on the same temporal plane. It highlights the coevalness of Buddhist elements with other features of sexual personhood, while *synthesis* designates individual ideological formations that result from the interaction of Buddhist and liberal elements.

Global Sexual Contemporaneity

The notions of contemporaneity and anachronism come to bear on Thai sexualities in yet another way. The question of how to situate Asian genders and sexualities in time has not entirely been adjudicated. The work of Tani Barlow, however, explains the uneven temporalities of sexualities and genders in Asia through the colonial histories and complex adaptations of Enlightenment thought. Throughout her work Barlow stresses the contemporaneity of Asian gender and sexual politics when she shows that Chinese feminisms, for instance, are not derivative or Western but represent prescient and primary ways of centering women.[39]

In the same manner I investigate Thai sexualities as contemporaneous with other sexualities in the world rather than as sexualities that remain before prohibition or lag behind liberation. This is of particular concern because, as Rosalind Morris points out, "few nations have been so thoroughly subject to Orientalist fantasies as has Thailand. Famed for its exquisite women and the pleasures of commodified flesh, the Thailand of tourist propaganda and travelogues is a veritable bordello of the Western erotic imaginary."[40] It is in this context that contemporary cinema's invocations of a Buddhist sexual contemporaneity contribute to a reparative, postcolonial resituation of Thai sexualities in time.

Chapter 3 traces how a shift in the understanding of the geopolitics of desire and sexuality may register also in the transnational reception of Thai cinema: for the first time Thai queer films—and thereby Thai sexualities—are recognized by some critics as avant-garde cultural products instead of as always only emergent.[41]

Sexuality

The past two decades in Thailand saw the emergence of novel modes of prohibition that exemplify a quintessentially neoliberal form of regulation. At this time questions regarding the normativity or deviance of sexuality became firm components of citizenship and national-cultural identity when Thai state agencies initiated a set of disciplinary actions and campaigns. In the context of a refurbished nationalism after 1997, the state developed seemingly moderate disciplinary campaigns that seek to regulate the sexualities of large sections of the population. Most notably the campaigns of *kan jad rabiap sangkhom* (social ordering) and *kan fao rawang thang wathanatham* (cultural monitoring) invented and promoted a new lexicon of sexual normativity. Rather than attempt outright prohibition, these policies, which aimed to streamline the sexualities of urban populations, created a unique combination of regulatory measures and discriminatory rhetoric that persists into the present. In the context of these struggles over exemplary Thai sexualities, sexual minorities were forced into a novel kind of publicity and—as newly outed *citizens* in need of reform—were no longer able to remain under the radar of the state. What is the significance of the invocation of same-sex desire in a film like Apichatpong's *Morakot* in this political climate? (The case of male homosexuality remains my example for the ways the new logics of minoritization operate. In chapter 1 I look more closely at how femininity figures in contemporary policy.)

Homosexuality ambivalently haunts the political and aesthetic present in Thailand, on the surface primarily as a trope of diminution—as a thing that uniquely instantiates either cultural loss or minoritarian injury—but ultimately also as a figure of creative talent, potential economic productivity, and affective abundance. On the world map of homophobia, Thailand represents something of an anomaly. Activists and scholars have long struggled to reconcile evidence of high tolerance and visibility of sexual minorities with the deep-seated antipathies and notions of homosexuality as diminished personhood that are also evident in the country. Finding expression in a few manifest legal ways, Thai homophobia more pervasively takes countless subtle and roundabout forms. Both in the national and the international imagination, Thailand—and especially its de facto national religion, Theravada Buddhism—circulates as a figure of social and political moderation, even where evidence to the contrary exists. Yet the current, seemingly moderate kinds of sexual politics in the country created a potent blend of new discriminatory rhetorics and regulatory measures.

In the 2000s the Thai state's sexual politics resided in a domain of policy and discursive activism that straddled the field of the law and new forms of public speech about sexuality.[42] While attempts at prohibition in the 1990s were understood to effect the exclusion of sexual minorities, the disciplinary measures of the 2000s created a mixed juridical-discursive form of sexual regulation aimed as much at the inclusion of sexual minorities as at their exclusion.[43] At the same time as sexual minorities emerged into the public sphere as subjects of rights, homosexuality was doubly burdened by rhetorics of loss in official politics and media discourses. My argument in this context is that the government measures of social ordering and cultural monitoring brought into being new kinds of subjection of kathoeys, lesbians, and gay men while retaining older notions of their existential damagedness. Just as scholars have argued that different conceptions of gender and sexuality overlap in Thailand, we can also understand several modes of stigmatization of sexual minorities to occur simultaneously.[44] Roughly, the literature asserts that in the past two decades forms of stigmatization expanded from the social censure of gender deviance to state condemnation of sexual deviance. However, still more is at stake. In addition the campaigns of the 2000s brought older notions of existentially diminished personhood into problematic relations with new understandings of the necessity of state "care" for and social ordering of sexual minorities.

State Sexual Politics: Problematic Inclusion

On June 4, 2004, the deputy undersecretary of the Ministry of Culture, Kla Somtrakul, threatened to eliminate queer civil servants from his ministry and called on the Thai public to "oppose homosexual behavior": "The Ministry of Culture is serious about mobilizing against homosexual behavior. Although it is not punishable by incarceration or sentencing as in the case of obscene media, I call on the public to oppose it, so that homosexual behavior does not spread further than it already has."[45]

Kla Somtrakul's attempt to sideline, and discriminate against, queer individuals within a legal framework that does not in fact criminalize homosexuality encapsulates a distinct trend in the Thai state's post-1997 sexual politics. In academic writing on homosexuality in the Thai political context, much attention has focused on a singular event of legal discrimination in the 1990s. In 1996–97 the Ratchaphat Institute attempted to ban primarily transgender but also gay and lesbian students from thirty-six teachers colleges across the country.[46] That the ban generated alarm both nationally and internationally was in part due to the fact that the Thai state had until then largely hesitated to intervene in matters of sexual orientation. Thai law historically criminalized neither homosexuality nor male prostitution.[47]

An antisodomy law adopted from British colonial legislation in India seems never to have been implemented and was finally scrapped in 1959. Thai society moreover was widely thought to be tolerant, though not accepting, of sexual minorities.[48]

Due to protests and the fact that some argued it was unconstitutional, the Ratchaphat Institute's ban was ultimately overturned.[49] In the academic discussion the Ratchaphat case was treated as symptomatic of a breach in the relative privacy that the state had previously accorded to homosexuality. I suggest that, more importantly, the Ratchaphat case was a first indication that sections of the administration were preparing to develop systematic conservative-regulatory agendas. These agendas not only represented continuity with older, less-publicized homophobic measures but also sought to establish new forms of inclusion. What occurred in the late 1990s, then, was not the emergence of homosexuality from privacy into publicity per se but rather a shift from one kind of public focus to another.[50]

Following singular attempts at legal discrimination such as the Ratchaphat Institute's were organized, long-term disciplinary campaigns put into effect under Thaksin Shinawatra in the early 2000s, which consciously aimed to align a new sexual order with cultural revival and economic recovery.[51] The campaigns primarily relied on existing laws, administrative change, and publicity work to create new understandings of sexual citizenship and were continued by all subsequent governments.[52] Although seemingly geared toward exclusion and prohibition, these measures also legitimized sexual minorities as national and economic subjects, albeit subjects in need of reform.

In the 2000s Thai state homophobia thus did not primarily present itself on the level of directly discriminatory legislation. What queer activists had to contend with were not antisodomy or age-of-consent laws.[53] Rather state discrimination proceeded on a comparatively lower level of legal applicability (of social and cultural policy) and of modes of institutional classification as well as via the initiation of a continuous defamatory discourse. The former included Thai psychiatry's failure until 2002 fully to endorse and publicize the declassification of homosexuality as a mental illness. Thus activist endeavors against the practice of categorizing kathoeys as mentally ill on their discharge slips from compulsory army service (So. Do. 43) continued until 2011.[54]

The declaration by Deputy Undersecretary Kla condenses several elements of new state attitudes toward sexuality: the state's will to instill sexual order, its desire to intervene in gender and sexual deviance, and its fear of (new) media in combination with the "contagious" character of nonnormative sexualities—but also its relative incapacity to do these things in the context of a strictly legal framework. Yet the greater significance of such statements lay in how homosexuality was sporadically yet repeatedly invoked as antagonistic to culture and nation. With the recurrence of threats such as Kla's it became clear that the state's relative oversight of homosexuality had ended. Homosexuality had now come fully under the purview of the state, was continuously brought into negative connections with notions of proper public personhood, and increasingly became a matter of national import. On the other hand, none of the exclusions that Kla had threatened were ultimately put into effect. In fact all state projects to date that sought to ban sexual minorities from the civil service, television, or other institutions were prevented or overturned.

To date, however, the creation of ever-new projects of regulation has not subsided.[55] The Ministry of Culture's Culture Monitoring Center (now Culture Surveillance Bureau) was formed in the early 2000s and has remained the most active state unit to attempt sexual regulation. The group developed a concept of cultural deviance (*khwam bieng ben thang wathanatham*) that included, most generally, "the decline of morality in society, undesirable values, and the crisis of language use." Its mission statement and subsequent public relations documents explain that the group's "main task is to monitor events of cultural deviance and to warn society about such occurrences as well as to correct and take preventive measures against cultural deviation."[56] As the group's director, Ladda Tangsuphachai, confirmed in an interview, cultural deviance mostly refers to activities in the domain of sexuality.[57] The group's activities are in principle restricted to monitoring electronic and print media and concentrate on infringements of Thai obscenity law, Section 287 of the Thai penal code. As the law forbids only the trade in pornography and does not clearly define obscenity, it remains open to the interpretation of the officials. The group does not possess executive powers but regularly prompts the police to take action. Although academic observers have failed to recognize this, it is precisely actions like the Ministry of Culture's continuous public reprimanding of sexual and bodily choices that at present constitute a coherent form of policy rather than single instances of interference.[58]

The disciplinary campaigns were framed as communal projects. Thus the social order campaign encouraged the "cooperation of all sectors," including the public's participation by watching, volunteering, and reporting incidents.[59] In such appeals the nation was invoked as a strict but benevolent sphere of paternal watchfulness over the intimate lives especially of its youth. In this way the disciplinary campaigns aimed to bring into being a public sphere of authoritarian "care" and prescription regarding the bodily, moral, and intimate comportment of Thai citizens.[60]

Much of the new public discourse on sexuality was conducted as a discourse of loss. Recent transformations in understandings of sexuality are thus closely tied to narratives of cultural decline.[61] In these contexts Thainess is described as constantly on the verge of vanishing and as requiring administrative protection; in the early 2000s this represented a rationale for the establishment of the Ministry of Culture. Michael Connors argues that by then official understandings of culture had shifted from a rigid Thai-centric perspective to a more refined, pluralist—though no less "hegemonic"—conception.[62] It is in this sense that cultural monitoring and social ordering sought also to identify, classify, and administer rather than only to exclude sexual minorities. Homosexuality appeared not only as a figure of diminution but also as a national resource—an unstable figure of talent, potential productivity, and economic abundance.

Despite the fact that it was rooted in dispersed action and largely reliant on the population's internalization of new norms of sexual exemplarity, what is thus distinctive about post-1997 sexual politics is the relentlessness with which it laid claim, at least in policy rhetoric, to a communally monitored and streamlined national sexual community in urban Thailand. Regrettably this was not a passing policy fad: the campaigns conceptualized in the 2000s carried such momentum that they gave rise to and institutionalized lasting discourses and state practices. While the Ministry of Culture's monitoring activities received more regular publicity, the social order campaign had furnished a blueprint for subsequent police actions that continued to target sex workers, sexuality in public, and entertainment venues.[63]

Injury, Arbitration, Liberal Thought

In a liberal framework imaginations of freedom and justice for sexual minorities are largely relegated to two domains: the law proper and the nation. Religion is another prominent domain in which concepts of justice are generated, but one that scholarship is largely unwilling to entertain on its own terms or recognize as legitimate for establishing criteria of justice.[64] Reliance on the law as the primary remedy for minoritarian injury proves to be a fraught endeavor, however. I review the current shifts in Thai cultural and political imaginations of minority sexual subjectivity especially in light of the still growing body of literature that critiques liberal notions of sexual citizenship. Of greatest relevance within this literature is the prescient critical work that concerns itself with the problematic relationship between rhetorics of injury and emancipatory politics.[65]

With regard to the injuries of those who are designated sexual minorities, Brown and Berlant show that the frame of legal repair is compromised not only in its application but also in its very structure. These authors' critiques focus on the fact that the law always already encodes structural injustice; that the law is uniquely focused on abstracted, universal personhood and therefore only inadequately suited to addressing the specificity of minority injuries; and, most important, that the exclusive belief in the law's reparative potential limits the imagination of justice since the law's conceptualization of justice is by definition restricted.

At a time when sexual majority-minority relations are being reframed in Thailand, these critiques of the law as the sole proponent of justice are of great relevance to political struggles in Thailand. The currency of injury in political struggles remains uncertain, however. The aftermath of state violence against the 1973, 1976, 1992, and 2010 popular uprisings against military politics was overwhelmingly marked by the factor of state impunity. This adds complexity to the question of whether injury-based claims constitute viable oppositional politics.[66] Concurrently the reluctance (before 2010) to make historical traumata, losses, and injuries into political factors is also documented.

On the other hand, the notions of injury and recompense represent integral parts of Thai civil law. The processes of drafting the 1997 and the 2007 constitutions further attest to the fact that the concerns of sexual minorities were articulated with notions of damage and injury in official politics.[67] The political efficacy of claims based on the pain, loss, or injury of sexual minorities nevertheless remains ambiguous. At present the grievances of kathoeys, lesbians, and gay men still frequently fall between a failure of protection through the law, on the one hand, and accusations of transgressions of Thainess, on the other. Notions of loss moreover currently inform official nationalist rhetoric in a way that allows for little recognition of minoritarian claims.

In "Wounded Attachments," Brown draws attention to the deployment of pain as a problematic that fundamentally troubles identity politics. She describes how the valence of pain in identity politics is subject to a logic rooted in liberalism that must ultimately defeat the object of emancipatory politics. She writes, "Certain emancipatory aims of politicized identity are subverted not only by the constraints of the political discourses in which its operations transpire, *but by its own wounded attachments.*" According to Brown, a politics that is premised on specific minoritarian injury can ultimately only work to reinscribe that wounded particularity. Hence emancipatory projects predicated on claims of loss and injury find themselves in a deadlock of never-complete and nontransformative remedy of that injury, on the one hand, and the affirmation of the primacy of the normative ideal that they were excluded from, on the other. Brown explains that the way identity politics pursue a politics of *ressentiment* thus works to perpetuate subjugation rather than to overcome it. In order to surmount this impasse, she suggests replacing the politics of "I am" with that of aspiration, a politics of "I want."[68]

In the Thai context this state of affairs is further complicated by the country's history of state impunity, the fact that the state's new, prohibitory gaze on nonnormative sexuality itself vitally relies on rhetorics of loss, and that older, distinctly local rhetorics of loss also factor into public discourses on homosexuality. In a political context in which whole administrative bodies were created to bolster a national culture supposedly on the brink of disappearance, both queer politics of identity ("I am") and of demand ("I want") are always already hampered by pervasive discourses of loss regarding tradition, religion, the monarchy, and other elements of Thainess.

In her critique of the politics of pain, Berlant sheds light on the detrimental function of the notion of national reconciliation with regard to minoritarian injury. She critiques a political model of "national sentimentality" in which subaltern pain becomes the true index of subjectivity and the assumption of its universal intelligibility the basis for its (national) adjudication.[69] She locates the detrimental effects of the deployment of claims based on pain in minority politics in the fact that "questions of social inequity and social value are now adjudicated in the register not of power but of sincere surplus feeling." Berlant moreover argues that *adversity* is a more appropriate term than *trauma* for the conceptualization of modes of continual suffering that mark minoritized existences.[70] This distinction between trauma and adversity is of particular relevance for Thai activist politics. The fact that Thai state and social homophobia largely rely on subtle yet pervasive forms of denigration rather than on outright violence or prohibition has long presented a major difficulty for conceptualizing both academic analysis and counterpolitical actions. *Adversity* thus better captures the experience of minoritized persons under the seemingly moderate yet comprehensive forms of discrimination prevalent in the country.

At the same time arguments derived from Theravada Buddhism continue to be mobilized in public debate in Thailand and mark vernacular perspectives on homosexuality as diminished personhood. Historically, local discourses about homosexuality and transgender positions were already strongly marked by rhetorics of loss, ascribing karmic determinants especially to the condition of kathoeys. As Peter Jackson has shown, Theravadin Buddhist arguments were habitually advanced to procure compassion for transgendered people, but in the recent past also to legitimate the outright rejection of homosexuality.[71] Most frequently a transgender identity was thought of as a karmically induced condition and therefore remained beyond religious reproach. As Jackson notes, being transgendered was not thought to accrue any more negative karma; that is, it was not designated a misdeed in the present.[72] Transgender identity therefore bore a stigma but drew no additional religious-political censure. The condition of being kathoey neither required nor permitted change. As a result the notion of social obligation toward kathoeys included elements of lenience and sympathy, or *metta-karuna* (mercifulness). While karmic explanations still have currency, such reasoning has been augmented by discourses about sexual acts as social acts. Official discourses now depict homosexuality and transgender positions also as (volitional) *social vice*. Conversely, in sexual rights discourses homosexuality and transgender positions are now figured as *social suffering*. With the declining credibility of the explanation of karmic determinacy, however, transgender positions and homosexuality lost the relative legitimacy that this explanation conferred while retaining some of its stigma.

Liberalism and Sexuality in Thailand

The multiply constituted model of minority personhood, adjudication, and belonging that *Ghostly Desires* investigates bears out the elasticity of the meanings that liberal notions of personhood and freedom take on across geographic locations. While the book's greatest focus is on the ways in

UNIVERSITY OF SHEFFIELD LIBRARY

which contemporary Thai sexual politics and cinematic representation exceed liberal positions, I nevertheless argue for the need to assess with precision the effects of liberal claims in a given legal and social context. Likewise my analysis seeks to prompt a discussion about which facets of liberal, Enlightenment-derived thought to retain in progressive sexual politics. In addition this analysis of the politics of artists and activists in Thailand might open anew the question of how to delimit the radical from the liberal.

The study of Thai political justice and arbitration is constrained by the fact that the majority of scholars do not question the desirability, legitimacy, or universality of liberal law as such, do not look for liberal thought outside of the operations of the legal and administrative systems, and only decry liberalism's imperfect application.[73] To overcome this constraint I argue that liberalism must not be positioned as extraneous to the operations of state, law, and discourse in Thailand. Instead it is necessary to recognize liberalism's relevance within the structures of the state and legal system as well as in oppositional discourses.[74] Without ignoring the failures of the Thai legal system, it is imperative to not merely designate Thailand an illiberal state in which proper application of liberal law would resolve the problem of injustice.

In their study of a series of tort cases in Thailand, David and Jaruwan Engel argue persuasively that liberal law has little relevance in the daily lives of people in Thailand.[75] The Engels do not, however, analyze the inherent shortcomings of liberal law. Instead they evaluate the situation in Thailand as representing a failure on the part of the state to guarantee adequate legal proceedings. Similarly much recent critical work has designated the Thai state illiberal and set it in opposition to the supposedly liberal operations of Western European states.[76] Such a juxtaposition not only fails to recognize the postdemocratic nature of Western states but, more importantly, elides the urgent question of the universality and desirability of liberal assumptions.

In opposition to dismissals of the relevance of liberalism in Thailand, I contend that it is not solely the workings of the legal system that we have to take into account but also the important position that liberal thought occupies in discourses about rights and justice. In the domain of sexuality activism—as in that of democracy activism—in Thailand today, liberalism furnishes a vital language of oppositional politics. Liberal notions of injury and recompense strongly mark public discourses on sexuality, if not always actual legal practice.

As the state began to conceptualize sexuality as a problem of Thai citizenship, its regulatory programs prompted activist and artistic responses in the liberal idioms of law and policy. With the new logics of minoritization promulgated by the state came the desire on the part of activists to organize and once and for all to step out of social negativity, both as it had been entrenched and as it was being newly defined. That the legal sphere is engaged for this endeavor is not a mere reiteration of mainstream Western LGBTQ activism, however. First of all, the context in which the liberal law is held out as a promise remains vital for any assessment of its impact. Thus an activist symbol, demand, legal proposal, or measure that seems merely assimilationist in one context may take on radical meaning in another.[77]

When we consider oppositional sexual politics also in the context of Thai democracy's as yet unrealized emancipation from military politics, the sphere of the law continues to hold out the promise of radical amelioration. In her critique of liberal belief in the law, Brown persuasively details how the law is structurally compromised and disadvantages those who need its intervention and protection most. Yet in "Rights and Identity in Late Modernity," she concludes her rigorous critique with the insight that the legal sphere is nevertheless able to outline a horizon of possibility for justice.[78]

Not only does the liberal-legal domain furnish an idiom of political possibility in Thailand, but queer activism also systematically designed a mode of engagement with the legal sphere that was suited to the Thai political and social context. A large number of lesbian, gay, and trans activist endeavors in Thailand thus prioritize depathologization across a variety of institutional, legal, and social domains. This differs from what is frequently characterized as merely a demand for upward social mobility in the context of North American and European mainstream activism. Rather than aspire to inclusion into privilege, as this mainstream activism does, Thai queer activism largely focuses on destigmatization.

With a queer feminist approach to intervening in local and translocal rhetorics of stigmatization, the lesbian activist group Anjaree has taken the lead in public representation, political protest, and policy work concerning issues of homosexuality and transgender rights in Thailand since 1986. In 2001–2 the group took up Thai psychiatry's failure to fully endorse and systematically publicize the declassification of homosexuality as a mental disorder. The taxonomy of homosexuality as a mental disorder had originally been adopted from American classifications of abnormal sexualities.[79] However, although Thailand followed suit after the American Psychiatric

Association and World Health Organization revoked this classification, Thai psychiatry did not publicize and implement this decision effectively enough to affect policy and public perception. Activist projects aimed at the declassification of trans positions as mental disorders continued into the 2010s.

Anjaree aimed to counter a notion of diminished personhood that was of transnational origin yet had become firmly established and blended with other local beliefs about gays, lesbians, and kathoeys. The push to revoke the classification sheds light on Anjaree's adaptations of a rights framework to the specific demands of the Thai situation as well as on the group's relation to a politics and "logics of pain."[80] The relative dearth of directly discriminatory legislation such as antisodomy laws in Thailand led Anjaree to conclude that rights advocacy in general also had to address the more diffuse forms of discrimination prevalent in the country. When Anjaree began to lobby the Department of Mental Health to revoke the classification of homosexuality as a mental disorder, the group relied on activities targeting policy and on media work, educational activities, and action-research projects intended to bring about broad changes in public perceptions of sexual minorities.[81] Having identified the source of injury in the juridical domain, broadly defined, as well as the social domain, Anjaree did not anticipate accomplishing its repair only through the law. While activists strategically engaged the legal sphere, the liberal belief in the law as the sole purveyor of justice was absent from their agendas, and Anjaree's politics addressed the psychological, vernacular Buddhist, and social negativity of sexual minorities in combination.

Buddhism

Ghostly Desires tracks the way a vernacular, quotidian Buddhism comes to bear on cinematic fantasy that relates to sexuality as well as on contemporary national politics. Most scholarly writing on Buddhism and sexuality focuses solely on the issue of toleration and its obverse, prohibition, and directs little attention to the relation of Buddhist stories, teachings, and images to sexuality as fantasy.[82] With the argument that Buddhist elements directly inform notions of sexuality and desire, I extend Justin McDaniel's claims about the counterdoctrinal qualities of Thai Buddhism into the sphere of sexuality.[83] More than foregrounding its counterdoctrinality, however, my concern is to emphasize that Buddhism is not only brought to bear on sexuality in a regulatory manner. Rather the cinema and art I examine bring into play a synthesis of ghostly return with Thai Buddhist motifs to elaborate the affective dimensions of sexual desire. Buddhism not only permits or inhibits sexuality here but itself plays a part in the constitution of desire. Thus the Buddhist-coded stories of Apichatpong's short films, *Luminous People* and *Morakot,* do not primarily impart a teaching about nonattachment; these defamiliarized Buddhist tales perform a kind of political advocacy and provide a framework for fantasy in the domain of desire.

Buddhism in this study denotes a broad spectrum of beliefs and practices that include Theravadin Buddhist orthodox forms as well as magic practices and popular Buddhist conceptions. I am less concerned with Buddhism as an ideological system that furnishes ethical precepts than with Buddhism's vernacular, quotidian, pedagogical, and pop-cultural forms. Thus my analysis primarily tracks the work that Buddhism performs outside of the domain of religious instruction. This focus enables a perspective on the largely nondoctrinal work that Buddhism performs within the everyday realms in which sexuality becomes a question.

While others have examined Buddhism's vital role in the production of national modernity and the institutions of state, *Ghostly Desires* takes into account how Buddhist-coded notions of loss currently strongly inform cinematic and artistic imaginaries, vernacular attitudes, public policy rhetoric, and activist interventions regarding sexuality in Thailand.[84] What further requires explicit articulation is that, from their historical constitution until the present, Thai national subjects have been understood as Buddhist subjects. In the Thai context the notion of "Buddhist subjects" thus always implies also a dominant conception of national subjects and subjectivities. This feature of Buddhism comes to bear on the analysis in the coda of interethnic intimacies in the documentary *This Area Is Under Quarantine.*

Theravada Buddhist concepts of attachment are rooted in an ontology of impermanence (Thai, *anijjang;* Pali, *aniccā*), or of constantly impending loss. To illustrate the futility of desire under these conditions, Buddhist pedagogy privileges the female body and horrific depictions of its constitutional impermanence.[85] In this context Buddhist hagiographies as well as contemporary teachings and visual representations deploy anachronism as their preferred pedagogical trope. In this pedagogy women and stories about their malleable, decaying bodies are exemplary of the impermanence of objects of desire. One is supposed to understand from these examples the fundamental incongruity of desires and objects of desire and, in the final instance, that attachment is as such futile. While women are always already karmically diminished, the notion of existential, ontological negativity also applies to gay men and kathoeys, whose desires and embodiment are in vernacular Buddhist discourses understood to be the result of unfavorable karma.

At the same time, contemporary Buddhist writers and activists deploy Buddhist notions for the purpose of advocacy. In "Ke-Lesbian Wibakkam Khong Khrai?" (Gays and Lesbians—Whose [Karmic] Adversity?), the monk and author Chai Warathammo criticizes the pervasive tendency to attribute adverse karma to gays, lesbians, and trans people. In an inverse move to such ontological diminution, Chai skillfully redeploys karma discourse to speak about social injustice, shifting the burden of *wibakkam* (adverse karma; Pali, *vipāka* and *kamma*) from stigmatized groups to a discriminatory social environment and faulting its oppression of sexual minorities.[86] He argues that karma cannot uniformly be connected to identitarian criteria (male, female, gay, etc.) but rather represents the results of individual action and intention. Chai instead attributes karmic burden to a society that discriminates in action, word, and thought against sexually diverse people. He argues that assessments of karma should shift their focus from phenomenologies of gender and sexuality to appraisals of the communal, beneficial value of actions and intentions.

Using Buddhist arguments to advance feminist-queer discourses, Chai reconfigures especially the key Theravadin Buddhist notions of karmic causality and impermanence. In "Phrang Chomphu Khatha" (The [Buddhist] Tale of Private Pink) he uses the concept of anijjang (impermanence) to adjudicate controversy over transgendered students' dress and instead deconstruct notions of sexual difference as such. With his redeployment of Theravadin Buddhist concepts, Chai reformulates both traditional and contemporary as well as local and transnational notions of diminished personhood.[87]

While the institutional home of the pedagogical trope of femininity-as-impermanence is the temple, popular cultural adaptations of it abound. The contemporary Thai cinema of haunting refuses the detachment that the sight and contemplation of the (predominantly female) dead are supposed to prompt; instead this cinema turns on exploiting the space of deferral that I call Buddhist melancholia. Among the materials analyzed, Nonzee Nimibutr's heritage film, *Nang Nak*, best exemplifies a contemporary Buddhist nationalist deployment of Buddhist melancholia in relation to Thai sexual subjectivities. In contrast the independent filmmakers Pimpaka and

Apichatpong tweak this predetermination of Thai subjectivities by invoking this and other Buddhist motifs to redefine sexual personhood according to feminist and queer parameters.

Thailand is the only state in Southeast Asia that was never formally colonized, a historical detail that singularly determines the state's self-definition and legitimizes its policies—and comes to bear on much post-1997 cultural production. This narrative leaves out the fact that, on the one hand, Thailand's modernization in the nineteenth and twentieth centuries occurred under colonial-imperial pressure and that to an extent this modernity was, on the other hand, "deliberately modeled on the colonial regimes in neighbouring British India and Singapore."[88] Critical historiography directs attention to the Thai state's semicolonial or autocolonial characteristics as well as to Thailand's status as an imperial nation in its own right.[89] Nevertheless, to this day the state relies on invocations of its noncolonized status to underwrite authoritarian nationalism, narratives of cultural singularity, and political exceptionalism. In contemporary cinema exceptionalist discourse comes to the fore especially in post-1997 heritage productions that recount historical events in a royalist-nationalist format, such as the film *Suriyothai* (Chatrichalerm Yukol, 2001), and also informs Nonzee's adaptation of the ghost legend of Nak.

As Apichatpong's description of his film *Morakot* at the beginning of this chapter indicates, the 1980s and 1990s were characterized by rapid growth as the Thai economy boomed under the influx of transnational capital and the expansion of the manufacturing and services sectors. While journalists, politicians, and intellectuals embraced discourses of *lokapiwat* or *lokanuwat*—the Sanskritic Thai coinages for "globalization"—that situated Thailand centrally in a continuous trajectory of Asian economic ascendancy and cultural parity, commitments to local and communitarian agendas and models also increased in this period.[90] Concurrently the four decades since the brutal crushing of civilian uprisings in October 1973 and 1976 have also been marked by political struggles against both military and civilian-populist state authoritarianism.[91] Rather than resolve these crises, Thai official political culture seems at present to register an increased authoritarianism and the further convergence in the 2000s and 2010s of military and populist forms of governance.[92]

Thailand's growth period ended with the 1997 Asian economic crisis, an event that led to programs for economic recovery and to the reevaluation of notions of Thainess and a resurgence of cultural nationalism. What marks the 1997 regional economic crisis as a watershed for histories of Thai modernity is the perceived loss of national sovereignty on the part of financial and political elites at this time. In the domain of official politics the financial crisis engendered an extensive ideological overhaul of modes of governance. In this context Thai culture functioned as a kind of raw material to be exploited for nationalist revitalization. It is in this environment that we must situate the rise to power in 2001 of the populist tycoon Thaksin Shinawatra, who remained Thailand's prime minister until September 2006, when he was deposed by a military coup. Thaksin tapped into political discontent and class differences in ways that ensured the continued reelection—and repeated overthrow—of his party throughout the 2000s and 2010s. Of special interest for this study, his administration initiated an agenda for Thai capitalist recovery that, although strongly tied to transnational economics, nevertheless bore a distinctly local, national imprint (sufficiency). As we saw, similar formulas also informed sexual policy. Restrictive sexual politics henceforth became a feature of policy of all subsequent governments and are by no means limited to traditional elite regimes or to those aligned with Thaksin.[93]

In this period the media landscape also diversified; new bourgeois modes of representation (such as heritage cinema) emerged in tandem with the return of many regional forms (such as *luk thung*, Thai country music) to mainstream media. The expression of new bourgeois desires and the centering of regional artistic forms coincided with a profusion of discourses about minority identities and desires. Thus while a vocal conservatism asserted its positions on sexuality, the turn of the century also saw a publishing boom of first-person accounts about sexuality by women, gay men, and kathoeys. Changes in media production, accessibility, and circulation brought further diversification.

The late 1990s saw the revival of a Thai cinema whose output had previously dwindled because it was unable to compete with Hollywood productions. The revival occurred in conjunction with the international exhibition of Thai films. In Chalida Uabumrungjit's estimation, the participation of Pen-ek Ratanaruang's *Fun Bar Karaoke* in the Berlin International Film Festival in 1997 may serve as an approximate starting date for what is sometimes termed New Thai Cinema.[94] May Adadol Ingawanij details how Thai directors at this time adopted new cinematic styles designed to increase Thai cinema's appeal to wider local as well as international audiences.[95] Much of the scholarship on post-1997 Thai cinema has focused on the subjects of Thainess and nationalism, while also addressing questions of this cinema's global intelligibility.[96]

I adopt an approximate distinction of genres into popular, commercial, or mainstream cinema; independent or art cinema; and a digital avant-garde. I make these distinctions on the basis of the films' modes of political address and their commercial performance as well as their venues of exhibition, largely within the national context. However, rather than fit neatly into predetermined conceptualizations, contemporary Thai films cross generic divisions, and their generic belonging may also change with exhibition across national borders. That I read the selected films in the national context does not disavow their transnational significance; my engagement with the transnational is accomplished through my focus on how Buddhist notions expand liberal frameworks, my investigation of transnational femininity in chapter 2, and my consideration of international viewership in chapter 3.

Cinema of Haunting

Much of post-1997 Thai cinema occupies itself with questions of ghostly return and other ways of drawing cultural pasts into relation with the present.[97] Although haunting constitutes the thematic commonality of the films under review, these works do not belong to a single filmic genre. In "The Ghostliness of Genre," Lim emphasizes the considerable tractability and generic mutations of the "Asian horror film."[98] In the films I review the trope of haunting proliferates across the heritage film, transnationally produced pan-Asian horror, independent cinema, video art, and the documentary. In my reading this body of work is internally differentiated by the degree to which it deploys haunting for more or less emancipatory visions of sexuality and gendered embodiment. The task is to find out under which aesthetic and conceptual conditions this trope's critical potential can come to fruition.

If the trope of ghostly return has in the past two decades been closely allied with concerns centering on the Thai nation, *Ghostly Desires* focuses on a period of significant reconfiguration of the national.[99] Highly diverse in its instantiations, this trope remains malleable enough to allow for such reconfiguration. Depending on their generic distinctions, the films stake very different claims to the nation. At the same time, the trope of haunting affords local (and regional) intelligibility and provides for intrigue in global exhibition.

The film scholar May Adadol Ingawanij has provided the most rigorous investigations of Thai cinematic genres and their political alignments thus far.[100] Her critique of a post-1997 heritage cinema that is closely connected to bourgeois nationalist interests comes to bear on my analysis of haunting and femininity in *Nang Nak* in chapter 1. May Adadol further uses the term *independent cinema* to classify the works of Apichatpong and his contemporaries in Thailand and in the region. She details the complex position of Southeast Asian independent cinema as dependent on intricate global and state funding mechanisms, logics of exhibition, and the parameters of censorship—much of which precisely detracts from this cinema's independence.[101] She nevertheless calls the present moment in Thailand a "period of production and circulation of a body of politically radical and aesthetically avant-garde 'Third world' films" and claims considerable possibilities for "a radical cinema movement."[102] For the purposes of this study, I understand as independent those productions that strive for "independence," or for alternate aesthetic and political worlds as related to the domain of sexuality, such as are envisioned in the cinema of Apichatpong, Pimpaka, and Thunska.

Jean Ma's consideration of Chinese art film provides further support in characterizing Thai independent or art cinema. Ma complicates the definition of the global art film by detailing how Chinese art films diverge from classical conceptions of the genre. Her analysis makes special reference to the cinema of Tsai Ming-liang, a director whose work invites comparison with that of Apichatpong. Ma draws attention to the ways in which Tsai's work expands the parameters of the art film, including its relation to national cinematic traditions and to auteurship: "Rather than attempting to distance himself from the tradition of popular commercial film, Tsai displays a more nuanced and ambivalent attitude toward this tradition, incorporating its conventions, forms, and popular icons into his practice even as he radically departs from its narrative approach."[103] With regard to auteurship, she notes that "Tsai's insistence upon an intertextual authorial presence constitutes one more way of reworking a traditional auteur position, by a multiplication and refraction across textual levels."[104] Thai directors' borrowings from divergent cinematic traditions and their improvisations on the notion of the auteur similarly complicate the idea of a global art cinema that merely follows a general template and gradually emerges in different places according to a "developmentalist logic."[105]

As the surveillance of public expression expands, independent cinema in Thailand is further vitally defined by its role in challenging the limits of cinematic representability. In the years after the 2006 military coup, the increasingly repressive application especially of the Thai lèse-majesté law and the Computer Crime Act has had devastating consequences for artists, activists, and other politically expressive—or even politically nonexpressive—citizens.[106] The Film Act of 2008 further inhibited cinematic possibilities of expression.

Although it is mostly sex scenes that catch the attention of cinema censors, the role of sexuality in the context of censorship has not received sustained analysis. We saw that the Ministry of Culture's Culture Monitoring Center (Culture Surveillance Bureau) tends to compound visual media with virality and "contagion" and that its director associates "cultural deviance" with "obscenity." Against this background the production and circulation of independent cinema frequently take on an activist component that includes political protests and court cases that center on the banning or censoring of films.[107]

The most organized protest against censorship to date was initiated when Apichatpong's 2006 film *Syndromes and a Century* (*Saeng Sattawat*) was partially censored in 2007. The censors demanded that Apichatpong delete scenes of a monk playing guitar, doctors drinking alcohol, a doctor kissing his girlfriend in a hospital (while having an erection), and an old monk playing with a flying saucer.[108] Galvanized by the censorship of *Syndromes*, the Free Thai Cinema movement formed to campaign for the liberalization of the conditions for film production under censorship laws that originated in the 1930s and to prevent the new restrictive Film Act of 2008. The ultimately unsuccessful struggles of the Free Thai Cinema movement with the screening (censorship) committee underscored the precarious position of independent Thai cinema. Ben Anderson notes an increase in film censorship after the 2006 military coup and attributes intensified politicization to Apichatpong's work.[109] May Adadol likewise relates the new, particularly onerous restrictions on filmmaking to the political resurgence of the military and to anxieties regarding the future of the Thai monarchy.[110] I cite this context to underline independent cinema's precarious imbrication with political expression and to call attention to the constant, genuine possibility of censorship for several of the independent filmmakers featured here.

My consideration of Buddhism in Thai cinema diverges from that of other scholars in that I do not primarily seek to find literal instantiations of Buddhist teachings in this archive.[111] Rather than assume the concordance of invocations of Buddhism in cinema with Buddhist principles, I pursue what I regard to be the more pertinent question of the political and conceptual functions of Buddhist content and aesthetics that exceed the purpose of religious instruction in contemporary Thai cinema.[112] Crucial to my study is that the Buddhist-inflected imaginary of contemporary independent cinema furnishes an additional idiom for queer and feminist advocacy. Because this cinema delves deep into the social and ontological negativity of sexual personhood, it is able to radically redirect the discussion of injury and arbitration, point beyond liberal impasses, and expand the frameworks in which we think about desire, sexual personhood, and the social.

Archive

In *Ghostly Desires* I trace current logics of sexual and gendered minoritization through the aesthetics of popular cinema, independent film, and avant-garde video as well as through social and political crises. For my analysis of state and activist sexual politics I rely on print and visual sources and also on ethnographic materials collected during extensive periods of research in Thailand between 1999 and 2015.[113] In order to understand the development of state sexual politics and activist strategies, I draw on data gathered through participant observation in public forums on the subject of sexuality in Thailand. The late 1990s and 2000s saw a proliferation of public "sex forums," as one event labeled itself.[114] In these conferences, seminars, activist meetings, student forums, and policy recommendation sessions, a diverse public of activists, administrators, professors, artists, NGO workers, students, civil servants, Buddhist monks and nuns, psychologists, and others discussed issues of sexuality, rights, and culture. In addition I draw on information compiled from participation since 1999 in events of Thailand's primary queer activist group, Anjaree.

This study further relies on data from interviews with artists, writers, film critics, academics, policymakers, practitioners of corpse meditation, patrons of the shrine of Mae Nak, activists, monks, and filmmakers such as

Michael Shaowanasai, Wannasak Sirilar, Nonzee Nimibutr, Pimpaka Towira, Kong Rithdee, Araya Rasdjarmrearnsook, and Anjana Suvarnananda. The particular makeup of this archive of artistic materials, literary and scholarly print documents, and ethnographic data and policy research allows me to investigate the composite blend of psychic, social, and ontological negativity that at present defines understandings of sexual personhood in official politics, religious discourses, and vernacular perspectives.

Chapters

The first chapter of *Ghostly Desires* centers on the concept of Buddhist melancholia. It shows how in Nonzee's 1999 heritage film *Nang Nak* desire and sexual personhood are rendered in the idioms of Buddhist pedagogies and economies of desire. Examining how the core Buddhist trope of the negativity of female embodiment works in present-day cinema and policy, this analysis of *Nang Nak* questions the relations of haunting to historical injury and repair. The chapter shows how new forms of cinematic representation take recourse to Buddhism and parallel the ways that sexual and economic sufficiency policies draw on Buddhist concepts. Thus the trope of Buddhist melancholia furnishes a convention that in mainstream film figures nationalist heteronormativity. The analysis therefore takes into account the extent to which Buddhist understandings of the temporal dimensions of desire in film concur with the "time of capital" and the "time of the nation."[115] Finally this chapter demonstrates how the temporal incongruity of haunting can be made available to feminist interpretation. When Buddhist stories highlight the difficulty of giving up attachment, they also become counterdoctrinal and highlight the persistence of women's desires. Bodies play a prominent role in this chapter, and the malleability of female bodies is shown to be at the center of Buddhist fantasy as well as of policy programs.

The second chapter investigates a historical shift in the intersection of gender, sexuality, and minority Chinese ethnicity in Thailand. This analysis of the anachronisms of haunting in the 2002 Hong Kong–Thai coproduction *The Eye* sheds light on the recent transformation of Chinese femininity from denigrated minority identity to trans-Asian, cosmopolitan ideal. I examine how this filmic text nevertheless mobilizes the moment of cultural revival also for the consideration of Chinese-Thai historical negativity. The film tells the story of an involuntary, Buddhist-coded seeing that occurs when a Hong Kong woman receives a corneal transplant from a Chinese

Thai woman. It is through this motif of prosthesis that the film gauges the commensurability of Chineseness across Southeast Asia and East Asia. In this cinema Buddhism is a transcultural formation that supplies essential knowledge for everyday coping and provides a map for coming to terms with loss across Asia. Notably this formation crosses the boundaries of Theravada and Mahayana Buddhist lines of thought. Rather than being set into relation to activities of the state, in *The Eye* haunting femininity is linked to transnational flows of populations and capital as well as to the migration of loss and concomitant flows of feeling and ideology. Significantly *The Eye* shows minority injury to be a matter of female agency as well as one that has to be approached transnationally. In the film women's desires are largely directed toward historical agency.

In chapter 3 I turn to the analysis of independent cinema. I examine how filmmakers such as Apichatpong make use of the Buddhist notion of impermanence to interrogate the notions of social wounding and recompense that inform liberal discourse on minoritarian personhood. The analysis of *Tropical Malady* focuses on how male same-sex desiring is situated in the rich affective environment of a cross-gender queer sociality as well as in an economic context of relative poverty that nevertheless translates into affective plenitude. The film makes its greatest intervention into the social negativity of queerness in its second half, in which it performs a queering of the Buddhist notion of impermanence. *Tropical Malady* thus succeeds in deploying the anachronism of haunting to proffer a model of how to make social, psychological, and Buddhist-informed notions of negativity available to queer critique.

The fourth chapter undertakes a queer-feminist analysis of the contemporary Thai artist Araya's videos about intimacy and exchange with the dead. From 1997 until the mid-2000s this artist returned repeatedly to a hospital morgue to perform with corpses in different scenes and arrangements. Focusing on conceptual and performative aspects of Araya's video work, this chapter follows the question of how scenarios of loss and invocations of scenes of intimacy are made to relate in the films. It examines how Araya's work defamiliarizes the popular conventions of depicting female death and attachment to the dead female body in Thailand. The modes in which this art engages the trope of femininity as impermanence stand in radical contrast to *Nang Nak*'s. In contrast to previous chapters, chapter 4's analysis concentrates on works in which longing and sexuality are situated in a highly abstracted and dehistoricized domain. Using death as a register of the sexual, Araya's videos aim to create feminist publics by rooting desire in a very literal form of negativity. They deploy Buddhist melancholia, or the conventions of depicting female death and the erotic, to extend our notions of desire beyond physical possibility and to previously unimagined objects.

The coda tweaks the question of Buddhism's relation to sexuality still further by investigating notions of Buddhist-Muslim intimacy in the independent cinema of Thunska. *This Area Is Under Quarantine* (2008) was produced in the context of the perpetual state of emergency since 2004 in Thailand's three southern Muslim-majority provinces. The analysis gauges the critical potential of interethnic intimacies in a situation in which violence is continuously perpetrated by a central state that defines itself as Buddhist. The coda thereby probes one additional positioning of Buddhism vis-à-vis sexuality and liberalism.

Ghostly Desires thus traces how Buddhist frameworks and contexts inform both normative and queer-feminist ideals of gender and sexuality through the heritage cinema, transnational Hong Kong–Thai coproductions, independent queer cinema, feminist video art, and queer documentary.

DESIRE, EMBODIMENT, AND BUDDHIST MELANCHOLIA
IN A CONTEMPORARY THAI GHOST FILM

A poster for Nonzee Nimibutr's 1999 film *Nang Nak* introduces the problem of the story in two lines of poetry: "Mae sin lom sin jai / rue ja sin alai sineha"—"Although she was dead / her desire persisted" (fig. 1.1).[1] The film poster summarizes the predicament of the ghost Nak, who aims to prolong her love life beyond her death. Throughout the film she faces a problem of temporal incongruity when she attempts to reclaim her lover, a situation that is productive of great agony for her.[2]

This chapter investigates how the temporal features of haunting in *Nang Nak* underwrite the symbolic work that femininity performs in the contemporary Thai heritage cinema as well as in the arena of nationalist politics. It begins by examining how Nonzee's tale of nostalgia for an invented traditional femininity can be correlated with new normative parameters for Thai femininity in the social and cultural policy of the early 2000s. I analyze the role that Buddhist concepts play in the film as well as in bourgeois nationalist visions of a contemporary sexual order and in state rationales for economic revival.

Nang Nak and other contemporary Thai horror-ghost films draw on a notion of temporal incongruity that is central to Theravadin Buddhist pedagogy. This pedagogy vitally relies on the double temporality attributed to

FIGURE 1.1. The film poster for *Nang Nak* (Nonzee Nimibutr, 1999) distresses femininity both visually and linguistically.

the female body that lets this body incarnate illusionary beauty as well as the fundamental Buddhist truth of impermanence, or constantly impending loss. This Buddhist-derived anachronism structures contemporary Thai cinematic renderings of ghostly femininity that are closely bound up with dominant national ideals of sexual culture after the 1997 Asian financial crisis.

My analysis argues against scholars who claim that the Buddhist tradition of depicting and contemplating (mostly female) death brings about uniformly progressive political effects. However, rather than declare the prominent trope of femininity-as-impermanence only a deplorable misogynist tradition, I delineate the conditions under which this convention may also enable feminist practices and conceptualizations. In contrast to scholars who have diagnosed a "silence" of female desire for Thai culture, I maintain that with its focus on Buddhist anachronism, the horror-ghost genre devotes itself precisely to parsing the vicissitudes of women's desires.[3]

I track two different operations of this anachronism. I first investigate how the deployment of femininity as impermanence in the heritage cinema parallels contemporary trends in social and cultural policy that aim to distress femininity. *Nang Nak*'s notion of an invented traditional femininity manifests in the embodiment and sartorial style of its protagonist as well as in the concept of privacy that it presents; this aligns the film with several of the features that contemporary policy demands of women. A subsequent level of analysis takes seriously the critical potential that the anachronism of haunting nevertheless offers and investigates how the invocations of temporal incongruity in the film can be made available to feminist perspectives.

To understand the operations of *Nang Nak*'s deployment of Buddhist anachronisms, it is useful to review Harry Harootunian's contextualization of anachronism in the historical present. Harootunian describes anachronism as the unprecedented compression of historical time into a "boundless present" after the Cold War. This present is marked by the coexistence of multiple, differing temporalities, or by a "noncontemporaneous contemporaneity." The form that anachronisms take in this historical present is that "diverse local times" resurface to coexist with the empty homogeneous temporalities of nationalism and capitalism. As Harootunian explains, what has thus attained greater visibility since the late 1980s "is the persistent identity of a different accenting of temporality usually effaced by both capital and the dominant narrative form of history, especially with regards to its nineteenth-century vocation to vocalize the achievement of the nation-state and what has been called modernity. What has constantly been suppressed and kept from view everywhere is the persisting figure of Gramsci's Southern Question and both its challenge to a dominant historical culture and its conception of progressive time driven by an anticipated future."[4] This statement seems to imply that the introduction of temporal difference will by definition effect a progressively transformative intervention into the temporalities of capital and nation. However, Harootunian proceeds to argue that current assertions of temporal difference do not represent a progressive challenge to nation and market but rather underwrite fundamentalist turns that have marked the recent present.

Although not necessarily globally applicable, Harootunian's perspective on post–Cold War temporality is useful for approaching a neoliberal political context that is simultaneously marked by great recourse to tradition and history. I argue that in contemporary Thailand, temporalities of nation and capital coexist in a troubling synthesis with those of Buddhism and cultural revival. What has reemerged with greater intensity in political rhetoric and artistic media since the 1997 Asian financial crisis are claims to Buddhist heritage and conceptions of economy and collectivity posited as Thai. At the same time, the biopolitical component of a refurbished nationalism positions bodies and sexualities as central variables in the development of a new, originary figuration of Thai citizenship and a revised approach to a world market now regarded as hostile to Thai interests. In this context Buddhist-inflected temporalities do not necessarily contest temporalities of market and nation.

In Nonzee's film it is Thai femininity that bears the burden of molding itself to the exigencies of the multiply structured temporality of the political present. What has been required of Thai female citizens since the late 1990s is thus to perform the labor of embodying a Buddhist-inflected, updated traditionality while at the same time hewing to the demands of capitalist revival. Although Nonzee's film does not deploy the language of policy, the femininity that the ghost Nak stretches to embody represents a radically contemporary model that bears both nationalist-capitalist inscription and Buddhist-folkloric components.

A look at the departure that Nonzee's *Nang Nak* makes from previous adaptations of the legend is instructive for understanding how the double temporality that the ghost inhabits elucidates the twofold structuring of Thai female sexual personhood in the present. Nonzee's film reinterprets the story of a woman thought to have resided in the Phra Khanong district of Bangkok over one hundred years ago. According to the legend, Nak dies in childbirth while her lover, Mak, is away at war. When the unsuspecting Mak returns to Phra Khanong, Nak awaits him as a ghost, accompanied by her ghost infant. The temporal incongruities that result—she's dead, he's alive; she knows, he doesn't; and both lovers want something that they can no longer have—usually produce comical effects in the story.[5] Nonzee's horror-ghost remake, however, brings an entirely novel perspective to the more than two dozen previous film versions of the story.[6] Nonzee's translation of the legend into a Buddhist parable excises many of the fearsome and sexual as well as comedic aspects of Nak's haunting and instead turns on the grand emotions of love, loss, and Buddhist detachment.[7] *Nang Nak*'s period setting in the nineteenth century, a feature that the director advertises as constituting the film's historical accuracy, further works to present the legend with the pathos of nationalist historiography.[8]

We can understand *Nang Nak* as a strong example of Buddhist-nationalist cultural recovery in the domain of sexuality. The film achieves this precisely by producing a historically inaccurate relation between the story's setting in the nineteenth century and an ideal of femininity in the present. In Nonzee's adaptation the revenant's desirous gaze from the ghostly sphere at the life that she could have had thus outlines a model of heterosexual femininity of the present. Nonzee's novel, Buddhist framing of the legend is especially instructive for understanding how, since the late 1990s, state agencies and bourgeois publics have imagined Thai sexualities as something that should and can be moored, however minimally, to historical elements. In this context bodies bear some of the burden of representing a baseline cultural good onto which national economic and cultural hopes could be mapped. *Nang Nak*'s deployment of a Buddhist framework in which women have to embody radical temporal difference elucidates the contradictions in the demands that this policy makes of femininity in the present.

The remarkable effect of Nonzee's translation of the legend into a Buddhist genre of stories is thus not only that it legitimates a contemporary nationalist outlook; the film's Buddhist framing also elaborates the affective dimensions of desire in the story and allows for a feminist perspective on the body, desire, and social negativity.

In addition to examining how the film makes Nak into a type, an icon of updated traditional femininity, I therefore argue that when *Nang Nak* renders the ghost's desire in a Buddhist idiom, a partial failure of typification, of the ghost's consistent performance of a contemporary feminine ideal, occurs. Thus while the ghostly fantasy becomes symbolic of collective, national life, the cracks in the fantasy also provide insight into the breakages of current dominant concepts of sexual cultural difference: the vicissitudes of Nak's haunting reveal the inconsistencies especially of new notions of exemplary femininity in Thailand.

A Distressed Genre: Buddhism, Nationalism, and Embodiment in the Thai Heritage Film

Nonzee's film is the first to present Nak's story in a significantly nationalist context, which is in turn underwritten by the Buddhist narrative of the adaptation. On first viewing, the film's nationalism may not be self-evident. What *Nang Nak* highlights after all is face-to-face community—to all evidence, in a prenational setting. On the level of its story *Nang Nak*'s nationalism becomes evident only with the dating of an eclipse and the appearance of the abbot Somdej Phuthajan To. The framing by this historically significant person and event marks the communal or local occurrences in the story as national.

According to Susan Stewart, the "nostalgia for the presence of the body and the face-to-face, a dream of unmediated communication"—and the articulation of the communal with the national—are marks of the "distressed genre." Stewart uses the concept of the distressed genre to describe literary appropriations of the folkloric and the oral and their ideological functions. A prominent passage in her work describes the temporal disjunctures that the genre relies on: "Thus distressed forms show us the gap between past and present as a structure of desire, a structure in which authority seeks legitimation by recontextualizing its object and thereby recontextualizing itself. If distressed forms involve a negation of the contingencies of their immediate history, they also involve an invention of the past that could only arise from such contingencies. We see this structure of desire as the structure of nostalgia—that is, the desire for desire in which objects are the means of generation and not the ends."[9]

Nang Nak's appropriation of folklore, its deployment of "the authority of the oral world," and especially its reliance on structures of "loss and recovery" situate Nonzee's film within the parameters of the distressed genre.[10] From its very beginning *Nang Nak* frames the legend as a story of personal and cultural partings. For all but a few minutes of the film Nak is already dead, but it is the ghost's unrelenting desire for the life and love that she could have had that enables the film's mode of nostalgia. In an early scene Nak stands on a pier taking leave of Mak, who has been drafted to go to war. This is in fact the lovers' last farewell while Nak is still alive, and a close-up shows Nak withdrawing her hand from Mak's grip, only to grasp his hand again with both of hers. As Mak descends into a boat, her hand slips from his grip for good, foreshadowing the final, Buddhist-coded parting of the lovers at the end of the film. In what follows, Nak waits for Mak's return on the pier over days and seasons. In the sequence's final shot the pier is bathed in blue, the color of the night and of the ghost. The color coding underwrites the temporal discrepancy that structures *Nang Nak*'s narrative. This temporal distinction is further substantiated by the fact that Nak is holding a baby now, which means, as we will understand later, that she is already a ghost.

As the opening credits appear, the theme of temporal disjuncture intensifies: a traveling shot over abandoned houses and interiors, human bones, and murals depicting Nak's story heightens the ambiance of loss, and its sepia tones distinguish this sequence from the green and blue hues of the opening sequence. The color-muted view of the abandoned locales indicates that a narrative of loss is to follow and that everything that is about to happen is already in the past. This sequence links the personal partings of the opening scene to a scene of cultural parting: all the qualities of historical Siameseness invoked by the film's beginning are marked as already lost. The love story is situated at the heart of this past, lending the relationship epochal significance and personalizing imagined cultural community.

The film's opening contains all the elements that will make up its vision of historically grounded sexual and cultural difference. For one, the scene introduces a contemporary rendition of traditional Thai femininity as embodied by Nak. Rather than model an ideal that demands literal emulation, however, the film's protagonist incarnates the capacity of bodies and persons to suture radically different temporalities. This is indicated by the synthesis of historical and contemporary markers of beauty and accoutrement that characterizes the ghost's femininity. A medium shot first shows Nak from behind, highlighting the fact that she is clad in (the latest design of) traditional wide *jong kraben* pants and a breast cloth, and her hair is cut short in a fashion resembling the historical *mahad thai* style (fig. 1.2).

In what follows, point of view close-ups further detail the ghost's historico-contemporary beauty (fig. 1.3). With a hint of betel that tints her lips red but does not color her teeth black as betel would, Nak exemplifies the allure and promise of bodies that reference an invented national tradition while accommodating contemporary standards of beauty and hygiene.[11] In Nonzee's adaptation, Nak's dress and embodiment thus actualize the detemporalizing effect of the distressed genre: the ghost's sartorial contemporaneity, her recovery of Siamese fashion and styles of embodiment, also signals to the viewer that nothing has in fact been lost. As this scene lets the desire for something national intersect with the desire for the feminine, the distressing mechanisms of the heritage genre come into close proximity with current biopolitical demands that require bodies to synthesize disparate temporal and ideological registers.

What links *Nang Nak* to contemporary sexual politics in my analysis is thus the extent to which especially female bodies bear the burden of having to encode Thainess as well as suture different temporal strata. My reading moves on the level of analogy and has thus far relied on visual and narrative analysis; however, the inscription of nationalism onto bodies is also evident in the sonic design of the film.

FIGURE 1.2. Nak's sartorial style is first introduced with a medium shot from behind. Nonzee Nimibutr, *Nang Nak* (1999).

FIGURE 1.3. The scene of parting introduces the ghost's historically inflected contemporary beauty. Nonzee Nimibutr, *Nang Nak* (1999).

While the point-of-view shots inaugurate the desirous gaze on the film's female protagonist, the soundtrack of the opening scene tells yet another story. Even before we see Nak, we hear her weeping, a sound that determines much of the mood of the film and the personhood of its protagonist. The sonic properties of the scene are further complemented by the film's haunting theme music. This composition by Chatchai Pongprapaphan and Pakawat Waiwitaya invents a traditional-style lullaby, the instrumental version of which gradually intensifies throughout the scene of the lovers' parting and the boat's departure, rendered in a traveling shot away from Nak, who is left staggering with grief. In the subsequent days and seasons of Nak's waiting on the pier, a female voice begins to hum the lullaby, doubly marking these as scenes of female melancholy. A male voice summarizing the legend of Nak in a register of literary prose that invokes the authority of custom briefly overlays the tune, before the female voice intensifies into song, this time articulating the lyrics, "Oh la he," the onomatopoeic beginning of a lullaby.[12] At this point the convergence of the male narration of history with the ominous yet captivating dirge presages that the film will predicate its recovery of the national on female suffering. While the narrative authorizes Nak's position within a sentimental national history, the theme music compels us to assume a desirous, nostalgic relation to the femininity at its core.

Nang Nak is the signature film of a reviving and globally circulating national cinema that emerged in the period of political-cultural recontextualization after the Asian economic crisis in 1997. When May Adadol Ingawanij describes *Nang Nak* as a "heritage film," she stresses that this genre's "distinguishing features include an emphasis on marketing, high production values, the presentation of Thainess as a visual attraction, the pastiche of historical personages and traumatic episodes in the biography of the Thai nation, and most significantly the wishful claim to quality as films of a *sakon* or 'international/Western' calibre."[13] As May Adadol argues, the heritage genre is inextricably linked to bourgeois nationalist hopes for economic recovery and the international recognition of Thailand after 1997. What links cinema to politics in May Adadol's investigation are *Nang Nak*'s new look as well as its production and marketing. Her analysis demonstrates that much of the film's appeal lay in its successful rendering of Thainess through a global aesthetic—rather than in the thematization of cultural loss per se.[14]

My analysis focuses on concomitant notions of embodiment in Thai film and politics and argues that the particular contemporaneity that heritage cinema creates for Thainess extends also to the film's presentation of bodies and sexuality. *Nang Nak* combined the new sakon filmic idiom with a highly conservative form of cultural recovery that took recourse especially to bodies and sartorial detail. The film thus aligns its presentation of a particular Buddhist notion of female embodiment with the distressing of bodies and identities in recent state sexual politics.

What further allows Nonzee to present the legend as a distressed genre is his novel choice of references. Rather than cite the nonbourgeois, filmic history of the legend, he draws on its textual versions as well as on histories of the fourth reign, early anthropology and photography, and European accounts of Siamese customs of the time.[15] A significant part of Nonzee's deployment of Buddhism and Thai history is concentrated in the persona of the monk Somdej To. As a high-ranking monk under Rama IV (1851–68), To is closely associated with the nationalist modernizing project of the monarch as well as with notions of national protection in the present.[16] Nonzee's is the first filmic version of the legend to reference elite, royally sponsored Buddhism. In his book about the making of *Nang Nak*, Nonzee further highlights To's trademark blend of eccentric independence afforded by his high monastic rank ("than ja tham arai ko tham tam khwam pho jai khong than [in all his actions, he would only do as he pleased]") with the humility of a popular preacher who never lost touch with the people ("athayasai khong than mi khwam maknoi pen thamada [his disposition was marked by natural humility]").[17] Nonzee thus uses the figure of To, in combination with that of the village abbot, to bring elite Buddhism into close connection with vernacular, popular Buddhist practices. This particular reference enables the articulation of elite, royally sponsored Buddhism with vernacular, popular Buddhist strains. It thereby lets Nak's updated traditional femininity appear in a seemingly specific and historically authentic context in which Buddhism plays a nationally unifying role.

The Social Ordering of Femininity

In the context of contemporary Buddhist-inflected efforts to reinvigorate Thainess, femininity bears some of the burden of organizing claims to coherent national identity. In contemporary cinema, I argue, the ghost, a distressed version of Thai femininity, emerges precisely at the moment when the heretofore dominant form of femininity—that of selectively Westernized, globalized, and economically startlingly productive femininity—had partially exhausted its symbolic effectiveness.

Nang Nak fell into a period in which official politics systematically realigned the connections between economy and culture after the 1997 Asian financial crisis.[18] Since the Ninth National Economic and Social Development Plan (2002–6), the strategy for reentry into economic stability has explicitly been tied to the revival of Thai cultural elements. Thai government and nongovernmental agencies began to espouse the royally initiated "sufficiency policy" (*nayobai khwam pho phieng*) in parallel with liberal, world market–driven reforms. Sufficiency was to apply to sectors of the economy but came to also designate social and moral principles that were to buffer Thailand from further economic and social upheaval. According to its proponents, sufficiency is essentially motivated by Theravadin Buddhist principles of moderation and detachment.[19]

Official bodies such as the National Identity Board, formed in the wake of the state's conflict with communism in the 1970s, initially promoted Thainess as a basis of national security. Since the early 1990s these bodies have sought to rearticulate the nation through an emphasis on culture.[20] The financial crisis of 1997 gave this project its new twist of harnessing culture to the project of Thailand's successful reentry into global competitiveness. The crisis had put an end to hopes for more than marginal participation in the global economy, on which the country had significantly staked its future. Thailand's subsequent "forced acceptance of a bailout from the IMF [International Monetary Fund] . . . led to a general feeling that the country was being colonized by the West, and more specifically by the IMF."[21]

The official postcrisis approach, that of NGOs, and even that of former political radicals banked on the recourse to local values and knowledge (*phumpanya*) as well as economic forms. Calls to look inward and fall back on the sufficiency economy stressed "the need to restrain foreign consumption, the need to harness local resources and capital, the need to withstand materialism and avoid moral decay." The Ninth National Plan therefore stipulated that "engagement with global capitalism is to be achieved while simultaneously maintaining national integrity and identity that 'incorporates local wisdom and retains Thailand's cultural identity.'"[22] The late 1990s and the 2000s were thus a time in which rhetorics of paring down, of rationing, and of exhortations to return to quintessentially Thai ways of living began to acquire high currency. At the same time, emergent conservative discourses on sexuality paralleled the logics of sufficiency in the demands of moderation that they made of femininity in public.

The rationing, national solidarity, and cultural recovery that the state now demanded from the broad population also came to bear on the performance of femininity as a cultural element sustaining national culture. While Thai modernity had once depended on a modernized, selectively Westernized concept of femininity, it now equally depended on the updated notion of an essential, transhistorical Thai femininity. As the political rhetoric after 1997 increasingly appealed to Thainess, a diffuse conglomerate of cultural values and behaviors, it demanded that women bear some of the burden of embodying its anachronisms.

When in the late 1990s national cultural identity began to be closely articulated with normative prescriptions for sexuality in Thailand, the public performance of femininity fell under the renewed scrutiny of the state but also came to stand at the center of new discourses about sexual rights and democratic principles. The state's campaigns of *social ordering* and *cultural monitoring* that were initiated in the early 2000s did not rely on new legislation so much as develop a new language for what femininity in public was (not) supposed to look like.[23] In great measure the efforts at gender and sexual streamlining relied on anachronisms that were anchored in bodies and sartorial detail.[24] Female bodies especially now figured as a baseline cultural good, a kind of heritage.

In this context it became common for intimate bodily detail and sartorial practice to be linked to questions of national-cultural identity and rights.[25] Instead of explicitly emphasizing marriage or reproduction or generating restrictive legislation on a large scale, the moral-disciplinary campaigns singularly concentrated on delimiting the propriety of gendered and sexual bodies in public. Existing legislation, such as zoning laws, was used to enforce these standards. Although it cruelly instructed some bodies— such as that of the actress Chotiros Suriyawong, who appeared in a revealing dress at an awards ceremony and was subsequently punished by her university—in the vocabulary of new Thai virtuous femininity and heteronormativity, state sexual politics concentrated primarily on aiming to control publicly visible forms of sexuality and gender identity. That Chotiros was not tried in a court of law—which would likely have acquitted her of any wrongdoing—but instead shamed publicly and subjected to an internal disciplinary procedure at her educational institution is indicative of current sexual politics' dependence on the development of moral publics rather than on new legislation. Rather than relying solely on active repression, the Thai "sex wars" thus focused on forging new lexicons of femininity and culture and on inducing behavior within certain newly staked-out limits of Thai propriety. While scholars have downplayed the significance of the Thai state's current sexual politics, these more than decade-long efforts to use sexual regulation to attempt control over urban populations can be correlated with and may be as detrimental as other contemporary authoritarian measures.[26]

The Ministry of the Interior's social order campaign furnishes numerous examples of how women's bodies have become targets of regulation. In the public relations publication *Six Months of Social Ordering by the Ministry of the Interior 2*, the deputy minister of the interior, Pracha Malinond, writes up his experiences of bar raids.[27] In the chapter "Tattooed All Over," Pracha begins his first-person account with the observation, "I remember this event very clearly. It is still vivid in my mind, because of the diversity of the kids, teenagers, and different revelers, and because one could see every aspect of the vileness of such an event for young people."[28] In this report Pracha provides a detailed description of the tattooed body of an eighteen-year-old woman. He describes her see-through clothing and the details and locations of her tattoos and piercings. After a team of police and volunteers interviews the club-goer about her history of relationships, the report turns to describing the bodies of other clubbers and closes in an appeal to the remedial "love of the nation." The love advocated by the social order campaign seems to be predicated on the invasive intimacy with female—and queer and transgender—bodies and the transmission of their specifics to the public. As a body of writing, the Ministry of the Interior's publications interpellate a public who will know and monitor these bodies intimately.

A look back at the reversals that have recently occurred regarding notions of femininity and their relations to Thai modernity is instructive. In the boom years of the 1980s and 1990s working women and their prominence in the labor force, service industry, and middle management as well as in distribution and consumption figured as icons of Thai modernity.[29] Since the 1997 economic crisis, however, the specter of an imagined traditional femininity has increasingly defined discourses of Thai modernity. In this context female icons of loss gained special popularity: historical warrior heroines, such as Queen Suriyothai and Princess Suphankalaya, became figures of veneration.[30] These changes in the conceptualization of femininity register in post-1997 Thai cinema's propensity for heritage and horror productions and in films such as *Tawipop* (Siam Renaissance, 2004), which negotiates the question of present-day femininity's capacity to incorporate Thainess through the theme of time travel.

Although the fantasy of a lost Thai standard for femininity now consistently circulates through social policy rhetoric, it is primarily invoked negatively, that is, through complaints about how present-day women depart from its ideal. The past two decades in Thailand thus saw substantial shifts in meanings attached to femininity and sexuality.[31] Legal controversy coincided with and helped to spark a new kind of public "sex talk." In the Thai public sphere sexual choices and behaviors henceforth increasingly came under the purview of the state and became determinative of full citizenship.

By contrast a broad public sphere of publishing, visual cultural production, and activist and academic events also developed emancipatory, liberal as well as radical models of the Thai sexual present. Thus in response to the state's ongoing moral campaigns, a September 2007 article strongly defends the latest trend that has incensed conservative opinion: the author suggests that young women's not wearing underwear underneath short skirts should be understood as an identity practice and a way of claiming space rather than merely spark additional disciplinary rhetoric.[32] A public sphere of alternative discourses about embodiment, sexuality, and public demeanor thus constituted itself as a counterpoint to the rhetorics developed by the state's moral campaigns.

Over Her Dead Body: Body and Pleasure

To an unprecedented extent, Nonzee's adaptation of Nak's story turns on a Buddhist soteriological theme.[33] I use *soteriological* in this context to mean a Theravadin Buddhist conceptualization of salvation that relies on the contemplation of the repulsiveness of the female body. This course of action leads to the realization of the futility of attachment and thereby advances the practitioner's quest for liberation from suffering. Nonzee tells the ghost legend as a story of spiritual realization and elevation, and in this narrative strain Buddhist notions of female embodiment play a central role.

In Theravada Buddhism horrific images of female death and decay figure centrally in a pedagogy that intends therewith to exemplify the truth of impermanence and the futility of attachment and desire. Like other contemporary ghost films, *Nang Nak* draws its references from this tradition of witnessing female death, but it is also indebted to the conventions of *sayasat*, Thai occult, necromantic practices. Both in Theravadin Buddhist soteriology and sayasat imaginaries, female death and sexuality are closely connected, and in both traditions the contemplation of female death contains a component of pleasurable viewing.

In magic, necromantic practices female death is important not only because it has sexual significance but also because the dead female body represents an object by means of which future events can be influenced. Female haunting is understood to derive its strength in particular from forms of suffering linked to the vicissitudes of reproduction or to violations of the female body in life or death. Especially sayasat's wrongful manipulations of the dead female body or fetus become popular themes of ghost films.

Ranging from independent productions to commercial films, transnational coproductions, and a B-movie soft-porn genre, ghost films employ motifs of female death borrowed from Theravada Buddhism and sayasat. These films feature ghosts that are modeled on traditional types—such as the *pop*, *krasue*, and *phi tani*—as well as ghosts based on legends of individuals, such as *Nang Nak*.[34]

In Nonzee's film one of the registers of pleasure is instantiated by the malleability of Nak's body. In Thai ghost films in general, female haunting is a significantly embodied condition: the ghost possesses a changeable, alternately beautiful and decaying body. Most frequently the ghost splits into a spectral body—a temporarily beautiful, resurrected body—and an actual body, that of her corpse. The spectacle of the ghost's changing bodies as well as the final, physical obliteration of the ghost and her desire provide much of the viewing pleasure also in *Nang Nak*.[35] At the same time, in Thai figurations of haunting the domain of the female ghost is also that of transgressive sexuality. In this context her changing forms of embodiment also stand for the persistence and variability of female pleasure and sexual appetite.

Female ghosts in Asian contexts have been understood to represent hyperfemininity. Bliss Lim affirms that in classical Chinese literature death is thought to heighten feminine allure.[36] In the case of Thai female ghosts, hyperfemininity is in large part connected to the ghosts' sexuality. By virtue of her ghostly negativity, the female specter's sexuality is unconstrained and can even be lethal.[37] What is noteworthy about the ghost Nak in Nonzee's rendition, however, is that a "domestication of desire" has occurred, in which the ghost has sublimated her unconstrained sexuality into the desire for a domestic ideal.[38] Only Nak's nightly killings of her enemies bear the trace of the traditional ghost's licentiousness.

Necromantic practices related to the female body are further connected to an economy of loss and material as well as immaterial gain. The magical plenitude that can be gained from occasions of loss, through the manipulation especially of female dead bodies, represents a motif that propels many films' plots; however, the fact that they are transgressions against women is also a concern of the films and is depicted as the cause of haunting and as the injury that demands redress. The fact that necromancy is used as an effect as well as problematized in these films makes for highly ambivalent outcomes regarding their perspectives on gendered violence.

The Sight of the Dead

Nang Nak further participates in a widely accessible and internally diverse public sphere of death imagery. Mark Seltzer has shown that contemporary "wound culture" collapses the boundaries between violent representation and psychic interiors.[39] Such a merging of images and interiors is anticipated in Theravadin Buddhist practices of visualizing death and meditating on corpses, although originally in a different historical context and for the purpose of spiritual advancement. The ways that contemporary Thai wound culture draws on Theravadin Buddhist practices of visualizing death carry broad social, psychological, and political significance in the present.

Alan Klima has interpreted the visual contemplation of death imagery as necessarily effecting progressively transformative results in the Thai political public sphere. Klima takes the ubiquity and speed of circulation of death imagery to be coextensive with the accelerations of technological modernity, violence, and political change in the country. Analyzing the circulation of images of death from massacres of pro-democracy protestors in the 1970s and 1990s, he goes so far as to contend that the Thai public sphere came into being with the emergence of photographic death imagery.[40] According to Klima, it was corpse imagery that brought about democratic change in 1973; he asserts that the intimacy with violent photographic representation continues to have potential for progressive political change in the globalized, capitalist present. He centrally bases his claims on the anti-individualist intent of the Buddhist witnessing of death.[41]

In contrast I argue that the contemporary sphere of public death imagery in Thailand is more variegated.[42] Death imagery does not function only as the guardian of a democratic public sphere. Rather, because it manifests not only in religion, magic practices, and leftist politics but also in the daily news and in leisure viewing, it becomes difficult to sustain the claim of its uniform political effectivity.[43] Thai feminists have criticized the eroticization of images of female corpses in daily print media, but widely available popular magazines such as *Achayakam* (Crime News), *Rueng Phi* (Ghostly Matters), *Trakun Phi* (Ghostly Relations), *Susan Phi* (Ghost Cemetery), *Sayawet* (Necromancy), and *Mae Nak* are a still more specialized niche for the pleasurable viewing especially of female death. These publications variously combine images of gore, ghosts, magic, and soft porn. In these viewing contexts death becomes a register of the sexual, and death images are for pleasurable consumption rather than religious instruction or anti-individualist contemplative practice.

Analyses of the public domain of death in Thailand therefore have to take into account especially the implications of gendered death imagery in the current public sphere as well as in Buddhist practices. As much as the view of the dead female body is supposed affectively to instill the lesson of impermanence, the many modes of pleasurable viewing that it currently affords in the Thai public sphere outweigh its intended religious significance. It is thus imperative to question the categorical assumption that Buddhist wound culture, even in its orthodox textual instantiations, is desirable and that the practice of achieving higher spiritual consciousness over the witnessing of female death is unproblematic.

The Politics of Ghostly Return

Nang Nak is not the only contemporary Thai film that features female haunting. Female death is a ubiquitous trope in the neofolklore of a reviving Thai cinema. The horror-ghost genre has made up a significant part of Thai cinema since 1997, and, as critics have noted, its specters are overwhelmingly female. This predominance of female ghosts in the genre stands in for current crises around femininity; as Adam Knee writes, "The hidden pasts by which these texts are haunted are primarily those pertaining to women's oppression."[44] But while the uncanny decidedly figures unresolved social and political crises in this domain, the manner in which female haunting is ultimately resolved in *Nang Nak* does not offer a feminist vision of social transformation. Focusing on an instance in which ghostly return is not primarily reparative, I thus interrogate notions of haunting's potential for progressive historical and political transformation.

Haunting is often described as the eruption of the past into the present in a manner that effects the reexamination of past injustices and possibly leads to reparation. In this context the ghost can represent a paradigmatic figure of minority subjectivity. Avery Gordon accords strong disruptive potential to such a figure: "Following the ghosts is sometimes about writing ghost stories, stories that not only repair representational mistakes, but also strive to understand the conditions under which a memory was produced in the first place, toward a countermemory, for the future." In this conception ghostly memory is charged with a quasi-redemptive mission, and haunting bears the promise of historical revision. Gordon hopes that the ghost will provide unequivocal testimony for that which conventional justice has overlooked and for those whose stories usually remain untold.[45]

But what of a ghost that does not retrieve suppressed aspects of history? In contrast to Gordon's ideal conceptualization of ghostly return, haunting figures as a more variegated and compromised field of historical and political signification in Thai cinema. In *Nang Nak* and a larger subset of Thai ghost films the ghost's testimony does not always furnish progressively revisionary historical accounts. Rather in many films the nonsynchronicity produced by haunting becomes the very structure through which historical specificity is evacuated from the past. Haunting is purged of any counterhistorical content as the Thai past becomes merely a certain kind of effect.[46] While ghostly return in *Nang Nak* is not primarily reparative, its narrative of temporal disjuncture comes to exemplify the contradictions in current state social projects that desire to moor bodies to recognizably Thai elements yet have them remain superbly malleable in the context of economic flexibility and productivity.

What makes Nonzee's tripartite mise-en-scène of the ghost legend (the brief sequence in which Nak is still alive, the long middle period in which she is able to uphold the ghostly illusion, and the denouement of her haunting) so compelling is that, all along, it is both a narrative of parting and the story of an extended exorcism. As Buddhist pedagogy it uses the story of the lovers' extended leave-taking for instruction in the *trailak* (Thai; the "three characteristics"): the pervasive, general conditions of all existence, constituted by *anijjang* (impermanence), *thukkhang* (suffering), and *annatta* (nonself, nonidentity).[47] For all but a few minutes of the film Nak is already dead and the separation between the lovers is final. However, it is in this space that the intensity of her desire unfolds. As much as she exhibits devotion to Mak, the ghost directs violence against anyone who tries to obstruct her idyll. The action of the film is propelled by the tension between Nak's desire and the villagers' attempts to exorcize the ghost, as well as by the pressures of the ghostly illusion that Nak has to uphold while the realization that his wife is dead slowly dawns upon Mak.

First, Synchrony

Nak and Mak's initial separation establishes the Buddhist-inflected gender politics of the film. Directly after the couple take leave of each other, the narrative proceeds to juxtapose their respective ordeals.[48] The synchrony of the couple's suffering delineates a notion of quintessentially Thai sexual difference rooted in an agricultural and faith-oriented past. Consistently framed by a Theravadin Buddhist narrative of impermanence and by sayasat occult portents, Nak and Mak's separation begins with a juxtaposition of the hard labor that each has to perform. Mak is called away to corvée military duty, while the pregnant Nak tends to the fields at home. The division of labor and synchronous suffering of the couple mark the simultaneity of the time of the nation, but in addition the sequence begins to play out notions of sexual difference in Theravadin Buddhist soteriology.[49]

In a charged scene symbolic of fertility, Nak plows a rice field in the rain. When the pregnant Nak loses her grip on the plow and doubles over in the muddy field, this is the first indication that her fertility, and by implication her ideal femininity, is compromised. Both the labor of pregnancy and the (also gendered) agricultural labor that she is charged with are disrupted at this point. Meanwhile Mak experiences war trauma; he lies wounded on the battlefield, witnesses the death of his close friend Plik, and is finally taken to recuperate at a temple. At this point the most intense juxtaposition of their suffering begins. As May Adadol writes, "[Parallel editing] emphasises the bond of love between them, especially the cross-cutting sequence where both simultaneously fight for their lives: the injured Mak being treated in a Bangkok temple; while Nak is in painful labour at home in Phra Khanong."[50] While the lovers' gendered, synchronous suffering highlights their devotion, it also indicates their divergent yet complementary functions in the social and religious orders.

The sequence ends with Nak's death in childbirth, and a later, repeat account of her demise is juxtaposed with a sex scene after Mak has returned to Phra Khanong. For Nak the sex is interspersed with memories of the pain of childbirth, and sexual climax is juxtaposed with a flashback to the loss of her hold on life. May Adadol explains that the scene thereby makes "the disquieting invocation of the conservative cliché that sex is a danger that a good, loving wife must risk for the satisfaction of her husband."[51] The model of femininity and gender complementarity that emerges thus seems a conventional one. From the beginning of the lovers' separation the film aestheticizes Nak's updated, traditionally inflected femininity in a way that resonates with current searches for a gendered, culturally specific precedent in state sexual politics.

At the same time, the sequence of the couple's initial simultaneous suffering indicates the implications of sexual difference for Theravadin Buddhist soteriology. While there is prayer for the man, as the powerful Abbot To tends to the wounded Mak in the temple, in Phra Khanong only an incompetent or malevolent midwife attends to the woman, invoking occult beliefs as she supervises Nak's labor and perhaps causes her death. This narrative of socioreligiously salient sexual difference will reach its conclusion in the soteriological finale of the film. It is in the charged domain between gendered, national simultaneity and soteriologically relevant noncontemporaneity, however, that the couple's exemplary conjugality attains the greatest symbolic density.

Temporal Incongruity and Sexual Difference

When Nak's death makes the couple noncontemporaneous with each other, the ideal of sexual difference is heightened further. When Mak first returns to Phra Khanong, he does not know that Nak has died and that the woman and baby that he comes home to are ghosts. It is at this point especially that the ghost's determination to uphold conjugal synchrony increases and comes to stand for a national, collective ideal. Now begins the long middle sequence of Nak's hard work to uphold the ghostly illusion. While hinting at its imminent unraveling, the urgency and temporariness of the fantasy also reinforce the dream of cultural-sexual difference that the film sets out.

In this sequence Nak's heartrending efforts to patch up rifts in the ghostly fantasy, her elimination of opponents, and her simultaneous car-ing for her husband and management of her own sorrow stand in for her commitment to new-traditional Thai femininity, as well as for the difficulties of inhabiting it. Always under fire, the urgency of Nak's desires and the intensity of her sorrow in this section also engage our sympathy most strongly.

In parallel, in the Theravadin Buddhist perspective of the film, the ghost's duplicity also represents feminine duplicity. As Liz Wilson explains, Theravada Buddhism depicts *samsāra* itself—the being in and attachment to the world—as feminine and duplicitous.[52] Ghostly femininity thus doubly points to the fact that the world is always bifurcated, simulating durability in an ontological reality defined by impermanence. In this sense the cracks in the ghostly fantasy also always point toward soteriological resolution. Read as Buddhist pedagogy, Nonzee's film sets the ghost up to lead Mak and the viewer out of the *māyā*, the illusory nature, of the world. The cracks in the ghostly world and the little private jokes that Nak makes moreover interpellate the viewer as someone who shares knowledge not only with Nak but with a cultural community that stretches from Southeast Asia to South Asia. The pleasure of recognition finds its culmination in the famous scene of the elongated hand, when Nak's arm stretches to a fantastic length to pick up a lemon that has dropped to the story below her kitchen.[53] On the other hand, temporal and spatial stretching is also productive of pain for the ghost. The radically separate temporalities and spheres of knowledge that the two lovers inhabit are mainly responsible for Nak's suffering. This noncontemporaneity provides the background for Nak's mourning of her own loss of life and love. Her mourning in turn furnishes the film's most compelling mode of remembrance: the fusion of desire and pain in her memory establishes a nostalgic perspective on cultural-sexual difference. The creation of this particular formula of cultural memory over Nak's dead body begins with her own consciousness of her loss.

In the period between her death and her exorcism, Nak has traumatic memories of her first death while experiencing the slow process of her second death open-eyed. In this part of the film the ghost's persona is constituted largely through the constraints and the violence inflicted on her and through a certain concept of female servitude to which she adheres. Significantly Nak's final words to Mak are that she will not be able to *pronibat* (take care of or tend to him) in this life anymore.[54] It is this concept of pronibat in particular that marks Nak's as a femininity that is anchored in tradition. That she mourns femininity at the fraught moment of national(ist) history in which the film is set establishes a historically inaccurate link of the femininity that she embodies to the nation.[55]

Buddhist Melancholia

In *Nang Nak* it is a Buddhist theme that "show[s] us the gap between past and present as a structure of desire."[56] The Theravadin Buddhist convention of figuring the female as horrific is particularly relevant to the history and causality of female haunting in contemporary Thai ghost films. Throughout *Nang Nak* we see Nak change back and forth between her beautiful spectral body and that of a decaying corpse. This kind of transformation figures prominently in Theravadin Buddhist pedagogy, where the dead and decaying female body at once represents the (temporary) object of desire and the object that is supposed to end all desire.

In Buddhism desire is central to an epistemology of suffering and to a soteriology rooted in nonattachment. The *patijjasamutpat* (Sanskrit, *pratītyasamutpāda*; Pali, *paṭiccasamuppāda*), the theory of dependent origination, provides an explanation of the causal chain that produces suffering as the basis of existence in the world. In this theory it is desire (Pali, *taṇhā*; Sanskrit, *tṛṣṇā*, "craving") that gives rise to attachment (*upadāna*, "clinging"). According to the Theravadins, it is at this point, between desire and attachment, that the chain must be broken.

One of the practices used by monks, as well as by a small number of lay practitioners, to break the causality of desire–attachment–suffering is a deliberate and protracted visual encounter with death: *asupha-kamma-than* (Pali, *asubha kammaṭṭhāna*), the meditation on corpses or images of corpses. This practice is supposed to let the beholder of death realize the illusoriness of desire and the futility of attachment. Both in practice and in text and image Buddhist pedagogy repeatedly turns to the female body in this matter.

In Theravada Buddhism the moment of witnessing loss is ideally the moment of realizing the illusoriness of desire. The visual is primary in this process, and horrific figurations of the dead female body are prominent catalysts in it. Examining the instructional use of horrific images of women's bodies in Buddhist hagiographic literature, Wilson notes that "confrontation with death and decay looms large in the history of Buddhism. . . . One of the lessons that the Buddha is said to have taught again and again in his capacity as the head of the monastic order (*sangha*) is the utter perversity of pursuing sexual gratification when the human body, in its natural state, emits substances as foul as those emitted by putrefying corpses." As Wilson shows, however, the moment of "perverse" attachment to the dead woman is also scrutinized for its erotic potential in many Buddhist texts before they end with a spiritual resolution: "The charming but ultimately cadaverous female forms that serve as object lessons for lovelorn monks beckon one moment and repulse the next. As in aversion therapy, the lust of the male spectator is initially engaged but ultimately subverted as an alluring spectacle is transformed into a repulsive one."[57] The sight of the dead woman is thus supposed to free the viewer from worldly illusion and affectively instill in him the lesson of impermanence.

The strength of Wilson's analysis lies in her critique of the extent to which Buddhist pedagogy depends conceptually on infractions of the integrity of female bodies.[58] Wilson concludes, "An integral female body is a threat to the integrity of the *sangha*."[59] I want to draw attention, however, to the conceptual possibilities, especially feminist, afforded by the deferral of detachment that occurs in the contemplation of the female dead.

What Wilson has shown for Buddhist hagiographies also holds true for contemporary Buddhist teaching in Thailand; here contemporary Buddhist didactics likewise rely on images of women as the horrific embodiment of impermanence and illusion.[60] However, the visual encounter with death that is so important in Buddhist disciplines of the self has also been exceptionally productive of other fantasies organized around the dead female body. Although its institutional home is the temple, the motif of the female horrific spills over into popular visual culture.

Instead of only exemplifying the Buddhist truth that all existence is suffering, the story lines of contemporary Thai ghost films write complex plots for female death, desire, and the nature of collective sentiment in this realm. In ghost films Buddhist closure is at least temporarily refused, and the moment of beholding death is drawn out and exploited for its erotic potential. The deferral of detachment provides a space of possibility, and the belatedness of desire in the realm of literalized loss creates a domain for fantasy. The witnessing of death thus precisely does not lead to detachment. The cognitive and affective experience of anijjang (impermanence) does not lead to leaving off attachment or inoculate against further *thuk* (suffering). Instead it sets in motion a persistent attachment to loss or, at most, the redirection of attachment. Thus is formed a whole mode of pleasurable witnessing around Buddhist melancholia, at times with the alibi of following a religious imperative or practice.

A particular form of Buddhist melancholic remembering is evident in the embodied narrative of loss, in which Nak watches her own body gradually fall apart and her hold on the world loosen. On the one hand, this feature of the film almost literalizes Buddhist orthodox expectations of how detaching is supposed to occur. Women especially are supposed to realize the truth of impermanence through contemplation of the repulsiveness of their own bodies. In a key scene set late at night while Mak is asleep, Nak combs her hair with the comb that was ritually broken after her death. When a lock of her hair falls out, she mourns for the dissolution of her body and the inevitable end of her fantasy. Instead of beginning to detach from this fantasy, however, she persists in her desires.

That Nak's body becomes the site and medium of gender nostalgia is most evident in three scenes of flashback memory. These flashbacks culminate in the scene of the ghost's final Buddhist exorcism through the powerful Abbot To.

DETACHMENT

The long sequence in which Nak finally acquiesces to leaving life can be read as providing closure on the incongruities of desire in the film. It is here that the film's Buddhist narrative most strongly underwrites the film's nationalist theme. For the final, successful exorcism, the community is arranged around Nak's grave. The cinematic composition of this scene is noteworthy for the relations it creates between the act of the exorcism and the community and, by extension, between the figuration of femininity-as-impermanence and the nation. A traveling shot from left to right establishes the male villagers and monks as the audience of the event. Slow motion underwrites the sanctity of the moment in which Nak, hailed by Abbot To, subsequently rises from her grave, while Mak, kneeling among the men, also raises his gaze. After traveling back across their attentive faces, the camera switches to a view of the grave from behind the villagers (fig. 1.4). From this position a tracking shot on a pivot indicates that the rebuilding of collectivity is to be achieved *around* Nak's grave: it is over the event of her exorcism that the villagers will reconstitute themselves as a community, with the Buddhist patriarchal authority at their head.

FIGURE 1.4. The community reconstitutes itself around Nak's grave, over the act of her exorcism by Somdej To. Nonzee Nimibutr, *Nang Nak* (1999).

In Stewart's terms, this scene exemplifies the distressed genre's "nostalgia for context, for the heroic past, for moral order, for childhood and the collective experiences of preindustrial life."[61] As Michael Connors explains, in official nationalism "the Thai nation is 'imagined as a happy and calm village.' An immemorial and morally bounded community of intimate ties."[62] The exorcism scene that ends *Nang Nak* replicates such a vision of national communality over the invasive intimacy with Nak's body and psyche.

In close-up mode, cross-fades from the abbot, who sits at the foot of the grave, to Nak, who looks up at him, inaugurate the unequally weighted transaction between nationally consecrated religious authority and female desire (fig. 1.5). As the ghost yields to the abbot's recitation and reasoning, the scene at the graveside invokes all the truisms of Thainess that in the past two decades have gained ascendancy over pluralist and egalitarian values. Around the grave an emotional economy of sufficiency—of communal harmony, the virtues of knowing your place, of graciously giving in, and of nonattachment—is restored as a communal-national characteristic.

In this scene Nak is positioned as the object of loss and the object that generates nostalgic desire. The power of this object, according to Stewart, "arises not from intrinsicality, but from the narrative of the subject [it] engender[s]."[63] The effects of the disciplining of the ghost, which culminates in the chiseling out of a piece of her forehead, and the deployment of femininity as loss in the film are then that they position the viewer as

FIGURE 1.5. Cross-fades indicate the transaction between male religious authority and female desire. Nonzee Nimibutr, *Nang Nak* (1999).

someone deeply and meaningfully connected to the femininity that Nak represents and to its import for perduring cultural community. It is our losing her that immortalizes Nak's femininity in this scene, and throughout the ceremony at the grave traveling shots away from Nak heighten this sensation. As we watch Mak and Nak take leave of each other, we are supposed to attach to the truth of Buddhist principles and to identify with the community that functions so beautifully under these principles.

For Mak the instruction in the trailak (the impermanence, distress, and nonidentity of existence) and in the necessity of detachment seem almost complete at this point. In the last scene of the film, cross-fades from Mak standing in yellow robes and shaved head, attending to Nak's corpse burning on a funeral pyre, indicate the soteriologically relevant transaction that has taken place. Mak takes the robes in order to transfer merit to Nak, but it is also over her dead body that Mak gains entry into one of the highest states of personhood that Thai society offers. The film's final scene highlights the serene beauty of the monastic male, acquired by Mak, in proper Buddhist manner, through the acceptance of his loss and the viewing of the final destruction of Nak's corpse in the crematory fire.

As we view the piece that was taken from Nak's forehead, the final voice-over informs us that it was passed down as an amulet to the historically significant figure of the admiral and magic practitioner Krom Luang Chumphon Khet Udomsak (1880–1923). The voice-over goes on to relate that the forehead-amulet was finally lost and that "only the legend of Nak's love and devotion to her husband is left, an eternal legend that is recounted until today." In the final scenes of the film the social and soteriological division of labor between the man and the woman thus reaches its end point. In this resolution *Nang Nak*'s sayasat, or "death magic"—its manipulation of a female corpse for a future end—lies in how it makes female haunting serviceable to a vision of contemporary gender ideals. Through manipulations of Nak's dead body *Nang Nak* further creates the vision of Thailand as a site of simple splendor and Buddhist-infused intersubjective and communal affective sufficiency. This lost world is cruelly accessed via the psychic and bodily trauma of the female ghost. The villagers' witnessing of the ghost's acquiescence to the ideal of sacrificial femininity seals the vision of the organization of Thainess around sufficiency and Buddhist ethics.

Nak's painful embodied remembering is critically important with regard to the role that gender plays in the film's Buddhist-nationalist vision. During the long process of her final exorcism the ghost flashes back to iconic scenes of her conjugal life. These black-and-white shots are interspersed in the sequence of events at the grave. The semicircular camera movement that marks these flashbacks aids in constituting bourgeois familialism as a cyclical, natural phenomenon. Nak's first flashback memory is of herself and Mak sitting on a wide tree branch as water drops off a leaf. The second flashback, to a moment of play with Mak in the canal, is followed by the view of a field of young rice. Tall trees follow the memory of Mak putting his ear to Nak's pregnant belly. The dream of fertility, growth, and lives unfolding across generations according to natural rhythms comes to an end only when Nak reaches the final memory, of her death in childbirth. A dead leaf falls at the abbot's feet, and he brings his recitation to an end.

Nak's flashbacks are in turn nested within the pivotal tracking shots that mark the sequence of communal restoration around the grave as a whole. The cinematic configuration of the scene thereby further aids in positioning the heterofamilial ideal that the ghost longs for at the center of community and nation.

On the one hand, the theme of Nak's embodied remembering culminates in the idea that the piece that was chiseled from her forehead during the exorcism has become an amulet that symbolizes, and literally embodies, her love and loyalty. The final exorcism would thus have domesticated excessive female desire and made it exemplary for the present. In the realm of ghostly fantasy *Nang Nak* thereby elaborates how cultural recuperation takes recourse to an invasive intimacy with female bodies in order to fashion futurity. On the other hand, the fact that the forehead-amulet was lost can be read as giving the trajectory of Nak's desire yet another twist.

BUDDHISM AND THE FAILURE OF TYPIFICATION

What perspective would a consideration of this ending from the point of view of the story's female protagonist provide? If we do not stop at the categorical resolution that Buddhism provides—the transcension of desire—then Buddhist thinking usefully parses the anachronisms of bodies and desires for us. Nonzee's narrative of love, loss, and detachment does not end with the social and soteriological foreclosure of Nak's desire. Despite the closure that its ending suggests, *Nang Nak* leaves the viewer with a profound impression of the details and persistence of Nak's desire. In this the film is reminiscent of the many Buddhist stories in which women furnish what Wilson calls "object lessons" that are designed to convey the truth of impermanence and the futility of attachment. Although this is the pedagogical intent of such stories, the viewer or reader will hardly (be able to) make the dhammic turn that most of its characters take at the end.

To illustrate this I turn to the hagiographic account of Upagupta and the courtesan Vāsavadattā, which cruelly literalizes Buddhist dynamics of desiring, witnessing, and detaching.[64] At the same time, the story furnishes an alternative account of sexual anachronism, or of how pastness adheres to sexual desire.[65] Valerie Rohy's strategy of "historical anamorphosis," or of "reading aslant" across time, helps to establish commonality between these two temporally divergent texts.[66] Rohy's argument that we can make critical use of a *Nachträglichkeit*, or belatedness, that is always already inherent in perception, psychology, and historical evaluation supports a feminist reading of the historical text.

In the hagiography the beautiful Vāsavadattā desires the perfume merchant Upagupta and repeatedly sends her servant to him to request a meeting. Upagupta's enigmatic response is that he will see her when the time comes. Cut to the scene when Vāsavadattā, who has been brutalized for reasons unrelated to Upagupta, is sitting mutilated and waiting to die in the cremation ground. It is at this point that Upagupta decides that he will see her. His soteriologically motivated pleasure lies in witnessing the fragmented, cut-up, and mutilated body that now properly literalizes the inherent repulsiveness of the female body and the futility of attachment. After seeing Vāsavadattā in this state, Upagupta attains *nonreturning* (the state of *anāgāmin*), while Vāsavadattā dies and also attains a soteriologically more advantageous position (that of a *srotāpanna*, one who has entered the stream), though not equal to that of Upagupta.

Before that occurs, however, much more happens. In addition to literalizing brutal social and soteriological inequalities, both *Nang Nak* and the story of Vāsavadattā fundamentally reflect on the anachronism of desire as such: what the actors in these two stories want is either already in the past, or not yet what they want it to be, or otherwise incongruous with them, in time or space. In the film and the hagiographic text the respective things that Nak and Vāsavadattā want are already in the past. Nak wants back her life as it was, and Vāsavadattā wants Upagupta as he might have been before he became a quasi ascetic. Upagupta in turn wants Vāsavadattā as she will be but isn't yet. Only his desire will ultimately be felicitous, because Vāsavadattā's body happens to change into a state that represents his ideal object of dhammic desire. Before he goes to see her he expresses the past incongruity of his desire, as well as its ultimate felicity, as follows:

When her body was covered with excellent clothes
and bedecked with variegated ornaments,
then it was better for those who have turned away
from rebirth, and are set on liberation,
not to see her.

But now that she has lost her pride,
her passion and her joy,
and has been wounded with sharp swords—
this is the time to see her form
in its true intrinsic nature.[67]

As for Mak, the trajectory of his desire is the opposite of Upagupta's; for him desire seems temporarily congruent: he wants Nak as he thinks she is, but he does not know that she *is not* anymore. When, before his eyes, Nak changes into an object that is not yet the object of his desire, Mak reluctantly adapts his desire to it; witnessing her cremation, he ultimately transforms his desire for Nak into a desire for the dhamma.

The women's desires have been the least felicitous in these scenarios. Yet it is their desires that furnish central themes especially of the film but also of the hagiography. In the text the temporal incongruities of the plot let Vāsavadattā consistently appear as a subject of desire. Even in the cremation ground, as she hears that Upagupta is approaching, she attempts to influence the scenario: "She told her servant girl to gather the hands, feet, nose, and ears that had been cut from her body, and to cover them with a piece of cloth."[68] Whether or not she does so consciously, Vāsavadattā aims to maintain a remnant of the image of her old body and thereby refuses entirely to embody Upagupta's ideal object of desire. What is more, when she addresses Upagupta, it is in the register of complaint. In the course of this complaint, it becomes clear that even at this point she has not entirely given up on her desire:

> Seeing him standing there, Vāsavadattā said: "My lord, when my body was uninjured and well-disposed for sensual pleasure, I sent a servant girl to you again and again, but you only said: 'Sister, it is not yet time for you to see me.' Now my hands and feet and ears and nose have been cut off, and I sit in the mire of my own blood. Why have you come now?" And she added,

> When this body of mine was fit to be seen,
> soft like the womb of a lotus,
> and bedecked with costly garments and jewels,
> then I, the unfortunate one, did not meet you.
> Why have you come here to see me now
> that my body is unfit to be looked at,
> plastered with mud and blood, causing fear,
> having lost its wonder, joy, pleasure, and play?[69]

Distressing as Vāsavadattā's discourse on the incongruity of desires and bodies may be, it also clearly articulates her desire and the pleasure that she took in her body in its former state. Rohy advocates a critical strategy that, on the one hand, plumbs the aesthetic (literary) properties of the historical text itself for access to meanings that may not immediately be evident. While she is referring to the temporal alterity of a narrative structure, we may also direct attention to other textual elements that provide an entry into its queer and feminist "shading[s]." Rohy enlists this strategy for a *queer* historical reading, promising that "the perverse effects of the text appear when observed from the wrong time, through the obliquity of belatedness."[70] Directing similar attention to the narrative properties of the hagiographic text, I argue that we can read it as saying something about women's relations to their bodies and desires. I cite Vāsavadattā's address to Upagupta at length to point out the degree of attention that the poetry devotes to the description of her body in its former state, performing a willful resurrection, at least in language. The extent to which she appears as a self-directed, speaking subject in this passage is particularly noteworthy. Before Upagupta arrived, in the hope that even at this late point he might actually want Vāsavadattā herself, as opposed to desiring her mutilated body only as a pedagogical tool, the servant girl had moreover said to Vāsavadattā, "My lady, that Upagupta to whom you sent me again and again has arrived; surely, he must have come impelled by passion and desire." As an extension of Vāsavadattā's hope for the gratification of her desire, the servant girl's utterance seems almost deliberate in its misrecognition of Upagupta's desire. Even at this belated point the women's narrative hints at the fact that Vāsavadattā's was a desire for pleasurable equity. The qualities that had initially inspired Vāsavadattā's attraction were Upagupta's beauty and honesty. Her fantasy is one of reciprocating these qualities with her own beauty and generosity: "She wished to pursue pleasure with him," the text says, and even waived her fee of five hundred pieces of gold.[71]

Like Vāsavadattā, Nak holds on to her fantasy until the very last moment. Just as Vāsavadattā's despair eloquently conveys also her notion of pleasure, the most significant affective quality of *Nang Nak*—Nak's melancholy—also impresses on the viewer the strength and qualities of Nak's desire. While Vāsavadattā in the end fully accepts the teachings of the dhamma and relinquishes her desires entirely, the nature and trajectory of Nak's desire are slightly different.

In the sequence at the grave Nak can be understood as slowly relinquishing her claims on bourgeois generationality.[72] But this is also the time when she formulates her wish for family and conjugality most precisely. She had expressed her determined adherence to a heterofamilial ideal earlier, when she threatened the villagers, "If you try to separate man, wife, and child, I will kill you." The ghost's adherence to her ideal culminates in the exorcism scene, when, during the Pali recitation that is intended to vanquish the ghost's desire, Nak reviews in great detail her love life as it was and as it could have been, presenting a retrospective summation of the tenacity of her desire.

Following this Mak is called to the graveside, and the lovers have a last conversation about karma and conjugality. Although both invoke Buddhist concepts of karmic predetermination that inform life trajectories, it is only to underwrite their wish for eventual reunion.[73] "Let's be born as man and wife again in a next life," Mak finishes. While we must read this moment as a powerful final invocation of a heterofamilial ideal, we may also understand the scene as one that persuasively details Nak's assertion of her desires. As Mak gets up to leave the grave, the minutely rendered final slipping of Nak's hand from his literalizes Nak's insistence on her desire until the last moment: a close-up shows the lovers' entwined hands and tracks the slow downward trajectory of Nak's hand as it slides from her lover's, attempts a final hold on his fingertips, and, after it has finally slipped from his grasp, still reaches in his direction.

In Buddhist stories such as these the presentation and witnessing of female demise thus also furnish the occasion on which women's desires—for something other than death and spiritual advancement and for a variety of sexual and social pleasures—are most clearly articulated. Read against the grain, Buddhist melancholy highlights women's protest against the trajectories of desire that have been scripted for them. What ultimately resonates long after the supposed end of desire in these two stories are the detailed accounts of what Nak and Vāsavadattā "would have wanted."

The Story of Two Ghosts

I began this analysis by describing how *Nang Nak* can be read as making the legend of Nak available to orthodox Buddhist and nationalist sentiment. Yet the trajectory of Nak's ghostly return provides insight throughout into the breakages of concepts of corporeality and subjectivity that are by force moored to "tradition." Especially the way that the film fuses personal memory with national memory relies on a notion of privacy that is precisely ahistorical and thereby complicates the notion of Nak and Mak's exemplary heterosexuality.

If Buddhist-informed anachronisms are at the basis of sexual difference in this film, there are also ways in which the story makes Mak and Nak semi-contemporaneous again. Mak's status of being alive has been contingent since he and Nak struggled for their lives simultaneously. After his postwar delirium he frequently appears ghostlike, barely hanging on in the realm of the living. Both his war trauma and Nak's passing into another realm have drained him too of some life.

As much as it is invoked in the early scenes, iconic cultural-sexual difference is already severely compromised from the moment Mak returns to Phra Khanong. As they "resume their lives together," the lovers exhibit a companionate ghostly sameness.[74] May Adadol calls Mak's masculinity unusually "credulous" and says that this type of masculinity was claimed as essentially

Thai in the context of the film's reception.[75] However, Mak's masculinity is not only defined by credulity but is also as exhausted as Nak's femininity is dissimulated. With both gender identities somehow bifurcated, theirs thus becomes a kind of ghostly male-female companionship that exemplifies the ultimate untenability of current dominant ideals of sexual difference.

When the first voice-over of the film informs us that Nak's soul lingers, waiting to resume life with her husband, the narrator uses the term *kin yu duai kan*—to cohabit or, literally, "to eat and live together"—invoking an ideal of conjugal domesticity. This is exactly what the two lovers will never do again, however, as they now inhabit different existential realms. In fact when Mak returns to Phra Khanong their short time together is riven with logistical problems for the ghost. For one, it seems as though they never eat together again (at least Nak doesn't—and, as a ghost, cannot—eat) and thus never fully cohabit again in the complete sense of the domestic ideal.[76]

Though described as heteronationalist, Mak and Nak's relationship is severely antagonistic, at least to the immediate community. The hostility of such a conjugal unit to community would then also extend to the implied nation behind it. The idyll that unfolds for a short embattled moment in the secluded forest location takes place in almost total isolation. The couple's domicile, a modest and tranquil traditional Thai wooden house, is located in jungle surroundings that completely cut the pair off from the rest of the community—something that would have been virtually impossible in the late nineteenth-century Siamese life that Nonzee purports to re-create. At such a time a Siamese household would have been distinguished precisely by the lack of such forms of privacy.

What further remains unclear in Nonzee's epic is how the flow of goods and services works. How does Nak shop? Where does their food come from? Where are their relatives? Inasmuch as *Nang Nak* represents an ideal of heterosexual complementary difference for the present, it does not provide a model of how this ideal would be situated in a system of economic exchange—a concern that is pressing for imaginations of sexuality in cultural-nationalist recoveries of viable Thai social models. Although Mak takes part in one instance of communal harvesting, on the whole the conjugal unit seems overly privatized and "sufficient," also in present-day terms.

Even in the context of Buddhist soteriology, sexual difference does not maintain its coherence entirely when both Nak and Mak pass into states of nonworldliness. Whereas Nak may have given up her life so that Mak may live, in the end he abandons worldly life after her exorcism. The idea that haunting hyperbolizes sexual difference and that ghostly return is nationalist can thus not be upheld so seamlessly. In this respect the temporal disjunctures that Nak's insistence on prolonging her love life until after her death brings into play shed light on the fissures of the contemporary notion of culturally inflected sexual difference. Nak's haunting thus also reveals the instability of the sexual forms that present-day culture monitors and policymakers are striving so strenuously to institute at the heart of new understandings of Thainess and Thai economic competitiveness in the world.

Ultimately we can read the nonsustainability of the ghostly fantasy also as marking the untenability of current official notions of sexual difference in Thailand. In the realm of haunting, *Nang Nak* exemplifies both in its aesthetics and its content the ironies of demands for bodies and identities that are required to reference pastness and traditionality, while at the same time having to function competitively for the sake of national economic and cultural futurity. *Nang Nak* thus shows—in sometimes gruesome detail—the impossible relays between modernity and historical mooring demanded of women in contemporary Thailand.

Two more instances of filmic and devotional engagement with women's social and ontological negativity center on the persona of Nak and depart from the Buddhist-nationalist structuring of personhood that *Nang Nak* introduced. While perhaps not globally intelligible as feminist, both cases provide the grounds for women's self-directed negotiations of desire.

The Shrine

I first want to draw attention to a contemporary psychodevotional practice that refigures conventional notions of female negativity. Through the observation of practices at the Bangkok shrine that is dedicated to Nak, we can gain an understanding of how the noncontemporaneous contemporaneity of female haunting contains within it the potential for feminist practices and pleasures. The activities at the shrine to Nak proffer a further example of how agency does not remain foreclosed to women within the necromantic domain.

The practices of the female patrons at the shrine of Mae Nak open up an entirely different perspective on what the ghost's gendered suffering may signify and accomplish. Every day a steady stream of patrons comes to the shrine at Wat Mahabut temple in Phra Khanong, Bangkok. Here Mae Nak is a ghost turned figure of veneration to whom the largely female patrons of the shrine appeal primarily with financial concerns and in matters of love.[77] While the general merit-making activities do not differ from those at other shrines, Nak's areas of competency as well as the gendered makeup of the shrine's patrons are highly distinct. It is precisely the accent on loss in Nak's life that is responsible for her status as a powerful purveyor of material and affective abundance. The women who come to the shrine *bon* (make vows) and thereby initiate a contractual relationship between Nak and themselves.[78] Should the requests they make of the ghost be fulfilled, they will bring previously specified offerings to Nak (*kae bon*).

The accounts of the women describe the trade in affect between themselves and Nak as a highly reflective practice of intrapsychic negotiation. In their activities at the shrine they make use of a semipublic domain in which affective transactions related to loss and abundance take place. Organized around Nak's and their own histories of loss, the women bring into being economies of loss and gain that allow for the alleviation of emotional pain and provide for (anticipated) affective and material abundance. Drawing on the necromantic potentials of femininity and loss, the female patrons of the shrine use a logic of entrusting and delegating, in which Nak (as well as the women themselves) becomes the arbitrator of the incongruities of their desires. While the women's activities may not be globally intelligible as feminist, they engage the nexus of gendered loss and recovery that marks such a significant portion of present-day politics and cultural production in Thailand on their own terms and frequently semicollectively.

Pimpaka Towira's *Mae Nak*

Pimpaka Towira's thirty-minute experimental film, *Mae Nak* (1997), reconfigures the story of the incongruity of gendered bodies and desires of the legend in yet another way. Refusing closure on the problem of Nak's haunting, Pimpaka makes the anachronism of Nak's desire available to feminist interpretation. As in Nonzee's film, in which the story of Nak's slow exorcism exemplifies the way bodies are torn apart by desire and by the political and religious demands that are made of them, in *Mae Nak* desire and social strictures also threaten, even literally, to split bodies.

Buddhist injunctions to detach appear only in the form of a voice-over, a gentle female voice that urges Nak to heed karmic determinacy, *ploy man pai tam kam*. In the rest of the film ritual is held almost entirely in the register of Thai Brahmanism. Although the Brahmin ritualist is hostile to Nak's desire,

FIGURE 1.6. Nak approximates a devotional stance as she scoops up the rice traditionally thought to frighten the ghost. Pimpaka Towira, *Mae Nak* (1997).

the prominent soundtrack of the Sanskrit recitation seems rather to invest Nak's pursuits with an aura of the sacred. Almost without speech, with varied sound effects and very slow movement, *Mae Nak* does not suggest a definite plot but juxtaposes a number of characteristic scenes from the legend. Three scenes of Nak's pleasure stand out. In one she (or someone who impersonates her) simply stands in the sunlight listening to the sound of a children's song, "Mae Sri Oei," that is sung when one "plays ghost." In the final scene of the film Nak stands in an open field, her body whole, signaling that she has survived attempts at obliterating her body and desire. These scenes of Nak's solitary pleasure suggest that in Pimpaka's version Nak has solved the problem of the splitting of bodies by separating from other bodies rather than relinquishing her own. The scene most emblematic of Nak's bliss, however, is one in which she bathes in rice, a thing traditionally thought to frighten the ghost.

The rice scene is preceded by one in which Nak lies on the floor while a female voice urges her to detach. The subsequent scene presents a strong

FIGURE 1.7. In a scene of atypical delectation, Mae Nak savors the rain of rice on her face. Pimpaka Towira, *Mae Nak* (1997).

counterpoint to this doctrinal injunction. Close-ups of falling grains of rice open the detailed rendition of the ghost's atypical delectation. After Nak rises slowly to a seated position, a close-up of the hint of a smile on her face introduces the theme of enjoyment. It is followed by a medium shot in which Nak scoops up rice from the floor. She does so slowly, as though relishing the grain's plenitude. The ceremonial bent of the carefully choreographed scene is further heightened by the monotone of ambient sound that lends Nak's movement an aura of the sacred. As she stands she lifts her hands full of rice and, raising her gaze to its source, approximates a devotional stance (fig. 1.6).

Subsequent close-ups of her feet and medium shots of her head present Nak slowly turning in the shower of rice. The scene ends on a close-up of her face with eyes closed, savoring the rain of rice on her face (fig. 1.7). The ambient sound ceases first, then the sound of the falling rice. The scene's culmination in the ghost's silent immersion in something that is usually associated with her obliteration sketches out a counternormative notion of pleasure for women. Rice in *Mae Nak* thus comes to figure something that, rather than abolish her desire, nourishes the ghost's delectation. The film thereby manages to make an intervention into the conventional positionings of women in relation to ontological negativity. Most provocatively this notion of pleasure includes a durational element, thus defying the notion of femininity-as-impermanence on a fundamental conceptual level.

Buddhist Melancholia: Trauma, Agency, and Pleasure

The figure of Nak and the convention of Buddhist melancholia furnish significant opportunities for feminist conceptualizations and practices. These opportunities are rooted in the ways each case arbitrates the question of detachment. In this context Buddhist temporalities of trauma and their conditions for agency also play an important role. Whereas Buddhist doctrine prescribes detachment, in Nonzee's mainstream *Nang Nak*, in Pimpaka's experimental *Mae Nak*, and in the case of the practitioners at the shrine, detachment is either deferred, does not remain final, or is not attempted in the first place. Rather than aim for the kinds of adjustment that doctrinal Buddhist or conventional psychoanalytic views of the correct relation to a lost object outline, these characters and practitioners persistently inhabit realms of deferral.[79]

Thus we saw how for the protagonist of *Nang Nak* the pull to remain in a relation with the lover and the life lost is much greater than the anticipated release that detachment promises. Buddhist melancholia in *Nang Nak* has nationalist overtones, but for the viewer it entails the ability to observe closely the temporalities, the trajectories, and the question of the durability of desire.

Not only does Buddhist melancholia afford the viewer or reader this vantage point from which to think about desire, but it differs from other notions of melancholy also in its understanding of the relations of trauma and agency. Thus the temporality of trauma within the diegesis of Nonzee's film becomes significant for an understanding of the agency of its protagonist. While it does feature singular traumatic events, such as Nak's death in childbirth, the film sustains an ambiance of traumatic loss throughout. Sonically the traumatic quality of the ghost's everyday is reinforced by the haunting lullaby that furnishes the film's soundtrack. As one of the dominant features of *Nang Nak*, the traditional-style song composed especially for the film is not only an elegy for the ghost baby but figures Nak's painful attachment to an idyll that is always already lost.

The intensity with which trauma is conveyed in *Nang Nak* ultimately references a noneventful conception of trauma.[80] According to this understanding, high-intensity loss and pain furnish a constant over a long duration—a paradigmatically Buddhist conception of the essential suffering, or unsatisfactoriness, of existence.[81] This affective and temporal configuration of the film allows for protracted contemplation of the possibilities of agency, cognition, and pleasure under extreme duress.

The possibilities of agency that Nak retains in this state are greatly reduced, to be sure. Yet the obduracy of her desire trumps religious prescript at the very end. Even when Nak is exorcised, her agency is still not extirpated but instead is displaced onto the intractable repetition of her haunting-desire. Throughout Nak has furthermore approached her trauma open-eyed, so to speak. Cognition is thus not evacuated from the event-duration of trauma. The subject is not rendered incoherent through trauma but rather learns to inhabit the traumatic state in ever more canny ways.[82] This perspective on trauma allows us to move toward a more refined notion of agency, in which agency is not entirely the domain of the subject but a conglomeration of structural conditions and of individual and collective affect—an understanding in which the responsibility for actions and effects is complexly distributed.[83]

In the case of the practitioners at the shrine, their psychodevotional practice also relies on a notion of dispersed agency. The women enlist additional help in their continued relation with various lost objects. The figure with whom agency is shared—Nak as a devotional figure—is not debilitated by her history of loss but instead becomes powerfully agentive because of it. The practitioners thus tap into the necromantic power of her experience of (ghostly) negativity.

It is the experimental rendition of Nak's story by a director whose work is singularly attuned to female figures that makes the greatest departure from the conventional logics of social and ontological female negativity. Pimpaka's *Mae Nak* provides the viewer with a notion of pleasure for women that, although rooted in negativity, does not hinge on sacrificial absorption into a collective. In this *Mae Nak* inhabits the sphere of loss as much as Nonzee's mainstream adaptation. What the experimental film recuperates from loss, however, is not the triumphant coherence of community but rather a form of pleasure that appears to remain solitary. Instead of being exorcised in the midst of community, Nak stands alone at the end of the film. *Mae Nak* thus draws on the temporal difference of haunting in order to create a zone in which the exigencies of community cannot fully encroach on female bodies.

Both *Nang Nak* and *Mae Nak* seek the adjudication of the problem of women's desires in realms ostensibly beyond the secular law, the nation, and other liberal domains. However, its feminist subtext notwithstanding, *Nang Nak* integrates Buddhist-inflected haunting into a nationalist framework, and the ghost's contravening of and eventual succumbing to religious dicta therefore also have national implications. The nation thus becomes vitally influential in the film's rendition of Nak's quest for pleasure.

In contrast Pimpaka's separation of Nak from community charts a very different route for the ghost's pleasure—decidedly one in which it is not defined by the exigencies of nationalism. Although *Mae Nak*'s ending appears to advocate separation from community, the ghost's pleasure never appears subsidiary or only circumstantial. The film does not link her pleasure so much to a male object of desire; rather, after highlighting Mak's betrayal of his beloved early on, it focuses on the modes of pleasure that Nak develops thereafter. In Pimpaka's rendition the scenes of Nak's pleasure let it appear complete in itself, a rendition that does not displace pleasure onto the desperate obduracy and cyclicality of female haunting. The film thus models ways of inhabiting the domain of female ghostly negativity that have as yet found no equal or precedent in the presentation of female pleasure in the horror-ghost genre.

Itself the product of transnational collaboration, the 2002 Thai–Hong Kong–Singaporean coproduction *The Eye*—titled *Khon Hen Phi* (The Ghost Seer) in Thai and *Gihn Gwai* (Seeing Ghosts) in Cantonese—tells the story of a transnational female and Chinese possession. The film's heroine, Wong Ka Man, does not choose to see the ghostly visions that appear to her with increasing regularity; rather they force themselves on her perception after a corneal transplant. As visions of the dead and those about to die encroach on her, all of Man's private as well as public spaces in her native Hong Kong turn into sites of spectral terror; the source that generates them, however, remains unidentifiable.

Ultimately the possession leads Man to Thailand, where a complex story of individual loss and ethnic denigration is revealed to be at the core of haunting. Man traces her new eyes to a Thai donor, Ling, a young woman who happens also to have been Chinese and who committed suicide because her gift of foresight remained unrecognized. Man's possession is moreover propelled by an additional, mass disaster that manifests only in the final scene and that further complicates the story of transnational haunting.

This chapter investigates how the directors Danny and Oxide Pang use the intersubjectivity between the two Chinese women that is established through the corneal transplant to interrogate a specific problem in the understanding of transnational Chineseness in Thailand. In particular I argue that *The Eye* enables a critical perspective on the recent transformation of Chinese femininity from denigrated minority identity to trans-Asian, cosmopolitan ideal in Thailand. The analysis thus takes up the question of whether the attainment of a position of desirability in the present is sufficiently reparative with regard to a history of Chinese denigration in Thailand.

If horror allegorizes cultural shifts, I propose that *The Eye* further uses the motifs of haunting vision and embodiment to gauge the commensurability of Chineseness across the diasporic constituencies of Thailand and Hong Kong in the present.[1] *The Eye* was produced in a distinctly transnational historical context, a period in the 1990s and 2000s, in which Chinese economic ascendancy was articulated with economic, political, and cultural realignment in Asia as well as with the increased validation of transnational Chinese communities.

While Chinese communities in Thailand (Siam) were historically subject to varying degrees of social and political exclusion, Chinese migrant labor and entrepreneurship were also central to the Thai economy. That Chinese Thais have today attained positions of social and political centrality results in part from the migrants' and subsequent generations' persistent labor as agents of modernization and national economic prosperity. Mainland Chinese economic ascendancy since the late 1970s and the resultant political and economic realignments in the region may be understood to accelerate this process further.

While this chapter investigates how *The Eye*'s theme of haunted witnessing parses the complexities of uncovering a minority history, it also asks what is at stake when this history is recovered under the sign of Chinese economic and cultural ascendancy. The previous chapter detailed how the femininity of *Nang Nak* became iconic of directions in post-1997 nationalist policy in Thailand; this chapter examines the salience of a transnational female subject position in Thailand. Rather than primarily determined by its relation to activities of the state, femininity in *The Eye* is, in further contrast to the preceding chapter's analysis, linked to historical and contemporary transnational flows of populations, capital, and affect. Tani Barlow has shown that femininity was historically inextricably linked to the idea of globalized modernity itself.[2] I argue analogously that *The Eye* addresses a contemporary context in which femininity retains its privileged relation to economic and social futurity, albeit under a different paradigm of globalization.

The analysis thus tracks the logics of minoritization and the arbitration of past injury in the context of a female ethnic subject's haunting across time and space. The two ideological contexts that this subject has to straddle in *The Eye* include a neoliberal economic order (in which determinations of value dominate, if not replace, history) and an ethical relation to history and past injury. To disentangle the logics of the haunting, the heroine, with the assistance of the ghost, has to reexperience the melancholy of a minority position, to unravel a history of assimilation, and to grapple with how catastrophe affects minority politics.

Much of my analysis is devoted to assessing whether *The Eye*'s deployment of haunted intersubjectivity lives up to the promise of establishing a progressive transdiasporic relation between Hong Kong and Chinese Thai communities as well as between the past and the present. What salience does Chinese femininity acquire with regard to a politics of transdiasporic solidarity and ethnic kinship in this story? I use *diasporic* after Gayatri Gopinath to examine a position with the potential to resist both nationalist as well as transnational capitalist logics.[3] I use *diasporic* in relation to Hong Kong to designate a position of commonality with Thailand vis-à-vis the People's Republic of China. In many other respects Hong Kong figures as a homeland or repository of a classical Chinese culture in the film. Finally I take into account how *The Eye*'s invocation of transdiasporic Chinese solidarity is troubled by the continued tendency in the Hong Kong cultural imaginary to view Thailand as a terrain of ghostly alterity.

The previous chapter detailed how female haunting is such an overdetermined force in the imaginary of contemporary Thai cinema that it would seem as though other cases would merely provide more variations on this theme. While much of Thai and coproduced horror does bring women's grievances to light, the genre's resolutions of haunting foreground the pleasurable witnessing of the elasticity and destruction of female bodies.

While the majority of scholarly investigations of haunting equate the shattering effect that characterizes Freud's notion of the uncanny with a nearly automatic shift in historical or political consciousness, the previous chapter showed that a substantial section of the Thai ghost genre neutralizes the progressively transformative potential of haunting. Although haunting appears as a shattering effect in such stories, it precisely does not bring about a transformation of historical consciousness on the part of the viewer or even within the diegeses of the films.

The Pangs' *The Eye*, however, occupies the tradition of female haunting with an entirely different relation to history, conscience, and embodiment. At the same time, the film continues to privilege the feminine senses as the collective aesthetic register for coming to terms with political subjectivity in the contemporary world.

Significantly the film's inquiry into trans-Asian Chineseness is transacted in the register of witnessing and experiencing the pain of another. "I saw and encountered the same kind of pain that she did," Man concludes upon her return from Thailand, where she followed Ling's story. As much as *The Eye* presents a story of and desire for Chinese transnationality, it tells this story in the frame of traumatic witnessing.

The film begins with a glimpse of Man's life before the cornea transplant and then cuts to a longer sequence in the hospital, after the operation. As Man slowly regains vision, "images of the recently dead, and of those about to die, keep breaking the surface of her everyday reality in Hong Kong." Man now clearly sees ghosts in all parts of the city and in her home. Even "her dreams are afflicted by grotesque and inexplicable visions, glimpses of what seems to be another, unhappier life."[4] Blind since early childhood, Man has to learn how to see all over again. The difficulties of this learning process blend with the incertitudes caused by the haunting visual intrusions. From the beginning *The Eye* uses this confusion to signal skepticism about the reliability of superficial cognition of the world as well as to bring into being a connection of compelling urgency between a middle-class woman in Hong Kong and a traumatic history in a faraway place.

With the motif of the organ transplant *The Eye* joins a long cinematic history of what Alison Landsberg has described as "prosthetic memory," an intersubjective transmission of memory and a process that several films represent through the motif of organ transplants.[5] In *The Eye* it is by virtue of the corneal graft that Man is affected not only by personal trauma but also by traumatic aspects of Chinese Thai history. Throughout the film the sense of seeing becomes a literalization of two problems: of being set apart through privileged knowledge and of being haunted by both a past and a future. Both problems become representative of minority Chinese positions in the story. Ultimately Man's prosthetic seeing of traumatic pasts and disas-

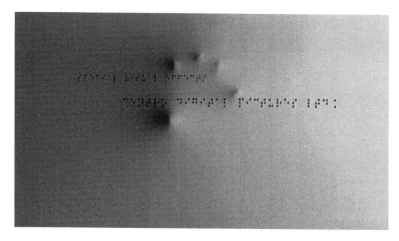

FIGURE 2.1. The opening of *The Eye* (Danny and Oxide Pang, 2002) signals that its mode of apprehending history will rely not only on the ocular but also on the haptic sense.

trous futures allows the viewer to gain a perspective on what happens to the past when an ethnic position shifts out of its status of minoritization.

Witnessing in *The Eye* is transacted not only through the sense of vision, however, but also through the embodied experience of another's life. Already the film's opening sequence habituates the viewer to a particular mode of access to the history that will be recovered. Hands press and move against a screen from behind, miming the quest of something as yet unseen to attain intelligibility. With their fourth movement across the screen, the hands begin to write the film's title in Braille; it is again touch that subsequently changes the Braille title into English and Chinese writing (fig. 2.1). This scene announces the subject matter of *The Eye* as one that has to be decoded and intimates that an understanding of history is to be accomplished also through "feeling" it. While the film's mode of *Einfühlung* (empathy or, literally, "feeling-in") in large part does rely on the sense of vision, *The Eye* complicates the notion that the ocular stands in for authoritative knowledge of history. The haptic sense foregrounded in the opening typifies a method of apprehending history that relies on multiple senses and is grounded in affective, embodied experience.[6] In the story this strategy of access to history is actualized by the melancholy possession that befalls Man and that allows her affectively to reencounter parts of a distant stranger's past.

The divergent temporalities of haunting in *The Eye* further inform a particular notion of agency. The collaborative action of the living and the dead woman across temporal zones indicates that the film considers the repair of minority injury to be a matter of female agency as well as one that has to be approached transnationally. Women's desires are largely directed toward historical agency in this story. In this context haunting is once again framed in Buddhist terms. Unlike in *Nang Nak*, the Pang brothers' cinema does not reference Buddhism in a nationalist context but presents it as a transcultural formation that furnishes the imperative for collective action on behalf of others. Notably this formation crosses the boundaries of Theravada and Mahayana Buddhist lines of thought. Buddhism is further depicted as a resource that supplies essential knowledge for everyday coping and provides a map for coming to terms with loss across Asia.

Rendered in the "'low' body genre of horror," the story that *The Eye* recovers makes an urgent claim on the viewer.[7] It compels us viscerally to apprehend Chinese Thai histories as traumatic. The mode of horror makes a case for the proper uncanniness of this history and attempts to shatter the resistance to engagement with its traumatic aspects.

Chinese Cultural Revival and the Visual Reclamation of Femininity

The premise of this chapter is that haunting's allegory in *The Eye* is both national and transnational. It is with the national story, the other "unhappier life" revealed by transnational haunting, that my analysis begins.[8] Scholarly accounts of Chinese Thai history in the twentieth century focus on the vicissitudes of Chinese belonging under the formation of an exclusionary nationalism. Since the beginning of the twentieth century, notions of Thai nationhood and modernity had in part depended on the exclusion of the Chinese, or what Kasian Tejapira has called an "imagined uncommunity."[9] On the other hand, since the 1950s the notion of assimilation has to an extent negated the continuity of a distinct Chinese culture in Thailand—as well as neutralized the critical potential of a position coded as antinational. In contrast the present sees the ascendancy of a Chinese transcultural identity, in particular feminine, into desirable subjectivity. In the past two decades articles with titles like "Sino Chic: Suddenly, It's Cool to Be Chinese" began to appear in Thai and regional newspapers, pointing to the fact that Chineseness was acquiring new status in Thailand.[10]

Kasian describes this emergence from a history of social negativity: "The Thai-speaking *lookjin* [ethnic Chinese] middle class, after many years of public reticence about their Chineseness, were now finally 'coming out of the closet.'" It is this established and educated middle class of Chinese descent that Kasian names the driving force of the revival.[11] In that sense the persistent move toward social centrality of the Chinese in Thailand would then have brought the project of integration to fruition for the second and third generations of Chinese immigrants. It is only after having reached this stage that the reclaiming of Chinese identities became possible, according to this analysis. Despite the giddy sense of having arrived that Kasian's account intimates, however, pop cultural and essayistic evaluations by no means address the immense shift in the valences of Chineseness only in triumphant tones.

In the context of the *krasae jin* (the Chinese trend) that evolved in the past two decades, Chinese femininity was reclaimed visually in lifestyle magazines and advertising and became fashionable. Whereas until then Chinese looks were frequently disparaged, in the early 1990s the phrase *khao suai muai sek* (pale, beautiful, Chinese, and sexy) became popular.[12] A text that exemplifies the gendered facet of new Thai-Chineseness as well as the consciousness of its historical negativity particularly well is the Thai lifestyle magazine *Dajiahao* (Hello Everyone!), which targets a readership that Francis Nantasukhon labels "indie-hip" teenagers.[13] The cover of the August 2005 issue features a young woman in jeans and a tank top, a model named Ja, who will present the issue's cover story about a trip to Shanghai (fig. 2.2).[14] The mix of the cover's global references is striking; the issue is titled "East Meets West," in English, with the subtitle "Ja's round [small] world in Shanghai" in Thai.[15] We can understand the cover as iconic of the current moment of aspirations to trans-Asian Chinese globality and Ja as embodying a femininity that is strongly linked to middle-class consumer sensibilities.

In her analysis of advertising ephemera in early twentieth-century China, Barlow argues against a reductive reading that understands femininity in commercial images either solely as representative or simply as exemplifying the logics of capital. Instead Barlow stresses that femininity in these ads performs a particular type of intellection and introduces desire into the scene of commodification, gender, and modernization: "This argument holds that commercial drawings do not exactly *represent* the social,

FIGURE 2.2. *Dajiahao*, August 2005, cover. The model reaches toward the horizons of the new global Chineseness.

but rather are pictorializations of the social experiences to come, dreams of the future, 'forms of thought whose ontological status is not that of thought.'"[16]

As a graphic and photographic document that is not drawn from advertising per se, the *Dajiahao* cover is positioned differently within the nexus of intellection and desire that Barlow describes. For one, Ja does not advertise a specific commodity but rather represents a physical ideal of Chinese femininity that translates across East Asian and Southeast Asian locations.[17] However, the representative function of the image is augmented by further performative elements. On the cover a red sun with the yellow stars of the national flag of the People's Republic of China radiates out from behind the model. Ja holds out her hand as though holding a globe, signaling an equally competent and enthusiastic stance toward the (future) world illuminated by the rays of this sun. Her gaze too is raised, as though toward the horizon of the new global Chineseness.

The August 2005 issue of *Dajiahao* includes articles on advertising, film, architecture, the Chinese economy, product reviews (for instance, of a Chinese dictionary that can be worn around the waist), Chinese history, magazine covers with Chinese themes, Chinese Thai coffee culture, learning Chinese, and an interview with a lesbian activist. Reader reviews and letters indicate that young, trendy Chinese Thais are ready to participate in Chinese cultural and consumer activities and to bring their own particular mix of globalized Thainess to this new trans-Asian Chinese world. Extrapolating from the magazine's content, the woman on the cover participates in an educated, already globalized femininity, to which are added facets of new transcultural Chineseness. Her gesture in the image performs a desirous reaching toward the economic and "social experiences to come"—the centering of Chinese communities across Asia.

However, *Dajiahao* also shows us that the investment in present-day trans-Asian Chineseness cannot forgo a consideration of the violence of its historical minoritization. Francis Nantasukhon writes that *Dajiahao* developed from a "community zine" into a fully commercial "lifestyle-driven" publication that caters to the emergent market segment of the "hip Chinese" or "indie-hip" generation.[18] As such the publication addresses a trendy, simultaneously consumption-oriented and newly heritage-conscious group. The magazine's commercial orientation notwithstanding, *Dajiahao* does not pass over the still recent fact of Chinese denigration in Thailand.[19] Thus the August 2005 issue reclaims some of the derogatory language around

Chineseness in Thai everyday usage, recontextualizing epithets such as *ta yi* (slit eyes), *muai* (Chinese girl), and *jek* (Chinese). Tracing the new valences of once-denigrated Chinese looks, the article "Regarding China through Slit Eyes: Looking at Chinese Women in Chinese Beauty (1)," undertakes a detailed consideration of how a history of disparagement of Chinese looks morphs into a present of appreciation.

As both a document and a product of current transnational Chinese flows, the Pangs' *The Eye* works within a similar logic. As such *The Eye* is one of the first contemporary films to mobilize the moment of cultural revival for the consideration of the traumatic aspects of Chinese Thai history.[20] The film performs this task through extended deliberation on the possibility of women's agency. In this context I pose a question about gender in horror cinema that diverges from those in previous analyses. While the predominance of women in Thai and other Asian horror and ghost films has been noted, the female ghosts' predicaments have largely been read with a view to critiquing notions of sexual difference. Queer and feminist analyses of U.S. and European horror films have likewise focused on tracking motifs of gender transgression and interpreted symbols of homosociality as homoeroticism. In contrast I argue that women's homosociality is primarily put to a different task in the Pang brothers' films. In *The Eye* as well as in *The Eye 2* (Cantonese, *Gihn Gwai 2*, 2004) and Oxide Pang's *Ab-normal Beauty* (Cantonese, *Sei Mong Se Jun*, 2004), women represent the main actors: it is solely women who are charged with social and historical agency, with acquiring knowledge of the past and competency in domains of loss, and with suturing past negativity to the present. In this cinema female collectivity becomes the basis from which problems of historical and political agency are worked through.

Hong Kong–Thai Coproduction

The move of Chineseness from denigrated minority identity to desirable transcultural capital not only registers in the history of Thai cinema but is determined also by changes in the industrial background of East and Southeast Asian film production.[21] At the same time as the status of being lookjin increased in desirability, the conditions of Thai film production diversified. According to Adam Knee, *The Eye* inaugurates a new mode of pan-Asian cinematic production and storytelling in the 2000s.[22] In a 2002 interview Peter Chan, one of the producers of *The Eye*, attributes generic openness and vigor to films from Korea and Thailand and the ability to fill the gap of an exhausted Hong Kong market and production scene.[23] Originally from Hong Kong, Danny and Oxide Pang began to direct and produce films in Thailand in the early 1990s and became the two most prolific and recognized filmmakers to engage in such coproduction. Most of their films are coproductions; some, such as *Re-cycle* (Cantonese, *Gwai Wik*, 2006) or *Ab-normal Beauty*, may have no obvious Thai content, while *Leave Me Alone* (Cantonese, *Ah Ma Yau Nan*, Danny Pang, 2004), *The Eye* (2002), *The Eye 2* (2004), and *The Eye 10* (Cantonese, *Gihn Gwai 10*, Danny and Oxide Pang, 2005) feature movement between Hong Kong and Thailand as a substantial part of their plots. The Pang brothers' films further exemplify Thai cinema's imbrication in a "pan-Asian coproduction sphere" not only in their industrial background but also with respect to the visual spheres that they occupy and the desire for trans-Asian Chineseness that they mediate. This is borne out by *The Eye* and its sequels *The Eye 2* and *The Eye 10*. The Pang brothers' films stand in a complex relation to invocations of transnational Chinese ascendancy. For one, this cinema itself participates in transnational flows of Chinese capital, cultural production, and validation. Yet these films' stories do not present exact parallels to their conditions of production.

My analysis takes as its premise the notion that both Thailand and also Hong Kong are featured as diasporic sites in *The Eye*. In the context of a coproduced story about Chineseness, Hong Kong's own history of oppression of Chinese populations and of forced de-Sinicization under colonial rule can be expected to contribute an informed empathetic view on Chinese oppression in Thailand.

As a coproduction *The Eye* also occupies a potentially critical relation to mainland Chinese hegemony.[24] Even after its return to China in 1997, the city-state's historical, political, and cultural makeup differs significantly from that of the mainland. During Hong Kong's phased transfer of sovereignty, its political activism and sections of its cinema have been strongly identified with resistance to mainland Chinese hegemony. What is more, in *The Eye* Hong Kong appears in a realist, quotidian mode, providing a counterpoint to prevalent depictions of the city as a glitzy economic powerhouse, thus undermining the triumphalist stance toward transnational Chinese ascendancy.

To get to the ghost and the ghost's story, it is necessary to understand how the past, even if it is just the past that flickered by a moment before, can be seized in an instant, or how it might seize you first.—AVERY GORDON, *Ghostly Matters*

After much torment and with much difficulty Man and her young psychiatrist, Wah, trace the origin of Man's new eyes to a small provincial hospital in central Thailand. When they finally arrive at Sayam Rat hospital, Wah speaks to the front desk to inquire about Dr. Ek, whom the transplant documents name as a contact, while Man surveys the premises of the hospital. The dark wood interior of the provincial government building and the low-key lighting of the scene make Sayam Rat appear abject, emphasizing the patients' disabilities, poverty, and frailty. A black crow's low caw and a curtain moving in the wind draw Man's attention to a corridor of the hospital and cue her in to a memory. Rather than repeat an exclusively visual memory, however, the scene actualizes a memory that is composed of several sensory impressions. A tracking shot of the corridor's ceiling makes sense of Man's heightened auditory and visual awareness: she is reliving an experience from the position of a patient wheeled along on a stretcher. Framed by point-of-view shots, the scene alternates views of Man's face and the corridor with close-ups of details, such as the shoes of a patient, the crow, and the curtain. The extradiegetic soundtrack of a drumbeat accompanied by metallic crescendo effects that signify apprehension further designate the hospital a site of the ominous. For Man the sonic properties and visual details of its hallway mesh with the sensory memory of what she calls her "nightmares." When the drumbeat segues into the rhythmic noise of an approaching stretcher, Man's disjointed sensory impressions cohere into the realization that Sayam Rat is the origin of the ghostly visions that came with her implanted corneas. When she sees the patient with bandaged eyes on the stretcher, Man identifies the multiple sensory memories that she is having as those of a patient in a state of traumatic injury—and as stemming from Ling's experience.

Dr. Ek, the physician in charge of the organ donation, at first refuses to divulge information about the source of Man's transplants. However, when Man blurts out, "I see the things that Ling used to see," he agrees to take Man and Wah to the family of Ling, the organ donor from whom Man received her corneas. It is at this moment that Man for the first time formulates that she is experiencing an instance of what Landsberg has called "prosthetic memory," the taking on of the memory of another—a memory that one cannot have because the event that precipitated it is removed in time or space. It thus enables the preservation of memories of others, even whole generations, who are or will soon no longer be alive. Landsberg describes the cinema as a technology of prosthetic memory, a medium that allows for the transmission of memory on a mass scale. With the motif of the corneal transplant, *The Eye* literalizes such prosthetic remembering and aims to bring to fruition its historical task. Through Ling's eyes and other sensory memories Man "remembers, responding to a series of questions, lost objects, languages and selves."[25] Gradually her ghost-seeing uncovers a story that would otherwise stop circulating. This remembering is not undertaken voluntarily, however; rather prosthetic memory is forced upon her through a kind of melancholy possession. The violence of this possession figures the unyielding claim that the other woman's history makes on Man across diasporic constituencies.

While until this point Man has had only disjointed, frightening glimpses of scenes that may be connected to Ling's life, she will now witness the history of the other woman in a more coherent form. As Ek tells Man and Wah, Ling had since childhood been able to predict disaster, but her gift of foresight only drew hostility from her community. A final instance of foresight occurred when, as a young adult, Ling foresaw a fire that would kill several hundred people. When her warning went unheeded, she committed suicide by hanging herself. Man and Wah spend the night at Ling's house, and a scene of exorcism of and for Ling's ghost—and what seems to be therapeutic catharsis for Man—follows.

Man recognizes Ling's room from her nightmares in Hong Kong. The exorcism proceeds through her verbal entreaty to Ling to reveal the conundrum of her haunting: "What is it that you have wanted to tell me?" In this scene the nearly black-and-white chiaroscuro close-ups of Man's face and eyes signal the clarity of cognition that she is about to achieve and announce the film's switch to the historical mode (fig. 2.3). The revelation takes the form of a discrete inset: a black-and-white flashback survey of Ling's life imparts the information to Man that with Ling's corneas she has inherited her gift for seeing impending death. Witnessing Ling's biography as a series of scenes of persecution, Man comes to understand the fraught position of a visionary and marginalized outsider—a position whose links to Ling's Chineseness the film continually highlights—as the cause of Man's haunting vision. Abruptly interspersed, the flashback sequence shocks with images of children running after Ling at the age of about six years, throwing objects and screaming insults. This is followed by several shots of adults chasing Ling away from sites of accidents as well as from play with other children and culminates in scenes of strife with her community as a young adult.

The quasi-documentary quality of the black-and-white flashback that discloses this story to Man marks this narrative as historical. Except briefly after the exorcism, Ling's character appears only in black-and-white episodes, as a historical person living through historical incidents. The story behind Ling's haunting is thus rendered in the idiom of "documentary evidentiality": these scenes deploy the documentary's "claimed capacity to reference the world."[26] However, the sequence endows what Man sees not so much with the authority of historical veracity as with the status of being an item of *collective* record (fig. 2.4).

Jean Ma notes "the flashback's potential as a device for representing memory beyond the parameters of an individual character's subjectivity" with regard to a sequence in Hou Hsiao-hsien's *A City of Sadness* (1989). Ma explains, "In this chain of overlapping remembrances, it is difficult to discern where one memory ends and another begins. The elliptical progression of this series of shots discloses a shared consciousness, a floating and heterogeneous subjectivity. By disarticulating the link between the flashback and individual character perspective, Hou captures the sense of a plural subject of memory emerging across time, collectively authored by an exchange of stories and objects."[27] Thus while Man "sees" the truth of Ling's predicament in the flashback sequence, the filmic characteristics of the sequence deprivatize this vision and endow it with the significance of collective historical memory.

While it is primarily due to her prescience that Ling is discriminated against, the resolution sequence in Thailand as a whole also clearly presents her as Chinese, and we can understand her position as allegorical of Chinese minoritization in Thailand. That the occurrences of haunting in the film stand in for the vicissitudes of such a position may not be completely self-evident at first. However, images of the abuse of a Chinese woman by a group of people in Southeast Asia strongly recall incidents of anti-Chinese violence in the region. The telescoping into biography thus records a local story of subordination, an internal social displacement that the film personalizes. Insistent references throughout the film to the Thai

FIGURE 2.3. Man is about to achieve clarity regarding the origin of her possession. Danny and Oxide Pang, *The Eye* (2002).

FIGURE 2.4. Man sees Ling's history of strife with and persecution by her community in the historical mode. Danny and Oxide Pang, *The Eye* (2002).

main character's ethnic background and her special powers substantiate this claim.

Ling's final attempt as a young adult to warn members of her community of impending disaster is again met with abuse. The biographic sketch culminates in a series of abrupt cuts that show Ling stepping up onto a chair and repeatedly hanging herself in a sling. At this moment the interspersing of still photographic images interrupts the continuity editing of the scene, indicating that Man has not yet achieved full cognition of the problem of Ling's haunting. Although the black-and-white inset has clarified Ling's story for Man, the scene's end intimates that (haunted) vision alone is not sufficient for resolution.

From the information divulged in the flashback sequence, Man realizes that Ling "is not dead" but caught in nightly repetitions of her hanging—a time warp of suicides. Her sorrow over her inability to save lives as well as unresolved conflict with her mother drive Ling's ghost to hang herself repeatedly at a certain time every night. Man fails to persuade Ling's mother, Aunt Chui, to come upstairs to reconcile with her daughter. Returning to the room alone, Man sees Ling step up onto a chair and hang herself. All subsequent shots of the hanging cut back and forth between Man's face in the sling, black-and-white shots of Ling's face, and Ling/Man's dangling feet. The fast-paced scene repeatedly cuts to shots of Aunt Chui in the living room and to an agitated exchange between mother and daughter. The dialogue ends in reconciliation, with Aunt Chui's Chinese exclamation "Ah Ling!" before she runs upstairs to release Ling/Man from the noose. Crying, Ling/Man apologizes to her mother.

Man's coming to Thailand thus seems to have quelled haunting and effected reconciliation between mother and daughter. As she relived Ling's trauma, Man also encountered an episode of Chinese Thai history. Ling's story allegorizes a Chinese Thai history marked by legal and social exclusion. Simultaneously, by allowing Chineseness to reappear as difference, it represents an anti-assimilationist move in the film.

Academic writing of the past two decades has struggled to provide accounts of the historical causalities of anti-Chinese sentiment in Thailand. According to Kasian, the history of the Chinese in Thailand is characterized by the expressly "imagined uncommunity" between ethnic Thais and Chinese since the reign of King Vajiravudh (1910–25).[28] Kasian describes the exclusion of the Chinese as a foundational element of the Thai nationalist project.[29] Yet he also notes the intertwining of Chinese and Thai cultural practices and identities and the uneven history of anti- and pro-Chinese sentiment in Thailand. Caught between histories of denigration, economic centrality, extraterritorial citizenship, conditional inclusion, denial, and current reassertions, Chinese-Thainess thus presents a challenge to historical description.[30] This is further compounded by the fact that narratives about Chinese assimilation in Thailand also negate the existence of a distinct Chinese identity in recent history.

Although not confronted with the violence that marked relations with the Chinese in other Southeast Asian countries, Chinese Thais were nevertheless subject to severe legal and social restrictions.[31] In addition to discrimination in the juridical domain, "throughout most of the twentieth century in Thailand, the category 'Chinese' has been inscribed with negative meanings."[32] A key trope of Thai anti-Sinicism is the association of the Chinese with extraterritorial loyalties and transnational networks, be they communism or, in the more recent past, transnational Chinese capitalism. In popular anti-Chinese rhetoric conceptions of Chineseness in Thailand remain strongly linked to ideas about economic roles, especially in notions of Chinese economic achievement or domination.[33]

Chinese immigration and the subsequent makeup of Chinese communities in Thailand are marked by a particularly gendered history in that the Chinese diaspora in Thailand was initially predominantly male. By virtue of this gendered history and ethnic plurality the Chinese diaspora in Thailand has therefore long been characterized by hybridity. Intermarriage, the adoption of local cultural and linguistic practices, and the simultaneous maintaining of Chinese traditions and, in some cases, transnational Chinese ties have led to the particular composite makeup of Chinese Thai cultures and communities.[34] Nevertheless Thai nationalist, anti-Sinitic discourse at the beginning of the twentieth century positioned Chinese Thai women as racialized and sexualized outsiders of Thai society. As Thamora Fishel observes, the literature of the sixth reign substantially defined Thainess in opposition to concepts of Chinese femininity.[35] Historically the Thai majority at times understood Chinese femininity as tied to commercial sex and female immorality.[36]

The new enthusiastic embrace of Chinese culture and identity only uneasily supersedes the legacy of historical denigration and ongoing hostility in Thailand. A minor but high-profile incident in 2003 that occupied the Thai media for weeks serves as a reminder that the trope of the sexualized, racialized Chinese female outsider still has significance—at least where noncitizens are concerned. The case of false allegations of rape made by a Hong Kong tourist, So Leong-ying, against a Thai *tuk-tuk* driver brought to the fore residual racist attitudes toward Chinese women in Thailand and was notable in the extent of nationalist rhetoric that it elicited.[37] Anti-Chinese attitudes thus seem to persist in the form of a buried sentiment that, under the pressure of nationalist rhetoric, is easily revived and adapted to new contexts. The apparent move of Chineseness from racialized minority identity to the status of desirable ethnic membership thus does not guarantee freedom from denigration.

Assimilation

In *The Eye* solving the mystery of Man's possession leads to an excavation of Chineseness, not only in the sense of uncovering a story of ethnic denigration but also in letting Chineseness in Thailand reappear as difference, thereby disinterring it from its supposed loss in assimilation.[38] Discourses of assimilation become particularly problematic when they deny a notion of agency to the ethnic subject yet fail to protect from violence whenever notions of ethnic difference are reanimated. Significantly the notion of assimilation obscures past suffering and trivializes ongoing discriminations.

Michael Vatikiotis assesses the Chinese revival in Thailand in light of the idea of assimilation: "The driving force is China's economic awakening, but the impact goes beyond money: Chinese culture is enjoying a revival among Chinese Thais, who only a few years ago seemed destined for near-total assimilation."[39] The vast majority of overseas Chinese reside in Southeast Asia; in the scholarly literature about this geographic context, Thailand has represented the paradigmatic example for the notion of Chinese assimilation since the 1950s. Yet it is currently this site from which notions of Chineseness are being reconfigured.

Not only academic perspectives on Chinese Thai history have espoused the idea of assimilation. In popular discourse denials of Chineseness stem from negations by the Thai ethnic majority of a history of denigration or can come from a refusal of essentialist notions of Chineseness on the part of Thais of Chinese descent. As Ien Ang writes with regard to Chineseness in Southeast Asia, "In these narratives, the very validity of the category of Chineseness is in question, its status as a signifier of identity thrown into radical doubt."[40] Chinese Thais have indeed generally passed beyond their historical status of economic centrality and social and political marginality.[41] Chineseness in Thailand today cannot always be distinguished by practices, speech, or names and has shifted from a racialized minority position to one of increasingly desirable ethnic membership. Yet the story doesn't end there.

We can understand haunting in *The Eye* as playing on notions of distinction and indistinction regarding Chineseness. When Man traces the roots of her haunting foresight, the film performs a recovery of Chineseness in Thailand. Already the first scene in Thailand sets distinction and belonging into stark relief. When Ling is introduced into the story it is expressly as Chinese. Upon Wah and Man's arrival in Thailand, a voice-over relates an earlier conversation in which he told her that her implanted corneas came from a "young Chinese woman who was born in Thailand" and whose *Chinese* name was recorded in the transplant documents as Chiu Wai Ling. This formulation, rather than "a young Thai woman of Chinese origin" or "a young Chinese Thai woman," as well as the stating of the woman's Chinese name in a country where for decades Chinese have used Thai names, tells us something about the perspective on Chinese Thai femininity that the film will put forth. It is a first indication that *The Eye*'s examination of the outsider's role of a young woman in Thailand will be coextensive with the examination of an ethnically minoritarian subject position in that country.

When Wah and Man fly from Hong Kong to Thailand, they do not entirely leave a Chinese world, however. As Sophia Harvey notes, the Hong Kong version of the film employs different Chinese dialects to underline the thematic of transnational Chinese identities.[42] While the Hong Kong version's main language is Cantonese, Man and Wah speak Mandarin whenever they converse with Chinese Thais. The Thai version does not use language in the same way; instead the characters speak standard Thai throughout the film, but Chineseness is indicated by the use of names and terms of address with which Thai viewers are conversant. Thailand is thus part of a Chinese Asia in the film.

While the film clearly marks the two diasporic locales as different, the use of Chinese language(s) indicates the existence of transnational community across both locations. On the one hand, especially from the perspective of a viewer in Thailand, Ling's Chineseness appears as difference. On the other hand, through the film's language politics, Ling is included in a larger transnational Chinese community, of which Mandarin becomes the increasingly likely lingua franca. However, the difference is that the relation between Ling and her community is cast in severely antagonistic terms, while that of Man to hers is not.

In disagreement with the assimilationist paradigm, Tong Chee Kiong and Chan Kwok Bun emphasize the "alternate identities" that Chinese Thais assume when they adopt local practices and identities while simultaneously maintaining Chinese practices, languages, or self-identification.[43] These authors argue for the "tenacity and survival of a primary Chinese identity" in Thailand and conceive of Chinese Thai identity as a field in which the "ethnic actor" is able to make strategic, variable choices.[44]

However, the way *The Eye* references Chineseness does not point to such voluntary association. This becomes clear especially in the resolution scenes at Ling's house in which her Chineseness figures as a matter of life and death. Thus at the height of the mother-daughter conflict in the exorcism scene, Ling's Chineseness is further highlighted by Aunt Chui's use of the prefix *Ah*. This Chinese term of address seals the scene's emphasis on Ling's Chineseness. The term serves to interpellate Ling as Chinese in the important moment just before her death, but also just before she is liberated from the time warp of suicides and reconciled with her mother.

Man's actions in this scene, in which she "sees" Ling's suicide and performs a benevolent exorcism, brings Thai-Chineseness to light in yet a different way. This scene is refracted in the doubling that occurs between Man and Ling. It is through the pairing with Man, who is clearly identifiable as Chinese, that Ling's ethnic identity is further substantiated. The first scene of Ling's suicide becomes accessible for the viewer only through the lens of Man's haunted vision. In the exorcism scene the doubling between the two Chinese women continues when Man and Ling temporarily fuse and Man succeeds in breaking the cycle of suicides. With this frame of repetition, the film seems to suggest that a Chinese witness is necessary for the uncovering and, subsequently, for the undoing of Ling's predicament. In both instances the various forms of repetition between the Chinese Thai woman and the Hong Kong woman—identification, traumatic witnessing, temporary identity, and the reenactment of the suicide—affirm Ling's ethnic identity.

The transdiasporic kinship that binds Man to Ling is so strong that it compels her to hang herself in Ling's stead in order to free both Ling and herself from haunting.[45] With the trope of doubling between the two women, *The Eye* also models an understanding of how Hong Kong might relate to Thailand in terms of diasporic solidarity and historical repair. The trajectory of identification, witnessing, and action between the two women suggests that Hong Kong may be allocated a leading role in the recovery of Chineseness and Chinese histories.

As the benign exorcism is completed, the enigma of haunting seems to have been untangled. Mother and daughter are reconciled, Ling is freed from the traumatic cycle of suicides, and we can assume that Man's possession has ended as well. The next solemn scene of merit-making, at Ling's grave, underwrites this sense of resolution. Chineseness is flagged prominently in this scene, in which Aunt Chui, Wah, Man, and Ek make offerings at Ling's grave. Located in a slightly elevated landscape, Ling's is a solitary grave. Although this represents a proper location for a Chinese grave, the scene reiterates Ling's remove from community in spatial terms: in death as in life, she remains set apart.

The film consistently presents the most significant crises of Ling's life and death as closely connected to her ethnic identity. Throughout, the film has thus suggested that it is Ling's Chineseness that is at the root of the haunting. What ultimately assuages haunting in *The Eye* is an act of transnational Chinese witnessing as well as the performance of Chinese ritual. This particular transdiasporic form of solidarity has brought relief to the scene of violent haunting that stems from Chinese memory in Thailand. *The Eye* thereby puts forth the notion that historical repair is to be accomplished through the praxis of Chineseness.

Possession and Female Agency

What is significant about the Pangs' treatment of female haunting is that, rather than only figure the violence of gendering, it also designates female collectivity as the basis for working through problems of historical and political agency. Queer and feminist analyses of gender in the horror genre have focused on tracking motifs of gender transgression and interpreting symbols of homosociality in ostensibly heterosexual plots. Thus Judith Halberstam winds up her queer reading of heterosexual narrative in the Western horror genre with a conclusion about horror's capacity to "mess up once and for all the generic identity codes that read femininity into tits and ass and masculinity into penises. The chain saw has been sutured and grafted onto the female body rendering it a queer body of violence and power, a monstrous body that has blades, makes noise, and refuses to splatter."[46] Whereas the genre had long been understood to produce merely misogynist reiterations of sexual difference, Halberstam's analysis makes horror available to (other) queer and feminist possibilities of interpretation.[47] Her analysis follows a tradition of feminist readings of sexual difference in Western horror that accorded relative fixedness to the female position. Her reinterpretation thus infuses female positions in horror with mobility and exceeds understandings that restrict the horror genre to dramatizations of sexual difference.

Thai and East Asian horror-ghost genres provide yet another perspective in that they always already feature the female body as one of "violence and power"—as well as one of abjection. Female figures in Asian horror have nevertheless most frequently been interpreted in terms of sexual difference, often building on the work of critics such as Barbara Creed.[48] However, while the haunting of women may well indicate crises around sexualized bodies and the performance of "feminine normality," the scholarship has passed over the fact that in the Thai and other Asian horror genres, these crises are also resolved by women collectively.[49] Although scholars have noted the predominance of women in the genre, the fact that horror frequently occurs in all-female terrains has been overlooked.

In the previous chapter's discussion of heritage film within the Thai horror-ghost genre, haunting was shown to be a predominantly female predicament and to derive its strength in particular from forms of suffering linked to being female, such as rape, pregnancy, abortion, and wrongful female death. Such female conditions provide occasion for the practices of *sayasat*, or Thai magic, for which the dead female body represents a particularly powerful necromantic tool. However, many of the transactions of loss and the necromantic abundance that can be gained from it specifically occur between women in the ghost genre. Not only are the ghosts of these films overwhelmingly female, but so too are the living main characters. Ghost film plots often turn on the theme of the possession of one woman by another, on its horrifying initial occurrence as well as on its role in the redress of the injustice at the root of haunting.[50] The relations between women that possession brings into being in these narratives can be violent but also serve to pass on knowledge or rectify past injustices. Thus in *The Mother* (*Hien*, 2003) the ghost of a mother haunts a young pregnant woman and ultimately instills in her notions of proper femininity and motherhood, and *Shutter* (*Chattoe: Kot Tit Winyan* [Shutter: Press to Capture Ghosts], 2004) uses female possession to uncover the story of a rape.[51] Although set up to interrogate past injustices affecting women, the transmissions that haunting effects can only seldom be read as critical. While many films' plots do include the redress of injustices endured by individual women, such resolution is not usually presented as social criticism. Instead exorcism or the resolution of haunting may lead to female sacrifice for a higher collective good that is rationalized through ethical-religious maxims. That is to say, most films end badly for the female ghost and diffuse the critical potential of haunting.

In this scripted fantasy space, female death and haunting more often than not bear the burden of linking contemporary rhetorics of loss regarding nation, sexuality, and conservative visions of collective futures rather than effecting a disturbance of the status quo. In order to produce such collective identifications with cultural loss, this subsection of the ghost genre relies on the evacuation of historical specificity from the past. In contrast the Pang brothers use haunting, melancholy, and the aesthetics of negative female embodiment to address a political concern of the present that relies on historical specificity. *The Eye* thus diverges from other ghost films by proposing a desirable relation to a past and a future, neither of which is primarily couched in terms of tradition. In the film women and their bodies are supposed to produce something other than children, magic fetuses, or substances from which material gain is to be culled.

In the Pangs' horror films there is also a gendered division of labor in which only women are charged with reparative agency. Men do not appear except in supporting or exceptionally destructive roles. In her study of Hou Hsiao-hsien's Taiwan Trilogy, Ma reflects on the gendered division of historical labor that becomes evident in the works of this director: while Hou's films invalidate the notion of men's historical agency—the patriarchs are either dead or have become ineffectual—it is women who witness history and become purveyors of alternative historiographies constructed from memory rather than official record.[52] *The Eye, The Eye 2, Re-cycle,* and Oxide Pang's *Ab-normal Beauty* register a similar phenomenon; here too women bear the primary burden of epistemological and discursive agency with regard to history. Women are primarily afflicted by haunting and horror in these films but are also charged with acquiring literacy and expertise in these domains. The Pangs' films diverge from Hou's treatment of women's historical tasks, however, in that women are also appointed with resolving the grievances that are at the heart of the uncanny in these narratives. In all four Pang films the events of haunting and horror transpire in the frame of affective relations between women: pairings of living and dead women, lesbian relationships, and mother-daughter relationships furnish central sites in which the problematics of the films play out. These relationships set the scene for resolutions that highlight female solidarities and in which agency is ascribed to women both in the psychic as well as the social and historical domains. Ultimately this agency is always significantly compromised, however; typically the Pang brothers' films set the scene so that no woman can solve the problematic of the story by herself. Their films use haunting and horror to adjudicate questions about the social or psychic origins of trauma and to debate possibilities of its collective resolution or alleviation. It is not women's gender that constrains their agency; rather the elements that qualify agency are the fact that it must be approached collectively. In addition women's agency is constrained by the ontological principles of a trans-Asian Buddhism that teaches the inevitability of loss.

The work that the Hong Kong woman performs in this context is closely related to Hong Kong's historical and political status. Man seeks out trans-diasporic kinship with someone who has experienced a different history of Chinese oppression in a diasporic location. Here Hong Kong's claim of privileged knowledge of Chinese culture stems from its history as a paradigmatic diasporic location.

According to Ackbar Abbas, Hong Kong is a majority-Chinese city that was never allowed to be Chinese, that was (almost) always already colonial and always already postcolonial.[53] Never having been nationally Chinese, the city has also resisted mainland formulations of Chineseness. Internationally oriented rather than oriented toward a motherland, Hong Kong enunciations of Chineseness are therefore quintessentially diasporic. In this the city also evinces a fundamental asynchronicity for Abbas, a kind of constitutional hauntedness.

In *The Eye*, Hong Kong bears the expertise of cultural recovery after forced de-Sinicization under colonial rule. What is more, the enunciations of Chineseness in the film present Hong Kong as the melancholy heir of classical Chinese culture also in view of PRC reformulations of Chineseness.

Buddhism

An early scene set in Hong Kong provides guidance on the question of action on behalf of others across Southeast Asian and East Asian borders and populations. A Buddhist ceremony is performed to lay to rest the spirit of the son of Man's neighbors, who committed suicide when his parents did not believe his story about a lost school item.[54] In this ceremony the monk declares the release of the ghost from haunting—and thereby the labor

FIGURE 2.5. Lanterns in her hallway enjoin Man to "make offerings to the dead." Hong Kong appears as a repository of classical Chinese culture and Buddhist-Confucian praxis. Danny and Oxide Pang, *The Eye* (2002).

of karmic amends—a collective matter and one that depends on others' recognition of the ghost's predicament. The explanations accompanying the ritual foreshadow how the haunting of the ghost in Thailand, whose redemptive prescience was also scorned rather than given credence, is to be approached.

While Jennifer Feeley traces a flattening of Confucian-Buddhist-Taoist aesthetics in transnational Chinese horror cinema, *The Eye*'s deployment of Chinese ritual and signification as central to the resolution of haunting offers a more in-depth consideration of the import of the praxis of Chineseness in the present.[55] One day Man opens her door to the neighbor's boy, who is already a ghost at the time and asks Man, "Have you seen my notebook? I've lost it." Man's vision is still not very sharp, but as she attempts to follow the boy down the hallway, she encounters two lanterns with the character *dian* at the door to his apartment (fig. 2.5). "Make offerings to the spirit of the dead" is the demand that the lanterns make, although Man may not understand this yet because her vision is still blurred and because she may not yet recognize all Chinese characters.

In *The Eye*, Hong Kong features as a place in which signs and symbols of Chinese ancestral worship abound, though their recognition may remain flawed. These signs and scenes from Chinese Confucian-Buddhist ritual appear as portents of the problem that Man will encounter in Thailand and presage its resolution. Although she does not yet realize this, Man is about to follow the injunction inscribed on the lanterns and to infuse it with new meaning. At the same time, these scenes reflect Hong Kong's authority regarding the recovery of Chinese histories in other Asian locations.

Another instance of haunting in Hong Kong occurs earlier, when Man attends a lesson in Chinese calligraphy, an art that, as the teacher tells her, no longer draws many students. As she makes her first brushstrokes, a ghost rushes in on her, demanding why Man has taken her place. The scene presents the recovery of Chinese cultural knowledge as perilous, but the film's first half also suggests that Hong Kong is a place that has accumulated knowledge in Chinese cultural recovery under precarious circumstances. In the Pangs' film Hong Kong features as a place in which praxes of Chineseness have endured under colonial rule and mainland parameters. These scenes indicate a difference in the knowledge about Chineseness and mark Hong Kong's authority in this matter. Yet they also connect East Asia with Southeast Asia as in principle united under a common Buddhist philosophy that informs cultural and psychic survival in the perilous present.

The Ghost Seers' Melancholy

Although Ling is not the main character, it is her story that centrally motivates the action of *The Eye*. The melancholy bind in which she finds herself is configured in the story of redemptive responsibility toward a community at whose hands the minority subject is suffering discrimination.

To understand Ling's condition, a look at Anne Cheng's concept of a "melancholy of race" is instructive. Cheng's formulation of dynamics of loss and retention that operate on individual psychic levels as well as in collective contexts sheds light on the affective binding of subjects who are defined as racially minoritarian and majoritarian. Most important, Cheng shows that melancholy is constitutive of more than psychic formations of minoritarian personhood. Transposed into the social realm, melancholy has a sustaining quality for uneven dynamics of power between dominant populations and those whose bodies and identities are racially marked. According to Cheng, the grief in question marks the psychic state of the minority as well as that of the majority: "Racial melancholia tracks a dynamic of rejection and internalization that may help us comprehend two particular aspects of American racial culture: first, dominant, white culture's rejection of yet attachment to the racial other and, second, the ramifications that such paradox holds for the racial other, who has been placed in a suspended position."[56]

Although the situation that *The Eye* allegorizes differs from U.S. racial dynamics, Cheng's notion of the suspension of the minority subject draws out a key element of Ling's psychic and social position.[57] In *The Eye*, Ling's haunting derives from her sorrow over her vexed relationship with her community as well as from her failure to prevent their disaster. What the film is then able to showcase with some urgency through Ling's story is the entangled relation between a minoritarian subject and a majoritarian community. Because she holds the key to their survival—and probably also because she has no alternative—Ling remains tied to a group of people who are responsible for her denigration. Even after her death Ling's ghost continues to be caught in this position. Because she cannot sever this attachment, she becomes stuck in a time warp of suicides. The violence of these repetitions illustrates the force with which melancholia binds a minoritarian subject.[58] While the film initially retains a notion of considerable—if only potential—agency for the minoritarian subject, the ending radically qualifies the possibilities of redemption, reconciliation, and communication. In the end *The Eye* allows the minoritized subject little room to maneuver within melancholia; not even Ling's suicide provides an escape from the impasse that she finds herself in.

Inasmuch as Ling's story also revolves around the vantage point of the minoritized outsider, the film adds still another dimension to the problematic. Through its deployment of the idea of haunting prescience, *The Eye* describes the Chinese Thai position as simultaneously privileged and denigrated.[59] With its attribution of foresight to Ling, the film is not only able to illustrate the necessary and painful ambivalence that characterizes the position of the minoritarian person vis-à-vis a society, the very constitution of which depends on the exclusion of this person; prescience in the film further seems to stand for insight into social relations, especially conflictual ones. What occult, special knowledge would also represent, then, is the painful hyperconscious awareness of the state of affairs of minoritarian melancholia.

MAN

With the difficulties of the melancholy possession that befalls Man, the film opens up a perspective on the complexities of remembering buried Chinese Thai histories. The intensity of Man's possession illustrates the problematic of remembering not only Ling's particular story but the history of injury to a Chinese minoritarian population more broadly. Especially the quasi-documentary quality of the black-and-white vignettes that recount Ling's story makes this narrative representative of a collective, Chinese Thai history. However, it is only in moments of Man's extreme duress that these scenes are disclosed. The symptoms of possession in *The Eye* thereby indicate also the fact that Chinese Thai history is in part not easily intelligible and that its excavation requires unusual effort.

Until this point in the story, *The Eye*'s insertion of minoritarian haunting in Thailand into a transnational context is successful. When the film appoints a Chinese witness to uncover the injustice perpetrated on a Chinese woman in Thailand, *The Eye* positions minoritarian injury as a matter that has to be approached transnationally. This particular invocation of Chinese transnational ties and of female agency promises to shift this instance of suffering from obscurity into public view. However, Man's melancholy possession by the memory of the other woman's past opens up an additional thematic when Man stands witness also to an event of mass disaster in Thailand in the present.

CATASTROPHIC LOSS AND THE MINORITARIAN POSITION

The pairing of the two women in *The Eye* initially seems to represent a radical form of solidarity on the basis of ethnic affiliation and personal empathy. When Man hangs herself in Ling's stead, she does so not only to free herself from possession but also because the knowledge of the other woman's suffering prompts her to do so. Deployed in this way, possession and melancholy represent forms of "'ethnic' communal mourning" and delineate at least limited possibilities of female agency within the domain of negativity and the political-historical context introduced by the film.[60] For the conclusion of its presentation of minority-majority relations in Thailand, however, the film chooses an ending in disaster. Its final scene of a gas tank leak references an actual event in the early 1990s on Bangkok's Petchburi Road.

After the appeasement of Ling's ghost, the narrative of the film appeared to offer a diversion from the arduous process of tracing the roots of Man's possession. Man and Wah's return to Bangkok on an orange cross-country bus provides scenes of simple harmony along the way: half-naked children, one with a topknot, jump off a pier into a canal; men play soccer barefoot in the dirt; small stalls along the roadside sell kites and fruit. Although

Man smiles at these views from the bus, they represent some of the saddest scenes of the film. In their position between two disastrous incidents, they seem to offer a brief respite from the witnessing of past and future trauma. Yet their slow motion, in combination with their representation of Thai poverty as idyllic, lends these scenes eeriness and also marks them as moments of nostalgia, already or soon to be located in the past. They echo the scene of a burning man that Man saw upon her arrival, and their uncanny quality points to the fact that the haunting has not yet come to an end.

As the cross-country bus enters Bangkok at night and is trapped in a traffic jam on a busy street, Man sees scores of dark figures walk past her window. She realizes that another disaster, this time of greater proportions, is about to happen. Her attempts to warn others go unheeded until the gas ignites. The scene of catastrophe that follows is cut with flashbacks to Ling's last attempt to warn her neighbors of disaster—the great fire that killed over three hundred people.

When Bangkok's Petchburi Road is engulfed by flames as the gas ignites, Wah throws Man to the ground and the flames pass over them. While the now slightly transparent figures of all those who died in the disaster walk away from the area, Man lies on the ground unconscious. One last time the film cuts to Ling, surveying the burning houses of her neighbors. The next and final scene shows Man and Wah together in Hong Kong in an intimate moment on a busy walkway.

Whereas the resolution of female possession in the Thai ghost genre usually has the double purpose of redressing the injustice perpetrated on the dead woman and of imparting essential knowledge to the living woman, in the case of The Eye this pattern of events does not come to as clear a resolution.[61] In the film the benign exorcism that the living woman attempts does allow the dead woman to escape a time warp of pain resulting from past injury; however, ghosts persist in Man's own vision and she retains the ability to foresee disastrous events even after she has freed Ling's ghost. With this continuation of haunted foresight, the Petchburi Road disaster provides the occasion for Ling's vindication: Man's successful prevention of the disaster would also have substantiated Ling's special powers as benevolent. But instead of providing an ending of reconciliation, the Petchburi Road disaster only reiterates the failure of communication between the Thai public and each of the Chinese women. The prescience of both women remains unrecognized. Neither can Man act out her redemptive position successfully, nor is the violence perpetrated on Ling effectively redressed.

The catastrophic ending of *The Eye* thus leaves doubt as to what the transnational migration of loss has accomplished. Although the specifics of the possession promise a more thorough resolution, *The Eye* does not carry through this project in a conclusive way. With its culmination in mass disaster the film ends in a condensed image of loss, posing the question of whether this resolution does not dissolve the specificity of minoritarian injury in a pronouncement about the general inevitability of loss. In the last scene of the film Man is shown to prefer blindness to the spectacular failure of vision that she has experienced. Her final sentence—in which she says that she does not mind being blind again because she has "seen the most beautiful thing in the world"—leaves open what kind of vision and which exact objects of vision she is referring to.

Man leaves Thailand behind as a place where redemptive action has failed, and with this the problematic of minoritarian personhood is to an extent left unresolved. That Ling's story ends in suicide and Man's in blindness can be read as strong criticism. Yet the trajectory of the doubling between Man and Ling still suggests something else. Does the direction that *The Eye* ultimately outlines for Chinese femininity in Thailand lie in the embrace of a globalized, middle-class subject position, an identity that Man embodies? This is intimated by the temporary identity of the two women that occurs in the course of the doubling. And the fact that Man survives—though not triumphantly—while Ling's life ends suggests that the fusing with this geographically and economically mobile subject is the film's final word on the problematic of this particular minoritarian position.

What is more, to neither of the Chinese Thai female characters does the film attribute effective agency with regard to their own histories. In contrast to Man's relationship with Wah, both Ling and her mother are single, perhaps intimating that their existence has no future. Aunt Chui in particular is portrayed as withdrawn, shriveled, gray, alone, and mournful. And the only relationship that the two women do have, that to each other, is marked by its ineffectualness, especially on the part of the mother with regard to intervention on behalf of the daughter.

With Man's evaluation of what she has experienced in Thailand, the plot takes a last, potentially problematic turn. The final scene, in which Man seems to turn away from the problematic she encountered in Thailand, makes the specters raised so evocatively in the story disappear in a propagation of the acceptance of the inevitability of loss. Yet the encounter between the two radically different subjectivities that Man and Ling represent is not entirely a one-way affair. Although there exists a hierarchy between the Hong Kong woman's and the Chinese Thai woman's experiences—a difference of mobility within their respective situations and of the extent of the disaster that befalls each—haunting intersubjectivity also establishes an interdependence between them. Man also leaves Thailand behind as a place that furnished existential knowledge. And while this knowledge has proven ineffective in reversing the problematic that she encountered in Thailand, the final scene in Hong Kong shows that the visit to Thailand has given Man privileged knowledge and a tool for the acceptance of loss. The urgent claim that Ling's haunting made on the Hong Kong woman has thus also provided Man with something essential. This is also the final instance in which it becomes clear that the film presents Buddhist knowledge as transcultural capital.

With the shift to the Thai context, *The Eye* thus delineates (historical) agency as essentially collective. Yet the ending also shows this agency to be severely compromised. It thereby lets Chinese haunting in Thailand remain irreducibly singular. Ultimately the vicissitudes of Buddhist-coded haunting exemplify the "immiscibility" of temporalities that Bliss Lim has outlined. In contrast to the heritage film's deployment of ghostly return, haunting in *The Eye* has brought into view "discrete temporalities incapable of attaining homogeneity with or full incorporation into a uniform chronological present."[62] The inassimilable quality of the story that Man uncovers thus lets haunting's potential for historical critique come to fruition in *The Eye*.

Rather than dissolving the specificity of minoritarian injury, irresolution preserves the uncanny quality of the history that Man witnesses in Thailand. Although the possession had bound the two women to each other as though by fate, in the resolution ethnic commonality as a single factor does not suffice to solve the problem. Rather the film ultimately suggests that a transnational Chinese consciousness must recognize the disparate histories of its constituents. It is women who have the privileged cognitive ability to witness these disparities; as in several of the Pangs' horror films, however, their limited agency is contingent upon collective recognition of the problem at hand and can come into effect only after great loss.

The imperfect adjudication of possession in *The Eye* rejects the notion that the globalized, privileged model that dominates representations of Chinese femininity in Thailand in the present can replace, without haunting, the legacy of oppression of Chinese immigrants and citizens in the country. With the incomplete resolution of haunting, the film suggests that neither successfully tapping into Chinese transnational desirability nor belated full inclusion in the nation carries enough reparative momentum to allow for disengagement from this local memory.

The Desire for Thailand as a Site of Loss

Koichi Iwabuchi describes a Japanese perspective on Hong Kong popular culture in which the particular object of longing is the vigor attributed to other Asian cultures, a quality that Japan is assumed to have lost. In the case under consideration in this chapter, it is not in media consumption but in the diegesis of a film that a transnational desire for a "different Asian modernity" becomes evident. As Iwabuchi writes, Hong Kong popular culture is able to fulfill the Japanese desire for an Asian cosmopolitanism that nevertheless retains Asian cultural specificity because the city-state is "temporally [and spatially] proximate enough to evoke a nostalgic longing for a (different) Asian modernity."[63] What distinguishes *The Eye* from the case that Iwabuchi describes is that in the film transnational desire concerns contexts of explicit loss.

In the Hong Kong imaginary of the region, Thailand is frequently relegated to a zone of radical noncontemporaneity, which enables the country to double as Hong Kong's historical or ghostly other. This is evident in Wong Kar-wai's films beginning with *In the Mood for Love* (2000), in which all scenes of old Hong Kong were filmed in Bangkok. Thailand also appears as a terrain of ghostly alterity and superstitious belatedness in Hong Kong cinema and media; this is most radically instantiated by the Hong Kong TV ghost-buster series *The Unbelievable*.[64]

The Pangs' *The Eye* establishes Thailand as a paradigmatic site of loss where accident and death are wired into the affairs and aesthetics of the everyday. Trauma is presumed endemic in the country, and the "'opening' of bodies and persons" occurs also toward the foreign visitor in the film.[65] It is in this capacity that Thailand can exemplify and impart essential knowledge about "a different Asian modernity."[66] Hong Kong is not devoid of occult occurrences in *The Eye* series but lacks the rawness and reach of what is found in Thailand.

In *The Eye* the buildup of suspense around Thailand as a place saturated with loss culminates in the Petchburi Road disaster. Counter to expectation, the scene after the fire has ignited is not entirely gruesome. Groups of people in buses, trucks, and cars who were portrayed in great detail before the fire have burned to death. Their corpses, however, are not horrific, and the soft piano soundtrack conveys resolution rather than horror. What seals the desirable character of the post-disaster scene in Bangkok is the way that it segues into what looks like a blue sky but is really the ground of the walkway to the ferry landing in Hong Kong. The sound tracks across both scenes and countries, creating continuity between the events in both locales and underlining the Bangkok disaster and the concluding scene in Hong Kong as commensurate events of closure.[67]

This use of the soundtrack also links the disaster to Man's romance. In the aftermath of the fire she is lying on the ground with Wah's arm around her, one of very few survivors. The lovers are the central point of this scene; the charred bodies around them provide the backdrop for their shared survival and mutual attachment. The connected final scene mirrors this setup when it centrally showcases Man and Wah's intimacy in the middle of the crowds on the busy Hong Kong walkway.

The Petchburi disaster represents the culmination of the need for Thailand constantly to burn and to exemplify accident in *The Eye*. Various forms of disaster are ultimately what enable the viewer's access to experiencing Thailand intensely, intimately, and profitably. The disaster scene is also closely linked to Man's final evaluation of her experience in Thailand. Although her survival is not characterized by explicit triumph, it stands in problematic relation to the events in Thailand.[68] With Man's return to Hong Kong, the divergence between Man's and Ling's lives, and between life in Thailand and life in Hong Kong in general, is further accentuated: Ling is dead; Man has survived, and with a lover by her side at that. Thailand has been left behind in devastation. As horror has been relegated to the other space of Thailand, the atmosphere of the final scene in Hong Kong is serene, and now that Man is blind again, Hong Kong is completely devoid of haunting. The repetition— the ghostly doubling between the two countries and two women—thus ends asymmetrically. The scene of abundance upon the return to Hong Kong depends on the large-scale losses that have occurred in Thailand—in short, on the country's ability to double as Hong Kong's abject other.

By pairing the Bangkok disaster with the final scene in Hong Kong, the film positions Thailand as a place from which one can extract knowledge about survival in the perilous (Asian) present. Not only did Thailand prove to be a site of revelation for the conundrum of the possession, but Man's journey to the country is also what provides her with the experience of loss on a large scale and thereby with the grounds for her new insight. The

Buddhist connotations of Man's acceptance of loss suggest that Thailand can provide superior religious-philosophical guidance.[69] The promise that Thailand holds in its proximity to loss, then, is that it represents a site in which the perils of Asian modernities are more distinct and in which pedagogies of loss are (still) in place. To attach desire to this territory of loss is also to seek to partake in this expertise in the domains of loss.[70]

It remains disturbing that to do the work of representing a "different Asian modernity" Thailand has to represent an extreme of accident and loss. As a terrain more saturated with trauma than others, Thailand consistently has to provide for points at which the breakdown of barriers between individuals, bodies, technologies, and epistemes can be experienced in radical, literal form. If, as in Iwabuchi's example, the Pangs' films' perspectives on Thailand include a desire for vigor, it would be for the energy that purportedly results from such breakdowns and from the disasters of Thai modernity. As Iwabuchi explains, where the desirous look to a different Asian modernity posits only a slight time lag, effortless identification and nostalgia—for what was lost as well as for what was never achieved—are made possible. In *The Eye*, Thailand is temporally and spatially proximate enough to provide invaluable clues to the problematic of (cultural) loss—a place from which one can obtain knowledge to confront the demands of a conflicted, explosive present. In its appearance as a proximate-distant reservoir of the modern-occult, it holds out the promise that there can still be magic in an Asian future. Yet Thailand is not depicted as a place where actual living seems possible, and a visit to its extremes of loss and horror must always remain brief.

THIS CHAPTER HAS EXPANDED the analysis of the logics of minoritization at work in the Thai present to the study of a transnational domain. Attending to how a past of injury relates to a present of cultural ascendancy, I have inquired into the transdiasporic commensurability of Chinese femininity and examined women's roles as historical witnesses and agents across the locations of Hong Kong and Thailand. I thereby demonstrated how the discordant temporalities of haunting bring to light a history of minoritization while also working through the vicissitudes of present-day globalized, gendered personhood.

In *The Eye* the Buddhist-coded anachronism of ghostly return functions as a historical corrective in the Thai national context, but it has one further transnational implication. Lim emphasizes that the ghost film presents a particular opportunity for mobility within time: "Whereas most stories serve up a beginning that is different from its ending, the ghost narrative has a tendency to transgress the principles of linearity without becoming antinarrative (as in avant-garde and experimental films)."[71] Such a departure from linearity affords *The Eye* the opportunity to move both forward and backward in time. By virtue of her possession, Man acquires the capacity to see both the past and the future. As its heroine enters a "lost" time of Chinese Thai history, the film thereby also disrupts the dominant, linear narrative of Chinese cultural and economic ascension that, in its present form, threatens to submerge historical cultural differences. The past of a Chinese Thai community that *The Eye* brings into contemporaneity is thus disinterred from contemporary processes that are gradually replacing diverse Chinese dialects with Mandarin and the complex histories of Chinese Thais with PRC-oriented narratives. Haunting in *The Eye* has thus made possible the reappearance of difference also in a transnational context, thereby countering PRC-driven homogenization.

The Eye conceives of arbitration in a Buddhist framework and ultimately delineates a Buddhist, gendered contemporaneity. Buddhist notions frame the imperative of action on behalf of the one who haunts and designate the labor of karmic amends a collective matter. At the same time, the Buddhist premise of the law of impermanence radically qualifies the possibilities of individual and collective agency. As a trans-Asian epistemological and ethical resource, Buddhism thereby furnishes a sophisticated notion of agency for the present.

But *The Eye* also tells its story of haunting as the story of a particular kind of femininity. In this context Buddhism furnishes an essential element of gendered personhood. In the wider cultural context that *The Eye* participates in, Chinese femininity is currently overdetermined by its relation to the future-present and its economic and social dreams. With Man's entry into the Buddhist-coded temporalities of haunting, this almost exclusive temporal orientation is augmented by a relation to the past. It is because Man follows the Buddhist-driven quest for historical accountability and schools herself in Buddhist modes of apprehending the world that she fully comes into her own. It is women who are at present appointed with this historical and epistemological work; by fully inhabiting this position Man attains a more complete kind of personhood that partakes of a Buddhist contemporaneity.

THREE. *TROPICAL MALADY*

SAME-SEX DESIRE, CASUALNESS, AND THE QUEERING OF IMPERMANENCE IN THE CINEMA OF APICHATPONG WEERASETHAKUL

A scene in Apichatpong Weerasethakul's *Tropical Malady* (*Sat Pralat*, 2004) shows two men licking, almost devouring each other's hands on a deserted street at night. When the younger man walks away, the camera remains on the older man and on two flags hanging over a fence behind him. The flags are Thailand's national flag and a yellow flag bearing royal or Buddhist insignia. When asked about the significance of the quasi sex scene of the two men in this setting, director Apichatpong says, "I wanted them to kiss for the nation."[1]

On first viewing, Apichatpong's feature does not appear concerned with overt political commentary or with homosexuality as politicized identity in Thailand. On the contrary the director's fourth film, a tale of pursuit and desire between the soldier Keng and a younger villager, Tong, seems at first to decontextualize the men's relationship from social and political meaning.

In *Tropical Malady*'s first, "social" half, Keng and Tong's courtship unfolds idyllically across the settings of an unspecified small Thai town and its rural surroundings. The men's relationship is portrayed almost entirely in an idiom of unconflicted bliss. *Tropical Malady* is a film radically split in two, however, and the scene of the men licking each other's hands marks the story's entry into loss; it is the last time that Keng and Tong meet in this context. When intertitles and new opening credits shift the men's relation-ship to another plane, an almost wordless, Buddhist-coded jungle fantasy about a tiger ghost recounts Keng's arduous quest to recover his lost lover in the film's second half.

The accent on bliss and loss in this description is significant. In contrast to other queer-themed Thai films, *Tropical Malady*'s fantastic-realist vision of working-class, male homosexuality in Thailand almost does not make *social* injury a theme at all yet is cognizant of the recent history of sexuality in the country. Significantly the film further deploys a notion of *existential* loss to make homosexuality the primary figure of subjectivity in its story. To achieve these goals the film draws on a variety of stylistic and rhetorical tools to reinvent a Thai nonurban, nonbourgeois same-sex publicity.

This chapter investigates the rhetorical strategies that Apichatpong's independent cinema deploys in relation to other Thai queer-themed films' understandings of the relations of same-sex desire, minoritization, and national community. I draw *Tropical Malady*'s trope of haunting, its deploy-ment of culture, its sparse references to same-sex desire in national public space, and its figuration of vulnerability in relation to the current coercive efforts in Thai social and cultural policy to moor bodies and identities to diffusely historical national elements. While May Adadol Ingawanij and Richard MacDonald have considered the politics of the "self-conscious marginality of [Apichatpong's] practice within Thailand" in relation to his films' transnational acclaim, my analysis seeks to provide a different per-spective on the confluence of local and transnational phenomena in this cinema.[2] My investigation of male homosexuality in Apichatpong's work focuses on how it counteracts the transnational and local, older and new rhetorics of loss and injury that collude in the new modes of sexual regula-tion in Thailand. I argue that, rather than reiterate conventional narratives of national clemency with regard to queer personhood, *Tropical Malady* puts notions of social, psychological, and ontological negativity to an en-tirely different, radical use. Both parts of the film are marked by nonlinear narrative and a filmic style that the criticism has described as "hallucinated documentary."[3] My reading thus also brings the film's avant-garde aesthet-ics and loose narrative structure to bear on an investigation of *Tropical Malady*'s queerness. My analysis concentrates on how the film's dominant register of casualness affects its perspective on homosexuality in Thailand.

While the analysis of *Nang Nak* introduced the concept of Buddhist melancholia and examined conservative appropriations of Buddhist tropes of loss, and the previous chapter on *The Eye* demonstrated how Buddhist-coded anachronisms provide a transnational idiom that helps to frame historical accountability, this chapter investigates how Buddhist temporal incongruity is put in the service of a queer reframing of the social position and ontological meanings of male same-sex desire in the Thai public sphere.

Queer Cultural Production

Much of the queer theater, cinema, art, and writing in Thailand at the turn of the century began centrally to engage questions of rights, privations, and national belonging. Whereas kathoeys had been stock figures of popular entertainment before, such performance, though not without subversive potential, had not explicitly been oriented toward political expression.[4] Before the late 1990s gay men had been underrepresented in performance and film—and lesbians even more so.[5] The queer art of the late 1990s and 2000s draws its material from contemporary instances of prohibition, and its contexts of reception also changed. Around the turn of the century the representation especially of kathoeys registers an instance of social mobility. This becomes evident in content, production, and venues of exhibition.

The post-1997 commercially oriented, mainstream new Thai cinema took up the themes of homosexuality and transgender identities in films such as *The Iron Ladies I* (*Satree Lek I*, 2000), *The Iron Ladies II* (*Satree Lek II*, 2003), *Saving Private Tootsie* (*Phrang Chompu*, 2002), and *Beautiful Boxer* (2004). These earlier features were followed by the teen drama *Love of Siam* (*Rak Haeng Sayam*, 2007) and the gay gangster melodrama *Bangkok Love Story* (*Phuean: Ku Rak Mueng Wa*, 2007), *The Blue Hour* (*Onthakan*, 2015), and comedies such as *Hor Taew Taek: Haek Chi-Mi* (2011) and *Iron Ladies Roar* (*Satree Lek Tob Lok Taek*, 2014).[6] Lesbians usually appeared in film only as minor characters until the 2010s, when the features *Yes or No* (2010), *Yes or No 2* (2012), *Yes or No 2.5* (2015), and *She: Their Love Story* (2012) were produced.[7]

To different degrees these films invoke a Thai multiculturalism that they demand should include also sexual diversity. I do not wish to invalidate these productions' divergent claims to familial and national belonging; however, their potential for radical figurations of queerness remains limited. In his nuanced reading of *Love of Siam*, Brett Farmer characterizes the film's political intervention as circumscribed by its liberal framing: "By thus encoding Tong and Mew with competing cultural differences [European Thai and Chinese Thai] that, like queerness, have also, at one time or other, been regarded as 'other' to traditional notions of Thainess but that have, more recently, been culturally assimilated, the film further underscores its liberal, pluralist agenda of (re)incorporating queerness as one difference among many in the ever-diversifying web of contemporary Thai sociality, a difference that ultimately does not make a difference to the familial integrity and harmony of Thainess." But Farmer stresses that the film's liberal, multiculturalist approach does not entirely foreclose its critical potential. This is largely due to Love's refusal "to furnish the conventionally happy, hymeneal ending of the teen romance." As Farmer argues, the film's indeterminate resolution opens it up to broader queer signification: "By keeping open the question of queerness and the eroticized modes of being it engenders, Love of Siam enables its diverse Thai audiences to imagine— which is to say, realize—queerness in variable ways."[8]

While commercially oriented films were not without critical import, independent productions provided very different formulations of queer personhood and its place in Thai society. In the 1990s Michael Shaowanasai began directing challenging queer shorts (such as Iron Pussy I–III in 1996, 1997, and 2000) that address the transnational commodification of Thai bodies before he codirected, with Apichatpong, and starred in a retro feature about a trans avenger, The Adventures of Iron Pussy, in 2003.[9] Thunska Pansittivorakul's signature combination of explicit same-sex materials with other contentious political contexts manifests in the banned documentary This Area Is Under Quarantine (Boriwen Ni Yu Phai Tai Kan Kak Kan, 2008) as well as in his subsequent features, Reincarnate (Jutti, 2010), The Terrorists (Poo Kor Karn Rai, 2011), and Supernatural (Nuea Thammachat, 2013).[10] In 2010 Insects in the Backyard by the independent trans filmmaker Tanwarin Sukkhapisit challenged familial nationalism with the story of a kathoey parent, and the film's banning once more invigorated the struggle against censorship.[11]

Several of the mainstream kathoey- and gay-themed films of the early 2000s revolve around instances of social and political discrimination and its redress on a national platform. Their endings turn on final, nationally mediated spectacles of recognition and overcoming. Thus Yongyoot Thongkongthun's popular first Iron Ladies film presented the story of a majority-kathoey volleyball team that fights its way to national victory and acceptance. What stands out in these new productions is that several films combine the theme of controversy over *sexual* deviance with the more customary (for Thailand) story of *gender* deviance. Portraying the struggles of kathoeys in the context of broader sexual rights advocacy and side by side with the stories of gay men, these films thus set older notions of stigmatization in relation to those that arose in connection with the new conceptions of sexual citizenship. At least some of their narratives are also constructed around the trope of the closet; however, the question of public speech acts around homosexuality is oriented not only toward the characters' social environments but also toward a national audience.

Allegedly recounting a true story, Kittikorn Liasirikun's *Saving Private Tootsie* locates its drama of minority sexual citizenship in an impossibly fraught scenario: after a plane crash a group of Thai kathoeys find themselves in a Burmese jungle region controlled by Tai Yai ethnic minority groups. A special forces unit is sent from Thailand to recover the kathoeys, including a trans- and homophobic soldier who is the father of a teenage kathoey. During the perilous journey back to Thai territory, the kathoeys and soldiers (as well as at least one Tai ethnic minority soldier!) put their differences behind them. Their negotiations of national belonging and mutual acceptance culminate in the symbolically fraught return to Thai territory when kathoeys and soldiers rescue each other across a river, reaching Thai soil under a waving Thai flag and deflecting the rifles pointed at them with screams of "We are Thais, we are Thais!" In *The Iron Ladies* state actors represent the bad guys while the general public is overwhelmingly supportive, and homophobia is eradicated when a homophobic official knocks himself out (and thereby eliminates his influence on a national volleyball competition). In *Saving Private Tootsie*, by contrast, it is the state actors, the soldiers themselves, who are reformed through their shared ordeal with the kathoeys in the jungle.

The final testimony to the sexual citizenship that the film envisions comes when one of the kathoey survivors speaks on a TV talk show. With tears running down her face, she says, "It was bad luck that I was born a kathoey, but it was good luck that I was born in the right place." Returning the care and commitment extended to her by "Thailand" in this publicly mediated statement, she invokes an older notion of damage—that of kathoeys as existentially diminished persons—while calling on a posthomophobic and posttransphobic Thai nation's potential and competency not to remedy its stigma but to assuage its pain. Explicitly and consistently framing its commentary on kathoeyness as a discourse on minorities within the Thai state, *Saving Private Tootsie* ends problematically when it affirms this minoritarian personhood as diminished within a national context in which, in reality, the stance toward sexual minorities remains volatile.

In thinking about gender, or any of the so-called identities, it seems to be extremely difficult to find a picture or a story that no longer needs the idea of exclusion.
—ADAM PHILLIPS, "Keeping It Moving"

Read against such invocations of homosexuality or transness as a kind of personhood that is temporarily diminished by imbalances in national regulations or by insufficiently enlightened officials, *Tropical Malady* stands out through its omissions: Apichatpong's queer film does not portray sexual explicitness or social struggle, privilege the theme of gender deviance, or bring into play the trope of the closet. I argue that the film mobilizes a radically different notion of publicity and engages Thai cultural specificity in ways that differ markedly from other independent and mainstream productions. Its deployment of loss further diverges from that of other Thai queer films. While the film's first, social half altogether eschews the presentation of homosexuality as a case of diminution, in its second half *Tropical Malady* improvises on the convention of haunting to establish homosexuality as the primary figure of subjectivity. In each case the film performs a deminoritizing move.

In both halves the film mobilizes notions of diminution and rhetorics of loss in ways that counter the dominant devaluations of queer personhood in policy, society, and religious discourse. In its realist social part, the film makes a precarious economic context the basis of social and affective plentitude. The film's second, mythical jungle half draws on Buddhist tropes to reconfigure the notion of the karmically determined existential diminution that is attributed to queer personhood. In Buddhist interpretations both homosexuality and the state of being kathoey result from misconduct in previous lives; as karmic outcomes of past lives, these states and types of personhood are thereby involuntary and remain beyond reproach.[12] On the other hand, the enduring validity of vernacular notions of karmic causality is also responsible for the continued stigmatization of homosexuality and trans personhood as deficient. The persistence of this notion in public discourse continues to mark queer and trans persons as ontologically or existentially damaged.

Tropical Malady transgresses the confines of the Buddhist-liberal synthesis that films such as *The Iron Ladies* and *Saving Private Tootsie* invoke, in which the notion of queer ontological diminution provides the occasion for staging scenes of national clemency. Rather than turn on single events of (national) learning and reconciliation, Apichatpong's queer fantasy creates a markedly different kind of publicity. To this end *Tropical Malady* combines a secular civic perspective on national sexual politics with conceptions that draw on Buddhist fantasy to expand conceptual vocabularies in the domain of sexuality.

While it does not ignore the issue of prohibition, *Tropical Malady* centers on the saturation of the social environment with highly public queer intimacies—a strategy of flooding the everyday with queerness rather than piercing it with traumatic or resolutionary events or single transgressive acts. A first observation on how *Tropical Malady* enters the fray over sexuality in the Thai public sphere thus regards the level of explicitness of the imagery. Apichatpong's previous feature, *Blissfully Yours* (*Sud Saneha*, 2002), encountered conservative-regulatory intervention, as did his subsequent *Syndromes and a Century* (*Saeng Satawat*, 2006).[13] When pressed on this point, Apichatpong stated that *Tropical Malady* originally contained explicit sex scenes that he cut because they did not fit the plot, not because he feared censorship.[14] Instead of pushing the boundaries of censorship, *Tropical Malady* presents Thailand as a "cruiser's paradise."[15] Although the criticism has neglected this feature of the film, we can read *Tropical Malady* as an homage to male bodies and same-sex relations in everyday life in Thailand—to men in public toilets, in the army, in the market, in the ice factory, playing *takraw*, or on stage leading public exercise. The film's first half registers many casual encounters, gazes, banter, and touches— exchanges between friends, acquaintances, and lovers that are usually not recorded on film.[16] As men look for and at each other as well as frequently directly at the camera, the viewer is implicated in a world of seemingly unopposed public homoeroticism. Sex is not explicit in *Tropical Malady*, but men who unequivocally signal their desire for other men are ubiquitous; sex between men seems always available for the taking and unquestionably part of ordinary, working-class, nonmetropolitan life in Thailand.

In contrast to other queer-themed films, Apichatpong's does not take on the more customary story of *gender* deviance nor explicitly that of current struggles around *sexual* deviance. Setting its portrayal of public homoeroticism squarely in the Thai present and repeatedly gesturing toward national sexual politics, the film surprises by skipping the logics of the closet as conventionally mobilized in mainstream cinema. In film the closet functions as a narrative device to thematize personal and social-national struggles over homosexuality. However, critiques of liberal gay politics show that the discourse of the closet also functions as an assimilatory trope that organizes a trajectory toward neoliberal citizenship.[17]

In Thailand the relations of homosexuality and publicity are configured differently, and both contemporary Thai cinema and political discourse present partial relocations of the logics of the closet. While same-sex desires and relations may have been public all along, what intensified since the late 1990s was the desire to come out of a closet that discouraged the explicit designation of same-sex desires as well as political speech about same-sex and transidentitarian issues. Although films such as *The Iron Ladies* also take up the issue of the disclosure of an individual's homosexuality, their greater emphasis lies on engendering national discourses of advocacy regarding homosexuality and transidentitarian positions. The coming out in such films is thus a coming out, in politicized speech before a national community, as an advocate.

In the diegesis of *Tropical Malady*, however, there is neither a coming out in the sense of an individual's disclosure nor any other verbal reckoning with the social negativity of homosexuality. Although the director asserts that he wants the film's protagonists to "kiss for the nation," explicit struggles over social or national recognition remain absent from the film's plot. Instead the director reclaims an unopposed public homoeroticism to contend with recent instances of national prohibition. *Tropical Malady*'s refusal to make the trope of the closet a central axis of the action further enables the film to trace a trajectory of desire rather than make of homosexuality a purely social or political occurrence.

With its portrayal of Keng and Tong's relationship *Tropical Malady* moreover foregrounds an aspect of male same-sex desire that remained underrepresented in Thai cinema: relationships between normatively masculine-presenting (*maen*) men rather than between one masculine and one kathoey partner. At the same time, the director does not present Tong and Keng's relationship as a "gay" relationship, with all the accoutrements of possession and aspirations to state recognition that this might include. *Tropical Malady* outlines a homosexuality that is neither the vilified one of state discourses nor the recognized consumer subjectivity that simultaneously came into being. Nevertheless the sexuality delineated by the film is everywhere linked to economic transformation and at times casually related to national politics.

Perhaps the most significant aesthetic feature of *Tropical Malady* is its dominant register of casualness. The slow, nonlinear unfolding of Keng and Tong's relationship makes a plot summary difficult. However, examining the social and material contexts in which the men's interactions occur provides a closer picture of the sexuality that the film seeks to address. The story strongly sets homosexual desire in the context of leisure time and modes of enjoyment. These in turn are intricately connected to a particular material environment and its economic determinants: *Tropical Malady* is set in the small-town periphery, a place removed from yet suffused with the effects of Bangkok hegemony and transnational capitalism. The sexuality in question is that of working-class men—of wage laborers like Tong and low-salaried state employees like Keng. Their relationship unfolds across meticulously rendered scenes of pleasure seeking, scenes of everyday queer sociability, and across a landscape of commercial, national-public, rural, natural, and small-town spaces. "Elliptical montage" loosely connects the first moments of courtship at Tong's house and a chance encounter in traffic to subsequent scenes that detail the unfolding of the men's intimacy.[18]

Keng and Tong spend leisure time in Tong's village, its natural surroundings, and the nearby town; they go to a restaurant, to the cinema, to a *sala* (a wooden structure in the forest where Keng lies in Tong's lap as they engage in lovers' talk), visit a cave with shrines, and spend time with two older women. The two men do not form a detached unit in these contexts but rather interrelate widely, in particular with older women who direct much of the social interaction and are influential in economic matters. In contrast to the homosexuality of urban nightlife targeted by state actors and to the heroic homosexuality that inspires national recognition in mainstream cinema, *Tropical Malady* establishes homosexuality in a nonurban social structure marked by relations of economy, gender, and pleasure that are particular to the Thai-global periphery.

Queer Aesthetics: Casualness and Ordinariness

In aesthetic terms *Tropical Malady* is a realist fantasy. The film renders the story of Keng and Tong's relationship through a documentary lens that admixes elements of fantasy, a style that James Quandt describes as a "documentary realism" that "becomes surreal, almost dreamlike in its matter-of-factness."[19] While many critics acknowledge Keng and Tong's homosexuality, most ultimately subordinate the issue of sexuality to investigations of the film's aesthetic or philosophical qualities. Yet it is precisely *Tropical Malady*'s narrative and cinematographic features that can be closely aligned with its queerness. The film's elliptical editing gives the story of the relationship between the two men a noncoherent quality that disrupts the linearity of conventional love plots. We can further discern queerness in what Cristina Nord calls "shape shifting" and Quandt describes as Apichatpong's general filmic "modus": "Stories morph, change course, or start over; genre slips moment to moment from fiction to fantasy to documentary; characters shift shape, male to female, human to animal, extraterrestrial to earthling, and what they report is often unreliable; time becomes suspended, and setting ebbs from landscape into dreamscape."[20] The most important aesthetic aspects of *Tropical Malady* in regard to queerness, however, have to do with the director's expert rendering of life in the Thai provinces and with the film's dominant register of casualness. On the level of content casualness takes three forms: the seeming absence of deliberate action, the social informality evinced by the story's characters, and the film's offhand political gestures all constitute important elements in its presentation of same-sex desire.

Critics have emphasized Apichatpong's unprecedented attention to the ordinary, referring to the director's proficiency in representing the Thai everyday and also to what he himself identifies as class.[21] Apichatpong expressly describes his films' devotion to the ordinary as a political project: "I am interested in class distinctions in Thailand. . . . Thai society to me is quite oppressive, no matter what class you are in. But it is like a mute oppression that occurs with the lower class people."[22]

Writers such as Thomas Dumm and Veena Das direct attention to the ordinary as the locus of agency and voice. Dumm claims the ordinary as fundamental to resisting processes of normalization and thereby as the main ground of political freedom in the present: "When the ordinary is invoked in reference to the conflict between the eventful and the normalized, it is usually considered to be outside politics, not a contestant in a political struggle regarding meaning and power. But the ordinary might come to light in the conflict between forces of normalization and events as an element that infiltrates events and opposes the normal."[23]

How can the ordinariness of provincial lives as depicted in *Tropical Malady* provide a counterpoint to the processes of normalization in the domain of sexuality in Thailand? It is precisely the detailed social reality that Apichatpong presents that opens the view onto the counternormative possibilities of a pervasive, quotidian homoeroticism in contemporary Thailand. First, because Apichatpong gets the specifics of the material environment and life in the Thai provinces right, meticulously detailing the provincial everyday almost in real time, he is able to give same-sex desire the status of a staple and even vital element of ordinary life there. Importantly, in *Tropical Malady*'s social landscape homosexuality, rather than representing urban decadence, is fundamentally rooted in rural and small-town life. It is thus something that the viewer can imagine as pervading all geographic areas and social strata of Thailand. While events of national prohibition lightly haunt its story, the film directs our attention primarily to the opportunities for circumvention, even resistance, that the everyday affords.

To examine how the film brings casualness to bear on queerness, it is helpful first to look at the social settings in which the men's relationship unfolds. One of the ways that casualness manifests is in the public nature of Keng and Tong's interactions and in the wholly unperturbed responses of the people around them. Throughout Keng and Tong's courtship, they are alone in an interior space only once. At most other times the men's intimacy is incorporated into other constellations—those of Tong's family, of other men, and, in particular, of women who are Keng and Tong's seniors.

On the level of *Tropical Malady*'s story, the summary effect of casualness (in the sense of social informality) is that everyone remains completely unperturbed by how Keng and Tong relate to each other. A dinner scene with Tong's family and members of Keng's patrol establishes this social attitude early on. The action of the slow three-and-a-half-minute scene is minimal, yet the scene is dense with intimations of desire. The dinner guests sit cross-legged in a circle on a bamboo platform outside, and a succession of point-of-view shots presents Tong's parents' observation of the budding amorous interest between Keng and Tong as well as between Keng's friend and Tong's sister. Each exchange is openly observed by Tong's mother, while Tong's father's witnessing of the goings-on is more discreet. Framed by medium shots of Tong's mother's facial expressions and eye movement, the scene sets the tone for a bemused laissez-faire attitude to homosexuality. Tong's parents stand in for authoritative seniority but refuse to interfere in a proscriptive way.

Throughout the film there is little evidence of aversion to or aggression against the two men. Keng and Tong show no fear or need to conceal their desire; neither do they assert it aggressively. When an unknown corpse the soldiers found and strung up in a hammock speaks up during the dinner described earlier, saying, "You don't have to chase me away. I may be a sweet talker, but my heart is sincere," he gives voice to the desires weaving across the dinner platform but also adds to the sense that anything is possible in this social context.

This permissive scenario acquires an added dimension in the continuation of the scene. As Tong disappears into a corrugated tin shed for his evening bath, the scene's final minute and a half concentrates solely on Keng's face and body. Seated alone on the bamboo platform now, Keng's attention is directed at the bath shed as he waits for Tong to reemerge. In a medium shot Keng smiles suggestively directly into the camera, sometimes turns sideways only to glance back flirtatiously, and bites his fingers in anticipation (fig. 3.1). Keng's direct look at the camera is also a direct gaze at the viewer, however, thereby implicating the viewer in an anticipated desirous exchange between men. Appearing as both object and subject of a desiring gaze, Keng reaches beyond the diegesis of the film to challenge viewers fully to enter the terrain of homoerotic license. Lacking all manifestations of external or internalized homophobia, Apichatpong's film thus outlines a queer utopian fantasy in the sense that homoerotic desire is almost in no way limited by its environment.

What does it mean that everyone remains untroubled by the desire between Tong and Keng and that their desire so easily incorporates the desires of and for others? In their conversation about *Tropical Malady*, Apichatpong and the film critic Chuck Stephens repeatedly consider this point. Referring to a scene between Keng and a fellow soldier in a public bathroom, Stephens points out the long, almost blinding smile that the other man gives Keng. As he notes, such interaction is ubiquitous in the film:

CHUCK STEPHENS: It gives you the sense that all of Thailand is one big cruiser's paradise.

APICHATPONG WEERASETHAKUL: Yes, it is . . .

CHUCK STEPHENS: . . . one big pick-up joint!

Stephens summarizes the multiple, crisscrossing interests in the film as follows: "There is a polymorphous sense of everyone being attractive,

FIGURE 3.1. Keng's gaze implicates the viewer in a desirous exchange between men. Apichatpong Weerasethakul, *Tropical Malady* (*Sat Pralat*, 2004).

everyone being a potential partner for someone."[24] Polymorphous desiring occurs not only in same-sex contexts in *Tropical Malady*, but also in a large variety of constellations. The film introduces this general social environment in an early scene in which Tong makes sustained, flirtatious eye contact with a woman in a pickup truck. When, at a traffic light, Keng's army truck pulls up alongside, Tong's nonverbal communication with the woman is cut off. Tong's subsequent banter with Keng remains entirely noncommittal, if not disinterested. While seemingly geared toward setting heterosexual desire in competition with homosexual desire, both flirtations remain inconsequential in this scene. Rather than indicate the thwarting of heterosexual desire, *Tropical Malady* thus suggests a casual coexistence and interweaving of desires.

What, then, is queer or, more precisely, critical with regard to Thai sexual politics in the landscape of casual desiring outlined by *Tropical Malady*? Does the way in which Tong and Keng's relationship is embedded in constellations of desire with other men and women not interfere with or cancel out homosexual desire? Does homosexual publicity in this context do more than illustrate the variance in attachments that has been identified for Thailand and that, in the case of male homoeroticism, is tolerated as long as it does not translate into domestic arrangements or sustained public intimacies?[25] And what does it mean that the film locates homosexuality in a social landscape of perfect harmony?

This is where the film's sparse references to queer desire in public space and in relation to national symbols come in. In at least two scenes the film gestures toward national politics and in several toward homosexuality's imbrications with the economy. Especially the long scene of Tong and Keng's outing into town becomes significant in this respect. Alternating between men's faces and bodies in commercial and national-public settings, this episode begins with Tong wandering around a Lotus department store. At one point he is framed under images that seem to declare the easy availability of men, or of masculinity, as objects of desire and consumption: for a long moment he stands under the large photograph of an attractive man in a tank top, to the left and right of which two signs declare a 20 percent and 50 percent sale.[26] Tong never buys anything, and the scene reminds us of the fact that he is a low-wage laborer and that Keng's position as a soldier and forest ranger is not much better. The scene signals the linkage of homosexuality with a market that recognizes it as a commodifiable terrain but eludes the economic possibilities of ordinary men—a point I will return to.

The view switches to the profile of Keng, who is smoking in the parking lot. Directly cutting to a muscular body on a stage, the next scene shows Keng's soldier friend with the blinding smile as a dance instructor leading public aerobics exercises. A medium shot shows Tong and Keng sitting close together on plastic stools on one side of the exercise area, sharing street food snacks. As they look at a photo together, and Keng finds in his pocket Tong's (or his mother's!) response to a love note that Keng wrote, they inhabit a measure of privacy in the clamorous public setting. Their conversation fades out as the exercise music dominates the scene and draws all attention to the movement of the male body on stage and to the nonverbal communication between the men: we cut back to the soldier–dance instructor moving on the stage in tight shorts and a tank top. The climax of the scene comes when he waves and smiles once again at Keng, who returns the smile over Tong's shoulder across the rows of the exercising public (figs. 3.2 and 3.3). Keng's smile is accompanied by a quick raising of his eyebrows, an appreciative gesture toward his friend's body in performance as well as an indication of his desire for Tong.

The scene thereby clarifies the notion of male homoerotic relations that the film puts forth. The exchange of smiles signals the friend's acknowledgment of Keng's desire for Tong, thus providing this desire with a queer

FIGURE 3.2. Keng's friend provides the relationship with a queer public. Apichatpong Weerasethakul, *Tropical Malady* (*Sat Pralat*, 2004).

FIGURE 3.3. Keng's smile indicates both his desire for Tong and its nonexclusivity. Apichatpong Weerasethakul, *Tropical Malady* (*Sat Pralat*, 2004).

public, while at the same time indicating its nonexclusivity. Homoerotic relations are not in any way depersonalized or anonymized in this scene, however. That it occurs in the location of the exercise area reveals yet another significance of the exchange between the men. Not only is this scene in which male desire is signaled nonsurreptitiously exemplary of a moment in which men "grant each other the illusions of privacy" in this public locale; its significance also lies in the way it centrally anchors male same-sex desire and the display of queer bodies in a public space marked as national.[27] When the scene ends with a long shot, we see that the public exercise occurs in front of a town hall or official building that bears symbols of the nation and the monarchy: six Thai flags draped from the building at mid-height, with the insignia of the monarchy above them. Further linking queerness to as quotidian, state-sponsored, and citizenship-forming an activity as the public exercise that was instituted across Thailand in the past decade, the scene casually gestures toward the relation of queerness and nation. The point, as we will see, is precisely that it does so casually. Apichatpong will repeat this particular move ("I wanted them to kiss for the nation") when he lets the men's intimacy culminate in the hand-licking scene underneath the symbols of nation, monarchy, and religion on the street at night. Precisely not building its story around a particular event of national sexual politics, the film thus highlights a different aspect of the politics of homosexuality in the country.

Tropical Malady's presentation of homosexuality as casually but inextricably built into the everyday in Thailand is not a regression to the notion of an idyllic preconflictual period—a time when homosexuality had not yet entered the political arena in the ways that it did in the 1990s and 2000s.[28] Rather it focuses attention on how gays, lesbians, and kathoeys contend with prohibition outside of the arena of direct political protest or policy reform in Thailand. In this context the casualness of political gestures matters. The offhand way in which the film invests homoerotic exchanges with political meaning represents an example of how the ordinary "infiltrates events and opposes the normal."[29] While events of national prohibition haunt the scene, they are overlaid with the detailed rendition of how men circumvent such prohibition and continue practices of pleasure in the everyday. Such opposition is here performed through a register, or a style of engaging with power.

The men's nonchalant flirtation under the flag represents a relation to prohibition that is also particular to Thailand. *Tropical Malady* shows that gay men in Thailand—in addition to outright protest—also engage in a kind of *play* with prohibition. Achille Mbembe has described play as a fundamental feature of how people engage with power in postcolonial situations. In Mbembe's account, however, play manifests in grotesque and obscene forms.[30] In *Tropical Malady*, by contrast, the register of play is subtle and the derision of power understated. The understatement of oppositional gestures accounts for the ways men contend with "moderate" regulation—that is, with the diffuse and insidious forms of discursive-juridical prohibition developed by state agencies over the past two decades.

The nonchalance of homoerotic performance in the scene described thus discloses something about the strategies and affective stances by means of which gay men have ignored, circumvented, and satirized the Thai state's various attempts at ordering. In the film men's reactions to prohibition are marked by neither direct protest nor evasion; rather the men evince a stubborn insistence on their desire and display their power to disregard its attempted prohibition. *Tropical Malady*'s perspective thus highlights the casual courage of men who continue to produce a public "world of virtually limitless erotic possibility," despite the fact that this intimacy may now appear deviant to state and society.[31]

The film also makes a statement about location. With its offhand, seemingly indifferent references to the nation, *Tropical Malady* insists on the persistence—in spite of the new prescriptions for sexual personhood—of a quotidian, nonassimilatory local queerness.[32] It thus portrays the fact that queer cultures in Thailand are ubiquitous yet dispersed, so that social ordering cannot entirely damage their informal networks, casual manifestations, and general resilience.[33]

Politics of Vulnerability

It is instructive in this context to review the state disciplinary campaigns' simultaneous deployment of vulnerability and strategies of inclusion that are in fact detrimental to gay men and kathoeys. When Pracha Malinond was in charge of the social order campaign as deputy minister of the interior (2002–6), he authored three books that lay out the campaign's rationales. Disseminated for public relations purposes, most of *Social Ordering* 2 is made up of vignettes that recount experiences during bar raids. These accounts document in great detail—and in the presumed idiom of youth culture—the very things that officials aim to banish from the public sphere.

Stories with salacious titles such as "Tattooed All Over, She Left Her Guy to Go Clubbing," "She-Male Show," and "Sexy Nights Gay Bar" list overt female sexuality, a transgender show, and practices in a gay sex venue as strains on Thai culture.[34] These accounts link Thainess to a certain performance of sexual personhood, always negatively invoked. Its transgression is described as occurring through homosexuality and transgender embodiment as well as through refusals of gender and sexual norms by women.

The report "From 'My Vagina' to 'My Penis,'" about the raid on a gay establishment, is characteristic of the campaign's attitudes toward gay men and trans persons. The report takes a familiar and even "inside" approach to the very modes of gendered embodiment and sexuality that the campaign aims to modify.[35] As in the case of the Ministry of Culture's stance on homosexuality, however, this intimate identification of and with a national civic, cultural, and economic "we" that includes sexual minorities ultimately paves the way for interventions into matters previously left unregulated. The report's novel, simultaneous recognition of suffering and rights, on the one hand, and the casting of gay men as a source of social disturbance, on the other hand, encapsulates something fundamental about shifts in understandings of minorities and majorities in the Thai public sphere.[36]

The disciplinary campaigns reinforced widespread beliefs about homosexuality as aberrant, ideas that Thai psychiatry also condoned both actively and tacitly until 2002, when activists prompted the Ministry of Public Health to act on the earlier declassification of homosexuality as a mental disorder. In addition the campaigns' designation of homosexuality and transgender positions as diminished personhood evokes vernacular notions of karmically determined inferiority derived from Theravadin Buddhist understandings. Yet, as becomes evident in Pracha's account, the campaigns' immense interest in and amassing of knowledge about the lives and practices of sexual minorities also result in the identification of gay men as a vulnerable population in need of protection rather than only regulation.[37] However, while gay men's vulnerabilities are exposed in detail by the campaigns, no concrete remedy or actual protection is offered. As a consequence the intimate knowledge garnered about the grievances of sexual minorities instead becomes the basis for a particularly invasive kind of quotidian regulation.

I have argued that the notion of existentially diminished personhood, loosely based on Theravadin Buddhist perspectives, continues to inform both official and popular perspectives on homosexuality. As we saw, even

Pracha's account of the inspection of a gay club invokes a notion of damagedness when describing the status of gay men and transgendered persons. When it speaks of gay men as vulnerable, Pracha's text further gestures toward the notion of social obligation to minority populations. When state bodies intervene in this sphere of vulnerability, however, the local, "traditional" stigma ascribed to transidentitarian positions is exacerbated rather than reduced.[38]

While Nord cites "damagedness" as an effective trope for portraying queerness in film, we saw how *Tropical Malady*'s social first half stands out precisely by refraining from presenting homosexuality in an idiom of loss or diminution.[39] Homosexuality is not subjectively experienced as traumatic. Neither does it figure at the center of a story about national injury and reparation, or even as a case of adversity.[40] Instead *Tropical Malady* presents homosexuality in the context of a story of social and affective bliss in which the characters often seem "suffocated with happiness."[41] Largely on the basis of this particular affect and through its replacement of the trope of the closet with an updated notion of unconditional queer publicity, *Tropical Malady* thus opens up a new avenue for queer expression.

At the same time, the film also acknowledges and addresses queers' vulnerability in the present political climate. When in the second half of *Tropical Malady* Tong reemerges in the jungle, his naked body and face are tattooed with *sak yan* designs conventionally applied to male bodies as a magic protective measure (fig. 3.4). Written on Tong's queer body is a popular Buddhist belief in male inviolability. The nakedness and animality as well as the Buddhist inscription of this body become significant with regard to how the film positions same-sex desire in the contemporary Thai political public sphere.

When read in the context of *Tropical Malady*'s sparse but explicit references to national sexual politics in its first half, Tong's form of embodiment represents a bold gesture toward national audiences: its animal element signals the unwillingness to desexualize queerness or to reduce it to a question of good citizenship ("We are indeed strange, queer beings"). In the context of Tong's human embodiment, his nakedness at once resembles a bold act of uncovering a queer body while simultaneously rendering it vulnerable— not least to censorship. Finally, this provocative gesture is supplemented by the protective tattooing, which signals the wish to reduce the vulnerability of queer bodies in a hostile political climate. The laying claim to a masculine, popular Buddhist quest for inviolability in combination with the risky act of visual exposure functions simultaneously as an irreverent gesture

FIGURE 3.4. Tong enacts a body politics of vulnerability and animality in the film's second half. Apichatpong Weerasethakul, *Tropical Malady* (*Sat Pralat*, 2004).

and a legitimating one. The film's innovative move here is that the tattoo signals an expectation of injury, but rather than seek to circumvent injury solely in the social and legal spheres, *Tropical Malady* situates the problem also on a broader existential plane. Tong's Buddhist-coded embodiment in this scene does not rely on notions of juridically effected repair, national reconciliation, notions of diversity, and psychological adjustment but nevertheless makes a social and political intervention. Casually signaling its engagement with state sexual politics, Apichatpong's work eschews liberalism as a language of oppositional politics and instead speaks in the registers of a defamiliarized Buddhism.

Women: Cross-Gender Queer Sociality in a Precarious Economy

Tropical Malady situates its model of male same-sex relating within a broader queer social vision in which male and female homosocialities intersect in pleasurable ways. The trope of manipulation of the economy is central to the director's vision of this queer sociality. In this social order men are the economic bottoms, and their economic receptivity is what constitutes their own pleasure as well as that of the economically more savvy older women.[42]

Keng and Tong's relationship is closely linked to the homosocial relationship between two older women, Samreung and Noi. The two women are representative of a particular kind of femininity marked by the intensity of the desires and fantasies that the women direct toward the economic sphere. Throughout the time of the men's association with Samreung and Noi, a constant narrative of the economy as a trope of relative scarcity *and* of potential abundance thus captions all their experiences.

From the beginning of the film's social half it is older women who literally set the scene for the men's romance. Women who are Keng and Tong's seniors provide the ambiance (a singer in a restaurant), the material settings (Tong's mother), and even the discursive framing for the men's relationship (Samreung and Noi). Yet their own enjoyment is also derived from these actions. What kinds of sexual subjectivities emerge from a world populated almost exclusively by gay men and older, economically savvy women?

Two scenes present the men's most significant interactions with women. In one of these the men's casual acquaintances Pa (Aunt) Samreung and her friend or sister, Noi, invite Keng and Tong, "Come, let's go drink Pepsi!" This invitation and the scene that follows it summarize the specifics of an environment where drinking Pepsi would still be a treat or constitute a social activity in itself. The scene also reveals how the women's desire is organized around male homosexuality and how material and affective economies of paucity and abundance interrelate. The women take Tong and Keng to Noi's village shop, an extension of her home that opens onto a dirt square. Here all four sit, legs folded, on a wooden platform at the front of the shop (fig. 3.5). Keng and Tong are offered Pepsi, and Samreung peels a pomelo for them—a combination of things to consume that is unmistakably particular to Thailand. In this setting eating pomelo dipped in a sugar, salt, and chili mix and drinking Pepsi just makes sense, as does the combination of goods and brands (small Sunsilk shampoos, individual cigarettes, small bags of snacks) that are sold in the shop with the view onto the thatched huts across the dirt square, the noise from passing motorcycles, and the stray dogs. In the little more than two minutes of the scene Noi casually offers her homegrown marijuana, Samreung playfully reminds her of Keng's status as a "defender of the nation," Samreung boasts about the shop's financial success, and the conversation turns to possibilities of securing employment.

When Noi produces a *palat khik* (wooden phallus) for Keng and Tong to look at, the scene reveals much about contemporary gender roles, desires, and social structures in the Thai-global periphery. Noi tells the story of the phallus, an object she acquired and had consecrated at the nearby Wat Ku temple and that has brought her unprecedented good luck in busi-

Business has been booming since I got it.

FIGURE 3.5. The men's homoerotic desire and the women's desire for capital gain coalesce around the phallic talisman of the *palat khik*. Apichatpong Weerasethakul, *Tropical Malady* (*Sat Pralat*, 2004).

ness. Keng and Tong look at the palat khik and smile broadly at each other and at the women. Although the appearance of the auspicious object cannot in any sense be said to represent a climax—in tune with the general mood of *Tropical Malady* the arrival of the phallus is met with the utmost casualness—the object condenses the desires for affective and economic abundance invoked in the scene: the women's somewhat patronizing fondness for Keng and Tong, the female economic prowess that makes this patronage possible, and Keng and Tong's desire for each other. In letting homo- and (perhaps) heterosexual desire, economic aspirations, and certain kinds of sensory enjoyment (Pepsi, pomelo, pot) come together, the scene presents a world in which it is women who attain expertise in (attempting) the control of an unstable economy, both men and women share its sensory pleasures, and the new gendered roles of aspiration, production, manipulation, and consumption also come to bear on sexuality.

How does the women's economic role relate, first of all, to their own sexuality? The women's relationship—it never becomes clear whether they are siblings or friends—is not explicitly erotic, yet the scene presents a female relationship that is characterized by intensity.[43] As minor characters in the film, Samreung and Noi do not represent its main sexual subjects, yet they are depicted as "complex, erotic beings, full of life and sex [and sorrow]."[44] Although not presented *in* actual sexual relationships—or are they lovers after all?—Samreung and Noi are nevertheless not desexualized. I would even argue that *Tropical Malady* presents the women's sexuality as a kind of queer sexuality. Most noteworthy in this regard is that the two are not defined by conventional forms of kinship but rather by the associations they choose voluntarily.

Samreung and Noi's relationship is marked by their shared commitment to commercial engagement and admiration of each other's successes in this domain. Although we do not know of their actual business involvement, what emerges from the hopes expressed in the scene with the phallic talisman is the women's intense desire for capital gain, exemplifying a moment of what Tani Barlow describes as women "creat[ing] . . . capital together"—even if only in fantasy. In contrast, in relation to men there is only talk of (un)employment but not of entrepreneurial activity—"the laboring subjects who produce wealth are all female," it seems.[45]

When Barlow writes about "women in transition" in Sinophone film, she is concerned with accounting for the historical specificity of a gendered, pan-Asian subject in the historical present. She describes the characteristics of this subject as follows: "Women rather than men are the producers of surplus value; the female agent engages in profitable and self-directed actions, though not actions that will ever emancipate her from the obvious political oppressions she experiences." The notion of "a singular economic subjectivity predicated as labor power" can be brought to bear on the socioeconomic world of *Tropical Malady*.[46] However, in this world, I argue, the female economic agency described by Barlow represents an element of a pleasurable queer sociality. Like the women Barlow describes, Samreung and Noi are consistently associated with commerce and (dreams of) surplus value, at times magically enhanced. As in the scene of a passive Tong in the sexualized commercial space of the Lotus department store, *Tropical Malady* points to a world in which men, by contrast, have become marginal in relation to the economic process.

The Asian economic landscape that Barlow investigates comes with restrictions for women's sexuality. Even though "women's productivity is increasingly sexualized," the women Barlow describes are denied "procreative sexuality" as well as "recreational sexuality."[47] As Barlow explains, women's access to social satisfaction does not parallel their ascendancy in the economic sphere.[48] She emphasizes that in the films she examines women are "forbidden to create anything but capital together"; that is, they are denied also a recreational homosexuality.[49] Rather than the question of whether

Samreung's and Noi's sexual possibilities are restricted in this manner, however, it is the women's homosociality that occupies the center of the film's attention. Although the characters of Apichatpong's film share the same general conditions of a globalized Asian economy, *Tropical Malady* is intent on portraying the social and affective pleasures that this female homosociality enables. The film's formula for how economy, gender, and sexuality interrelate contains the additional elements of magic as an economic factor and bliss as a dimension of all desiring.

While structures of social hierarchy are not absent from Apichatpong's docudrama, seniority is presented as overwhelmingly feminine. Keng and Tong's elders are independent women and male authority is not in evidence, with the brief exception of Tong's father, who extends an invitation to Keng to move in with the family. *Tropical Malady* thus presents social structures significantly marked by changing valences of female labor and femininity. In this space male homosexuality is permissible and even taken for granted, though perhaps not understood as exclusive. The picture that emerges is thus one of differently eroticized male and female homosocialities, the pleasures of which are heightened by a queer sociality across genders.

But what is the women's investment in Keng and Tong's relationship? The women seem to derive pleasure not only from witnessing the men's pleasure but also from the chance to display their expertise in matters of love and their ability to direct the men's relationship and to frame it discursively. Their first appearance in the film begins with a scene of instruction in which Samreung sketches out an economy of affect, magic, and market for the men. In the sala in the forest Keng lies on Tong's lap while they engage in the most intense lovers' talk of the film. After a while a middle-aged woman, Samreung, approaches with the question "Do you want flowers?" When Tong replies, "If they're free, sure!," she sits down and seamlessly joins in the men's intimate conversation with the assertion, "To acquire merit, you have to invest. And the same goes for binding a person's heart." Samreung then proceeds to tell them a fable about spectacular, magical material gain and loss. Her story of a *nen*, a Buddhist novice who turned stones into silver and gold for two poor farmers, ends badly when the farmers' greed prompts them to gather more stones, whereupon their riches turn into toads.

Concluding her story with a Buddhist-inflected exclamation, "Khwam lop khong khon, na!" (Oh, human greed! [*lop*, from Pali, *lobha*]), Samreung proceeds to tell of a woman in a game show who would not stop playing and therefore lost all but 30,000 Baht of her winnings. Keng's reply,

"Pa, I don't even make 10,000 Baht," and Tong's, "I really want to meet that little novice, Pa," underline their lack of access to finances and their economic bottomhood.[50] What seems to provide Samreung with the greatest pleasure is her ability to display her knowledge and to frame the men's relationship as subject to larger systems of investment and returns. Drawing the men's desires for each other in relation to Buddhist, magic, and market economies, she brings an element of caution to the men's exultant relationship and foreshadows events in the film's second half.

This conversation is also important because it lets the viewer begin to fathom the women's affective investment in male homosexuality. When Samreung recounts how she came to the area with her husband thirty years earlier, when it was a jungle, Keng says that it must have been romantic. She quickly discounts this idea—"What romance, with malaria?"—perhaps signaling skepticism also about the heterosexuality of her past. In contrast, in all the time that they spend with Keng and Tong, the women seem to partake in the men's affective states by proxy. Homosexuality is indeed contagious here, an infectious figure of affective abundance. Not strongly bound up in the economy or in familial life building, Keng and Tong's relationship represents a model of bliss and complementarity and of a pure and carefree form of love. Samreung's contentment and frequently even radiance in their presence testifies to the fact that these are transmissible elements.

Tropical Malady thus develops Keng and Tong's relationship with strong reference to these sexual-economic subjects and the world they delineate for the men. While the film consistently brings into play a notion of diminution through its persistent alignment of the men's lives with their failure or irrelevance regarding the economic process, this does not translate into feelings of diminution. This refusal to portray gay men as economically potent is significant in light of cultural policy's understanding of gay men's roles in the economy.

A look back at Pracha's report on the raid of a gay establishment reveals that in another twist of policy reasoning, gay men are also identified as a direct source of economic profit. Homosexuality figured ambivalently in the project of ordering sexuality that became so significant to "national fantasy" in the 2000s: it was not only vilified but also came to stand in for the potential for national (economic) betterment.[51] It is thus not surprising that in his report Pracha also designates gay men as consumers and customers.[52] And not only the deputy minister linked homosexuality to economic matters. In response to an electronic version of the newspaper article reporting Deputy Undersecretary Kla Somtrakul's 2004 declaration that he would ban lesbian, gay, and trans employees from serving in the Ministry of Culture, readers appended more than 1,500 comments. Although several readers held conservative views on the position of sexual minorities in Thai society, most wrote to protest Kla's actions. A large number based their opposition to the antigay and anti-transgender declaration on the argument that gay men, kathoeys, and lesbians represent especially productive populations.[53] In a gesture of radical refusal of queer productivity, *Tropical Malady* instead consistently highlights the communicability across genders and sexual orientations of affective, sensory, and material pleasures. Although the economic expertise and success is all on the women's side, it seems to produce pleasure for all.

The Buddhist sexual contemporaneity that *Tropical Malady* fleshes out thus also relies on the subversive engagement with economic models. Both the idea of gay men as potent economic actors and the notion of sufficiency—of a general, Buddhist-coded paring down on the part of the population—are turned in a radically different direction in *Tropical Malady*. For one, the relative poverty of the context invokes neither traditionality nor modesty in sexual or relational terms. On the contrary gay men figure as catalysts in a scene largely devoted to pleasure-seeking, countering the sobriety of sufficiency with wasteful affective abandon.

The film constantly highlights the sensory richness of Keng's and Tong's lives. Thus ultimately even the trope of relative material scarcity stands in for affective abundance; some of the scenes of purest bliss visually exploit an aesthetics of relative poverty. Thus at the height of his bliss, in the morning after the hand-licking episode with Tong under the flag, Keng rides in the open back of an army truck, in close physical proximity to the other soldiers. The soundtrack of a popular love song underwrites this as a scene of homoerotic enjoyment, yet it is the long traveling shot of the dust cloud behind the truck—a visual instantiation of the aesthetics of relative poverty—that represents the scene's most intense figuration of pleasure.

Unlike what Jonathan Hall describes for the gay Japanese boom films of the 1990s, *Tropical Malady*'s homosexuality is not misogynist, nor does it ever become competitive with women.[54] And while writers such as Mary Beth Mills have described Thai women's sexualities as eliciting intense anxiety in conjunction with women's new economic subjectivities, such conflict over sexuality and gender roles is simply absent from *Tropical Malady*'s society of younger gay men and older women.[55] The film does not label this as a feminist or queer ideal, but this sexual and economic landscape of the Thai-global periphery nevertheless comes to bear utopian characteristics. In this realist-fantastic world there is no zero sum of desires, and neither male homosexuality nor women's superior economic positions detract from anyone else's pleasure.

Instead of being connected to a central event of loss, queerness in *Tropical Malady* is, in contrast to other Thai queer films, skillfully woven into the uneventful flow of the everyday. The threat of loss that comes into play from economic fluctuation never translates into paucity of feeling. Rendered as a singularly unproductive economic subjectivity, male homosexuality represents a source of contagious affective abundance. Keng and Tong's relationship, far from threatening social disruption, enhances pleasure and strengthens nonfamilial and family bonds in a society in which gender roles are "in transition" in various ways.[56] In the idiom of fantastic realism, Apichatpong thus succeeds in sketching out a mode of being and relating that does not make social injury a theme at all yet is cognizant of the recent history of sexuality in the country.

Queering Impermanence

It is in *Tropical Malady*'s second half that Apichatpong makes the Buddhist ontology of impermanence available to queer interpretation. Rather than make the notion of impermanence subservient to the nostalgia of nationalist historiography, the film defamiliarizes Buddhist pedagogies of loss to broaden the interpretation of central psychological and ontological questions. Rather than primarily impart a teaching about nonattachment, the Buddhist tale of the tiger ghost performs a kind of queer advocacy, provides a framework for fantasy in the domain of desire, and reframes queerness with regard to the social and karmic negativity that it is so inextricably linked with. The tropes of loss and injury in this story do not work to minoritize but move queerness to the center of a reflection on attachment, loss, and creaturely existence.

Tropical Malady's second half transposes Keng and Tong's relationship from its social setting to the jungle. All the film's references to figures and genres of loss are crowded into this section. A reinvented folktale frames the story of two men—or of a man and a male being—tracking, pursuing, and fleeing each other through the forest night, a "macabre man/beast pas de deux that evolves into a hallucinatory episode of self-discovery unlike anything we've witnessed in Thai cinema."[57] Sakda Kaewbuadee, who played Tong in the first half of the film, reappears in this sequence as the jungle being who hunts and is hunted by Keng.

On Keng's journey to recover his lost lover, the jungle becomes invested with a spiritual, cultural, and emotional semiotic; it is symbolic of Thainess, mythology, and the spirit world as well as of Buddhist spiritual advancement. In *Tropical Malady* this cultural semiotic, especially the figure of the ghost, delineates the psychic dimensions of a male homosexual relationship. Ultimately the investment of the jungle with religious meaning also becomes instrumental in making homosexuality the primary figure of human existence.

Narratively the jungle sequence is linked to the first hour of the film in the following way. The first half ends with Tong sleeping in his room. When Keng enters the room, however, he finds Tong's bed empty. Keng hears a villager outside the house relate the news of a beast that preys on livestock: "I found a paw print this morning." For Keng this news kicks off a long stretch of sweat-drenched, malarial jungle roaming. Focused more on Keng, the episode recounts the pursuit of the mysterious beast as Keng's search for his lost lover. It is with this search that a notion of loss comes into play and that the film explicitly places homosexuality in relation to ontological and psychological negativity. While the first half of the film began to gesture toward the ominous, it nevertheless presented queerness as nontraumatic. The motif of pain thus appears only in the second half. Even here, however, the story of Keng and his animal–spirit–human counterpart portrays existential, not social, suffering. The nature of this existential suffering also differs from that invoked in mainstream films; rather than depict it as suffering that is connected to marginality, *Tropical Malady* universalizes homosexual pain in this sequence.

Vitally responsible for shifting the relations of homosexuality and negativity in this way are the film's interpretations of Thainess. While critical evaluations of Apichatpong's renderings of Thai culture stress his fidelity to the indigenous, the exact nature of his cinema's relation to Thainess requires further scrutiny. Kong Rithdee writes of *Tropical Malady*, "What confirms Apichatpong's status as a fresh and vital force in global cinema is the way his movies remain steadfastly rooted in the rich soil of his native culture and derive their innate power from its artistic history. His are not 'Asian films' cloaked in some exotic orientalist fantasy but wholly indigenous conceptions infected by tropical maladies cultivated at home."[58] Lauding Apichatpong as a truly Thai filmmaker, Quandt likewise notes the director's "marked debt to the indigenous—Thai soap operas and ghost stories, love songs, talk shows, children's tales, and Buddhist fables."[59] However, this emphasis on the director's faithfulness to "the indigenous" leaves unexamined the complex manipulations that cultural references undergo in this cinema.

Kong's appraisal implicitly contrasts the director's treatment of culture to that of mainstream Thai cinema and its "'Asian Films' cloaked in some exotic orientalist fantasy." Like the contemporary mainstream heritage films that Kong alludes to, *Tropical Malady*'s second half also makes use of tropes and genres associated with a Thai cultural past.[60] In his borrowings from tradition, however, Apichatpong tends to draw on minor genres and highlight cultural strains that until recently have not enjoyed high prestige. While I agree that Apichatpong's style of referencing Thai culture differs from that of mainstream cinema, it is important to note that the director's citations do not stand in greater proximity to a purported real culture, and to stress that the director is not engaged in a quest for authenticity.

The shift into the jungle fantasy is inaugurated by the screen going black for several seconds, which marks the story's entrance into a more somber affect. The episode opens with and is framed throughout by intertitles consisting of images that imitate a folk style of temple murals on which writing is superimposed. "Winyan" ([A] Spirit), reads the first, the word superimposed on the drawing of a tiger, "Inspired by the stories of Noi Inthanon. Once upon a time there was a powerful Khmer shaman, who could turn into various creatures. He roamed the jungle and played tricks on the villagers."[61] What Apichatpong does here is improvise on a 1950s adventure story and turn it into a Buddhist-coded folk tale. What is more, his story refigures the conventionally female tiger spirit of Thai folklore as a queer male being.

Before that happens, however, in an additional instance of intertextual borrowing, he revives an earlier style of Thai cinema and temporarily complicates the gender identity of the tiger. In the filmic vignette of the story, which comes complete with exaggerated acting, the tiger spirit enters the forest at night in the guise of a woman. She persuades a hunter or soldier to climb down from a tree and follow her. The hunter-soldier's eyes widen when he sees the tiger tail sticking out from underneath the woman's sarong. An intertitle informs us, "The hunter shot the tiger and trapped the shaman in the tiger spirit. The tiger corpse is on display at Kanchanaburi Museum."

The intertitles and the filmic inset of the story about the tiger spirit are significant. Already at this point we realize that Apichatpong deploys

"Thainess" unconventionally. Rather than recuperate ideal images of the past, Thai folklore throughout *Tropical Malady*'s second half functions to delineate the psychic processes of a man engaged in a quest that has to do with desire, and homosexual desire, no less. With his choice of filmic references the director continues to privilege ordinary Thainess in the second half of his film.[62] The filmic vignette of the hunter and the tiger spirit emulates a tradition of early Thai horror-comedies.[63] Apichatpong thus frames the action of the jungle sequence in the tradition of a low-budget, comedic, nonbourgeois genre. His use of tradition stands in contrast to the heritage genre's deployment of high, courtly forms of culture and of recuperations of the folkloric for national-culturalist purposes. Apichatpong thus eschews the conventional distressing of culture and the pathos of nationalist recovery that have become the hallmark of Thai heritage cinema. In this he also diverges from the genre's treatment of gender and sexuality; heritage cinema tends to freeze notions of traditional Thai femininity, conjugal complementarity, and sexuality in idealized iconic forms. Apichatpong instead uses the old horror citation to draw out the gender ambiguity of the tiger spirit.

What is thus missing from assessments of Apichatpong's deployment of Thainess is an account of the defamiliarization that Thai traditions of visual representation, folklore, and something that we can recognize as Theravadin Buddhist form—and, in close connection, models of gender and sexuality—undergo in his films. Instead of a quest for authenticity, *Tropical Malady*'s playful use of intertitles and mural-like images as well as the restaging of the folk tale represent self-conscious remakes of Thainess. Apichatpong's distressing of culture is thus by no means directed toward the performance of authenticity. Rather, in contradistinction to a cinema of origins, *Tropical Malady* reshapes Thainess in highly ironic ways. The scene in which a spirit rises from a dead cow is a case in point. As much as this scene will remind viewers of older Thai films, it also does so through the use of highly specialized effects technology, consciously and self-evidently displacing the cow spirit from its original context.

The mise-en-scène of Tong's body in the jungle episode represents another example of Apichatpong's playful exploitation of Thainess. Tong, or the jungle being, is naked throughout and moves like an animal, yet his entire body and face are covered with intricate patterns that invoke traditional protective tattoos conventionally applied to (male) human bodies. As the director reveals, the tattoos were specially designed for the film from Khmer, Lao, and Thai patterns. Thainess, although this is not immediately evident in the diegesis, is then self-consciously presented as an agglomeration of several cultural strands. More important, a defamiliarizing deployment of Thainess occurs, when it is (over)inscribed on a male body that we can also understand as a queer body. In summary, instead of competing in cultural authenticity, Apichatpong's oeuvre can more closely be described as opting for culture bending.[64] This queering of cultural forms also disrupts the conventional links between temporal incongruity and gendered and sexual formations that I described in my analysis of *Nang Nak*. In *Tropical Malady* the ghost of custom finally fulfills the critical task that she or he is charged with.

As Keng slowly enters the forest in pursuit of the beast, the tale of the tiger ghost figures the descent into the intrapsychic workings of loss and desire. Supertitles propel the story further when they inform us, "Now every night the shaman spirit turns into a tiger to haunt travelers." And "The villagers and their livestock have started to disappear." The next intertitle bears an image of the tiger spirit that is reminiscent of a hungry ghost, a *pret* (Pali, *peta*; Sanskrit, *preta*), introducing the motif of devouring into the story and signaling the psychic dangers of emotional and sexual appetites.[65] The image is captioned, "As the tiger ghost tries to enter his dream, the soldier thinks about the missing villager." Cutting back to Keng, the text continues, "Suddenly a strange feeling gripped the soldier's heart."

From its lightness in the first half, Keng's desire in the film's second half acquires the elements of obsession and pain that come with loss. On his journey through the jungle his pain is in no way alleviated; rather the isolating, primordial setting intensifies it further. Once "the tiger ghost tries to enter his dreams," Keng's tranquility is shattered. In the jungle Keng freezes, sweats, suffers leech bites, becomes frightened and hungry. Rather than delineate trajectories of social conflict and resolution, as it would in mainstream Thai cinema, haunting here figures an existential vulnerability that is in large part related to the workings of desire. Both Keng's bodily sensations as well as his facial expressions reveal the uncertainty, doubt, and fear that now mark his feelings regarding the elusive other. Even the morphology of the jungle comes to figure affect. The eerie moment when the camera traces the twists of vines in the jungle at night while Keng waits to be attacked is an instance in which his fear and confusion become particularly palpable.[66]

The film's second half deploys an entirely different cinematic style to signal the relationship's shift into a primordial, affective domain. Filmed largely at night, without artificial lighting, the jungle sequence lives on the play of shadow, light, human silence, animal sounds, and special effects. All language is suspended, save for Keng's abortive attempts to communicate with headquarters via his radio and the utterances of a baboon, a firefly, and finally the tiger spirit himself. The baboon conveys essential information about Keng's counterpart: "Soldier! The tiger trails you like a shadow. His spirit is starving and lonesome. I see you are his prey and his companion. He can smell you from mountains away. And soon you will feel the same. Kill him to free him from the ghost world. Or let him devour you and enter his world." At this point the relationship has become as antagonistic as it is desirous. The camera briefly cuts to the naked Tong sleeping between trees like an animal. In the jungle, and in Keng's mind, homosexual desire, almost not recognizable as such anymore, becomes predatory and potentially deadly.

Both the cinematic style and the infusion of the relationship with animalistic features make possible the focus on the psychic destabilization that desire brings with it. Roland Barthes emphasizes the shared affective state produced by "amorous loss" and loss through death when he glosses *catastrophe* as a "violent crisis during which the subject, experiencing the amorous situation as a definitive impasse, a trap from which he can never escape, sees himself doomed to total destruction." In *Tropical Malady* the amorous crisis crystallizes in the one occasion on which Keng and his elusive lover/enemy meet and struggle. The struggle culminates in the jungle being's throwing Keng down a hillside. At this moment the placidity of the relationship evident in the first half of the film is shattered for good. While Keng is slightly injured, Tong, or the jungle being, sobs and howls in the forest. Rather than present a resolution that relieves suffering, *Tropical Malady*'s second half is thus dedicated to elaborating pain's full range.

It is through its enactment of pain that the film's second half is able to do something remarkable with how it positions homosexual desire and personhood in relation to human subjectivity. The pursuit culminates in what may be a scene of obliteration: an exhausted, feverish Keng finally meets with the tiger spirit. As Keng crouches on the ground, the tiger stands on a tree branch looking down at him. To shots of a real tiger, the fable resumes in a voice that comes from the tiger/Keng's lover: "Once upon a time there was a powerful shaman who could turn into animals. A creature whose life exists only by memories of others." As Keng shakes before the tiger, the voice continues, "And now . . . I see myself here. My mother. My father. Fear. Sadness. It was all so real . . . so real that . . . they brought me to life. Once I've devoured your soul, we are neither animal nor human. Stop breathing. I miss you . . . soldier.

FIGURE 3.6. The improvised temple-style mural lends spiritual-ontological significance to the final scene of Keng's obliteration or fusion with the tiger/lover. Apichatpong Weerasethakul, *Tropical Malady* (*Sat Pralat*, 2004).

Monster." An intertitle appears with a drawing of the scene—of Keng crouching before the tiger, with a broad string connecting them (fig. 3.6)—again in the style of a temple mural, as the voice continues, "I give you my spirit, my flesh . . . and my memories. Every drop of my blood sings our song. A song of happiness. There . . . do you hear it?" To the extended view and sound of trees rustling in the wind, the closing credits roll.[67]

Rather than in coupling—one of the film's designated endings—the episode seems to end in Keng's being devoured. In his English-language review, Kong provides a persuasive reading of the film's ending as nibbanic obliteration—a termination of the cycle of rebirths and suffering: "If the Buddhist objective is to shed all suffering in order to attain spiritual purity and a kind of peaceful nihilism, then the film's impressionistic ending is a remarkably daring depiction of that goal."[68] Kong offers another Buddhist interpretation in his Thai-language review when he considers the "malady" of the English title: "Is it the malady of homosexuality? Or is it the malady that all of us whether homo- or heterosexual suffer from the moment we attain consciousness, namely the malady of *thuk* (suffering) that we spend our whole lives trying to cure (without ever succeeding)?"[69] In these interpretations Kong presents a relatively doctrinal understanding of desirable progress toward the highest spiritual goal of Buddhism. Although he takes *Tropical Malady*'s queer thematic into account, he ultimately subordinates it to what he considers the larger philosophical-spiritual meaning of the film. However, even if one agrees that the ending in obliteration supersedes the depiction of same-sex desire in importance, the spiritual drama and its nibbanic resolution are still borne out by a male-male relationship, and homoerotic desire is used to illustrate a fundamental tenet of Theravada Buddhism, namely that of the Four Noble Truths, the *Ariyasat Si*—a teaching that delineates the fact and origin of suffering as well as the path to its cessation. Read as a Buddhist parable, the ending would then make homosexuality the primary figure of spiritual subjectivity.

A consideration of Kong's doctrinal evaluation of the film proves highly instructive for discerning the manifold interventions that *Tropical Malady* makes into understandings of how same-sex desire relates to negativity. Two of the questions that this book set out to investigate were these: If in Buddhist formulations negativity describes an ontology that foregrounds the impermanence of existence, how does this understanding of negativity translate into contemporary logics of minoritization? If negativity includes an understanding in which desire is always already destined to fail, how do artistic materials reinhabit this notion? If we take Kong's interpretation of *Tropical Malady*'s orientation to nibbanic resolution seriously, we find that homosexuality assumes an astoundingly central place in Buddhist reasoning. Placing gay male subjects at the center of its existential, Buddhist-coded parable, the film thus performs a vital deminoritizing move. Rather than negate or even supersede the importance of the film's queer thematic, the iconic Buddhist ending can thus be read as deploying negativity, or the notion of impermanence, to grant full creaturely status to its same-sex desiring protagonists.

Considering the film's invocation of negativity and affect beyond the domain of religious interpretation, what is singular about *Tropical Malady* is that it ultimately tells the primal story of loss and attachment *as a homosexual one*. In the primordial yet culturally significant setting of the jungle, homosexuality becomes the story's primary figure of subjectivity. The film's final event of loss is cast not as a matter of social wounding but as a discrete occurrence of existential consequence, primarily outlining psychic dynamics of attachment and loss. The story's motif of ghostly return thus has no direct social purport, and haunting and its exorcism are not mobilized to remedy social destabilization, as they generally are in mainstream Thai cinema. In fact although the tiger designates its finale an instance of happiness, *Tropical Malady* does not tell a reparative story at all.

Viewed from a psychoanalytic perspective, *Tropical Malady*'s deployment of loss performs the rectifying move that Judith Butler calls for in her critique of heteronormative subject formation. Butler highlights the extent to which gendered subject formation depends on the disavowal of (even the possibility of) homosexual attachment. She argues that the unavowed, a priori loss of such attachments gives rise to a particular type of melancholic gendered identification: "The accomplishment of an always tenuous heterosexuality . . . mandat[es] the abandonment of homosexual attachments or, perhaps more trenchantly, *preempt[s]* the possibility of homosexual attachment." She suggests a rectification of psychoanalysis's tendency to tell the story of loss and attachment only as a heterosexual story: "We would lose a vital terminology for understanding loss and its formative effects if we were to assume from the outset that we only and always lose the other sex, for it is as often the case that we are often [*sic*] in the melancholic bind of having lost our own sex in order, paradoxically, to become it."[70] In making same-sex attachments a vital part of human affectivity, *Tropical Malady* brings about the psychological completeness that the heteronormative account suppresses. Apichatpong's film performs a still more radical move than merely one of completion, however; in *Tropical Malady* nearly nothing else appears alongside same-sex desire. The story centers on homosexual desire to such an extent that queerness exemplifies the human (and creaturely) as such.

The universalization of homosexuality attains the most gravity in the scene in which Keng trembles before the tiger in the final moments of his life. As the tiger delineates their imminent fusion ("Once I've devoured your soul, we are neither animal nor human. Stop breathing"), distinctions between bodies, desires, and consciousness give way: "I give you my spirit, my flesh . . . and my memories. Every drop of my blood sings our song." As divisions between self and other and between animal and human are erased, the taxonomizing power of the homo- and heterosexual binary also wanes. The film has thus countered the social negativity conventionally attributed to queerness precisely by fully inhabiting the negativity of the existential condition that Buddhism ascribes to human (and animal) existence.[71]

While psychoanalytic and doctrinal Buddhist readings of *Tropical Malady* open up fruitful perspectives, I suggest that we assay one further understanding of the film's ending. In the introduction of this book I noted that the films under review tend to focus on a domain of deferral rather than on the radical instantiation of negativity. I would argue that *Tropical Malady* is much more concerned with infusing prescriptive affective trajectories with elasticity than with telling a story in which attachment is the mere foil to inevitable expiration. As much as *Tropical Malady*'s ending gestures toward obliteration, it intimates fusion in equal measure—a possibility that the tiger expressly holds out in the voice-over. In a sense the ending is the film's most dramatic sex scene, the climax of the pursuit between Keng and his shape-shifting counterpart. The conceptual strength of *Tropical Malady*'s resolution is that it turns precisely on the indistinction of obliteration or fusion and the indistinction of desire fulfilled or desire foreclosed. Apichatpong's film thereby fully actualizes the potential of Buddhist melancholia, which operates as a trope of mobility with regard to desire rather than only as one of abnegation.

At a time when notions of diminution predominate in policy, psychiatry, religion, and cultural production about nonnormative sexualities, the film's manipulation of notions of negativity represents a discerning intervention. Viewed together, the film's two halves also instantiate a Buddhist-secular synthesis. However, *Tropical Malady* counters the potentially injurious effects of the Buddhist-liberal synthesis that is invoked in mainstream films such as *Saving Private Tootsie* with a more radical conception.

Tropical Malady outlines a vision that directs us away from dimensions of official citizenship, queers' particular karmic deficiencies, and notions of national clemency. The film's simultaneous intervention into secular and religious rhetorics regarding the negativity of queer personhood has shifted the perspective away from notions of corrective inclusion to a greater focus on homosexuality's position in a realist utopian sociality. Here Apichatpong's cinema reframes queer personhood as ordinary, though not obedient, and as socially central, though not assimilated. In contradistinction to a mainstream cinema that does not make room for more than toleration, *Tropical Malady* conceives of a social plenitude that is centrally anchored in homosexuality. On the other hand, it has invested this rich queer sociality with psychological and ontological depth.

Reception

Tropical Malady has reconfigured the conventional linkages between temporal incongruity and desire in the national context, but how does the film engage with transnational perspectives on Thai sexualities? In the transnational imagination of Thailand, temporally inflected fantasies abound, and for English-language audiences the *tropical* in Apichatpong's title alludes to the expectation that Thailand represent a gay paradise before prohibition—a place of sexual excess and limitless tolerance—while *malady* might suggest the idea of a site of pathological decadence.

I argue, however, that the reception of *Tropical Malady* registers a shift in global perspectives on Thai sexualities. Not only did the international criticism recognize the film as an avant-garde cultural product, but for the first time Thai queerness has also come to represent an avant-garde sexual culture. I will consider just one aspect of *Tropical Malady*'s global significance here. The film's approach to homosexual publicity, which eschews the presentation of overt struggles around individual or national disclosure, is one element that seems to have affected the film's global reception. As Hall writes, Asian queer films and Asian sexualities are generally read through the trope of competing national closets. In the criticism the manifestation of homosexuality in Asian cinematic and political public spheres is thus almost invariably subjected to international comparison—read: comparison with the West. The closet then comes to stand in for national time lags, so that Japan, for instance, is always behind in terms of homosexual publicity, and Japanese queer cinema is forever "emerging."[72] Alternatively the time lag may be ascribed to the prohibition of homosexuality; for this, Western projections of Thailand as a gay paradise are a good example.

Through the omission of the trope of the closet from its plot and its organization around an alternative mode of publicity, *Tropical Malady* seems to have succeeded in redirecting critical attention. When Nord reads *Tropical Malady*'s very form as performing queerness and casts the shape-shifting figure of the tiger ghost as a paradigmatic figure of queerness, Thainess, instead of standing in for a temporal lag in homosexual publicity (or homosexual prohibition), comes to represent a queer avant-garde, at least for this global critic.[73] If in the reception of *Tropical Malady* Thai sexuality is subjected to periodization, it thus comes to represent something that is "ahead," or coeval, rather than a thing that can always remain only "before" prohibition or "behind" liberation. At least for a moment, then, this reading unmoors Thai sexualities from the rigid temporal positioning imposed by transnational gazes.[74]

THE DEFAMILIARIZED BUDDHIST FRAMING of Apichatpong's film provides a perspective on the status of male homosexual personhood that exceeds the binaries of liberalism and illiberalism. While mainstream Thai queer-themed films present scenes of political damage and damagedness and conciliatory, national resolutions in response to seemingly moderate policies on sexuality that targeted the lifeworlds of broad sections of the population, *Tropical Malady* pursues the strategy of reanchoring homosexuality in the mundane, public, and collective aspects of life in Thailand, in an affectively shaped social environment, and in a final, not entirely transparent scene of existential annihilation or fusion. With this evocative finale *Tropical Malady* has occupied the domain of Buddhist-coded haunting in another provocative way.

The film also takes the questions of the Buddhist permission or prohibition and of the Thai social acceptance or nonacceptance of homosexuality in an entirely different direction. In this story homosexuality does not stand out as a disruptive event or as something that requires protective or regulatory intervention. Rather it merges in and out of other social relations and does not stand in opposition to nature or religion. At first glance seemingly nonpolitical, *Tropical Malady* carefully reclaims cultural, social, and political ground.

While acknowledging the existence of social and political threats, the film presents homosexuality in a setting of social pleasure and of a wholly "nonsufficient" affective plenitude. Rather than focus on the dramas of couplehood, *Tropical Malady* maps out a queer ideal that is located within a cross-gender sociality. This sociality is closely connected to an economy reliant on women-in-transition. Unlike in other gay male ideals (and unlike in the imaginary of the contemporary Sinophone cinema described by Barlow), women possess not only economic but also social centrality and occupy positions of pleasure in Apichatpong's vision.

The way in which *Tropical Malady* inhabits Buddhist ontological negativity adds a further dimension to secular, liberal formulations of arbitration. It does so by centering queer personhood within a Buddhist ontology of human and other living beings. Apichatpong thus succeeds in joining a realist social fantasy with a queer cultural fantasy to outline an imagination of freedom that does not make secular sexual citizenship its primary referent but provides a counterfantasy about how sexuality is imagined or could be lived in the Thai and global present.

FOUR. *MAKING CONTACT*

CONTINGENCY, FANTASY, AND THE PERFORMANCE
OF IMPOSSIBLE INTIMACIES IN THE
VIDEO ART OF ARAYA RASDJARMREARNSOOK

Making Contact is the title of a collection of video works on death that the contemporary Thai artist Araya Rasdjarmrearnsook presented at the 2005 Venice Biennale. Her performance videos were exhibited in the Thai Pavilion, where they were juxtaposed with the work of the late Montien Boonma. The title of the joint Thai exhibition, presented at the Convento di San Francesco della Vigna, was *Those Dying Wishing to Stay, Those Living Preparing to Leave.*[1] Araya's performance videos were installed in the cloister walk of the convent, where they were projected onto screens hung just slightly above the memorial slabs that cover the walk's floor. In the video *This Is Our Creation*, the artist can be seen lying on the ground among six corpses, softly speaking a poetic text and singing a children's song (fig. 4.1); *Conversation I–III* shows her sitting with and humming to corpses in a carefully timed video collage; and in *The Class* and *Death Seminar* Araya teaches classes to the dead on the subject of death.

Making contact with the dead was not new work for Araya; the Venice videos culminate the artist's almost decade-long occupation with death. In this chapter I investigate Araya's willed, long-term history of intimacy and exchange with the dead not for her treatment of mourning but rather for how the artist sketches out a feminist anatomy of desire in an idiom

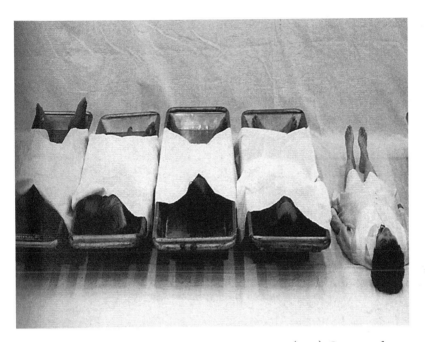

FIGURE 4.1. Araya Rasdjarmrearnsook, *This Is Our Creation* (2005). Courtesy of
Araya Rasdjarmrearnsook.

of negativity. In so doing I take into account the artist's explicit pedagogic
intent to initiate public discussions on femininity and sexuality in Thailand.

Since 1997 Araya has returned over and over again to a hospital morgue
in Chiang Mai in northern Thailand to film corpses in different scenes and
arrangements. Having stated at one point that she could not make art about
life anymore but only about death, she takes the viewer through recurrent
scenes of primarily female death in these videos.[2] The artist reads passages
from Thai classical literature or from her own erotic writing, sings to, con-
verses with, and dresses the corpses. While her performances have typically
been read as expressing affects around grief, I argue that, more fundamentally, they draw loss and death into relation with issues of femininity, desire,
and sexuality.

The Venice exhibition's Thai title, *Khon Tai Yak Yu, Khon Yu Yak Tai*,
translates slightly differently, to *The Dead/Dying Want to Stay/Live, the Living
Want to Die*. The title is instructive in that it invokes the reversals between
the dead and the living that are essential to Araya's video work and the ways
it deploys inequalities of gender, longing, and agency. In this context the

verb *yak* (to want) further substantiates that what the artist delineates in these scenes—which are ostensibly scenes of ritual action around death—is a feminist aesthetic and anatomy of desire. In addition the Thai title indicates that the desire that is the subject of this project is riven by ironies of possibility and boundedness.

Focusing on conceptual and performative aspects of Araya's video work, I thus consider how scenarios of loss and invocations of scenes of intimacy are made to relate in the videos. These works from the late 1990s to the mid-2000s situate longing and sexuality in a highly abstracted and dehistoricized domain, yet they proffer critiques of women's current erotic possibilities and defamiliarize popular conventions of depicting female death and attachment to the dead female body in Thailand.[3] All of Araya's videos on death and desire are approximately four to ten minutes long. Most frequently exhibited in the mode of installation, the videos at times incorporate site-specific elements and position the viewer in certain spatial relations to the works.

Thus far I have tracked the anachronisms of haunting through heritage cinema representations of female desire, Hong Kong–Thai cinematic renderings of female agency and historical accounting, and independent cinema's reworking of same-sex desire and queer personhood. This chapter culminates the analysis of the relations of Buddhism, sexuality, and temporal incongruity by examining Araya's feminist improvisation on the Buddhist convention of depicting the female body as horrific. While in the preceding chapters haunting took the form of stories of ghostly return, Araya's work situates desire in a highly abstracted scene of loss and unrelenting attachment. In her videos with corpses in the hygienic, clinical environment of the morgue, the artist directs discourses of longing toward objects of desire who can no longer respond. Her reconfiguration of relationality thus relies on eroticizing contingency and performing reversals between the living and the dead. The particular status of the dead—their inability to give consent—allows the artist to push questions of desire and agency to unfamiliar limits.

Since the 1980s Araya's work has continually problematized what it means for women to make their desires publicly known. Lisa Rofel has described the China of the 1990s as a place where the public expression of "private" desires constituted a new development, one that was in concordance with economic restructuring and neoliberal privatization.[4] In Thailand the novelty of the 1990s lay in the fact that the kinds of public expressions around love and sexuality diversified to a great extent. As the preceding chapters detailed, this occurred during a time when the Thai public sphere became increasingly explicitly sexualized and national cultural identity and citizenship began to be more closely articulated with normative prescriptions for sexuality. In this context the public performance of femininity fell under the scrutiny of new disciplinary measures.

Against this background Araya's work on death uses the frame of a particular, culturally located form of continued attachment in the wake of loss to outline counternormative possibilities of attachment. The artist avails herself of Buddhist form, without however reproducing orthodox pedagogies around death. Chapter 1 demonstrated that in Theravada Buddhism the female corpse represents a privileged pedagogic tool, the contemplation of which is supposed to let the viewer understand and affectively experience the futility of attachment. However, Thai practices of engaging with the dead are marked by enduring attachments to the deceased. It is this domain of tension between the actual practices and Theravada doctrine's categorical demand for detachment that Araya mines for her performances. In dwelling on the erotic and extending desire beyond its physical possibilities, the artist issues a complaint about the possibilities of sexual choice and pushes the boundaries of expression for women toward more explicitly sexual forms.

Araya Rasdjarmrearnsook

Araya is one of a relatively small number of nationally and internationally recognized Thai women artists and at present the most widely exhibited.[5] Her background is important because the content of her work is intimately tied to her biography and her professional development in national and international art circuits. Her video work is part of a larger pedagogic project that includes fiction and nonfiction writing, photography, and performance.[6]

Araya's art emerged from active engagement since the 1980s with German conceptual art, Thai artistic traditions, transnational feminism, and critiques of development policy rhetoric. In subsequent years she developed her sculptural, video, and installation work to a high level of national and international visibility. Prolific as an artist and writer, Araya focused on issues of femininity, sexuality, and publicity long before she began her work on death in the late 1990s.[7] Her installation art before 1997 as well as her later video work about women in a psychiatric hospital (*Great Times Message* [*Thoi Khwam Jak Huang Wela Phiset*], 2006) and performances in a slaughterhouse (*In a Blur of Desire* [*Nai Khwam Phra Mua Khong Prathana*], 2007) are marked by an abiding focus on feminist issues, by conceptual complexity, and by approaches that involve the performance of self-revelation.[8] Holding several advanced degrees from Thai and foreign art universities, most notably that of *Meisterschülerin* from the Hochschule für Bildende Künste in Braunschweig, Araya is also a professor at Chiang Mai University's Faculty of Fine Arts, where she has developed a highly effective pedagogy and nurtured a new generation of Thai artists. As a public voice of considerable influence, Araya is a regular contributor to the Thai print media and in 2005 published a volume of essays and polemics on art, *(Phom) Pen Silapin* ((I [masculine pronoun]) Am an Artist). Among other fiction, she has written a collection of erotic short stories, *Khuen Sin Klin Kamarot* (The Night the Scent of Desire Ceased).[9] As an artist, public intellectual, and writer Araya has continually initiated controversial public discussions of gender, sexuality, and affects around loss in Thailand.[10]

In the past decade Araya exhibited widely in Asia, Europe, and the United States.[11] Her 2002 exhibition at the National Gallery in Bangkok, *Why Is It Poetry Rather Than Awareness?* (*Thamai Thueng Mi Rot Kawi Thaen Khwam Ru Than?*), was still self-funded, but in 2005 she was chosen to represent Thailand at the Venice Biennale. A decade later the SculptureCenter in New York presented a comprehensive retrospective that accorded a central place to Araya's work on death. When the title of the Thai exhibition in Venice, *Khon Tai Yak Yu, Khon Yu Yak Tai*, was announced in Thailand, however, one critic reacted with the comment, "Well, if she wants to die, she can."[12] The remark exemplifies the hostility and derision that her work with the dead has drawn, work that has on the other hand elevated her to the status of one of Thailand's most recognized artists.

In the context of the Thai arts scene, Araya opposes herself to current neotraditionalist trends in art that recuperate national or religious symbols, a phenomenon that she terms, somewhat derisively, *thai-phut*, "the Buddhist Thai," not even bothering to make the compound into a real noun (*khwam pen thai-phut*, Buddhist-Thainess). She elaborates, "Artists who work in the genre of tradition are lauded as preservers and protectors of the Buddhist-Thai. The wind never blows in the wrong direction for their work in this country."[13] However, although she opposes a certain opportunist use of Thainess and Buddhism in art, and although her work uses cosmopolitan and global references and media, it retains a central concern with speaking from the Thai context and relies on Buddhist forms of engaging with the dead. Thus, as much as her work can be aligned with feminist video and body art such as that of Carolee Schneemann, Tracy Moffatt, Mona Hatoum, Louise Bourgeois, and especially Joan Jonas, it relies in equal measure on Thai literature, music, bodies, and social contexts. What the artist ultimately aims to outline by combining a particular "transaesthetics" with the very located foci and references of her work is a Thai-inflected feminist model of desire with universal salience.[14]

In *(Phom) Pen Silapin* Araya writes in a masculine voice about the difficulties of making radical art for women. While male artists ran naked through exhibitions (Utit Atimana and friends), peed at their openings (Kamol Paosawasdi), or railed against society and politics (Vasan Sitthiket), Araya writes, women artists, "even at the slightest cough, hurried to cover their mouths." Further complications arise from the fact that feminist art fails to achieve critical intelligibility in this context. As Araya writes, the social relevance of feminist art that took a bolder approach was consistently misunderstood: "Oh . . . it happened also, *khrap* [masculine particle], that a Thai female artist stood up and took off her clothes. She had just come back from France then. She did it to make a statement. But the viewers were not in step with her progressiveness. Instead they criticized visual aspects of her body just like they analyzed drawings. They talked about proportion and form and color, her weight and her skin, more than about social content."[15]

In contrast Araya's video work situates women's sexual expression in the sphere of death and literary language. Her work never features complete nudity, and her language, though explicit regarding sexual details, remains within the registers of poetry and literary prose. This is of relevance for the national reception of her art. Scholars of Thai literature have stressed the preeminence of form in classical literature. As Craig Reynolds argues, the registers of Thai literary works bore considerable political import, to the extent that charges of sedition against the author of a nineteenth-century poem were based on his transgressions of the poetic order rather than on the critical content of the work per se.[16] The significance of form also translates to contemporary expressions of women's sexual desire in visual and print media. While writers of erotic fiction such as Kham Phaka, who use everyday, "vulgar" language, are subjected to severe criticism, Araya adheres to the formal criteria of high literary language in her written and video work. No matter how sexual its content, her work is therefore spared the censorship that other visual work has been subjected to and the censure that other women authors have received.[17]

Lament of Desire

In the few lines that reviewers have to date devoted to Araya's work, they have overwhelmingly taken it to express Buddhist understandings of life and death, to portray care for the dead, nostalgia, and loneliness, or to interrogate "spiritual realities of the afterlife."[18] However, while they may do several of these things, Araya's videos more centrally link their scenes of death to desire, as her catalogue titles expressly indicate. The relation between loss and desire in this art deserves further scrutiny, and close attention to the relation between the sonic, visual, and conceptual aspects of her performances reveals a proliferation of affective registers besides grief throughout the oeuvre.

Without explicitly referencing contemporary representational, political, or ritual contexts, Araya's art consistently brings into focus the absence of a state in which "love and yearning do not have to hide."[19] Evident from the works themselves, from Araya's catalogue texts, and from interviews with the artist is that her videos contemplate possibilities of attachment by investing the domain of longing and mourning with feminist meaning and by expanding it to previously unimagined objects. On the most immediate level these performances convey the attachment to lost objects, or to loss as such: video after video shows the artist engaging with corpses in a morgue. As scenes of loss and performances of continued attachment persist across frames, videos, and installations, Araya's work initially indeed seems overwhelmingly concerned with conveying sorrow.

Sorrow, and longing for those who have passed, are clearly part of the sentiment expressed especially in Araya's early work. In these videos, often shown under the title *Thuk Haeng Prathana* (Lament, or Lament of Desire), the artist's engagement with the dead is solemn and her movement in the morgue is marked by restraint. At their most sparse, the mise-en-scène of the early videos is completely unadorned and highlights the contrast between the hygienic properties of the brightly lit morgue with its hard surfaces and the details of the bodies of the dead in their various states. In addition they focus on the artist's body, the symmetrical setup of the scenes, and frequently on the material qualities of the books that the artist reads from.

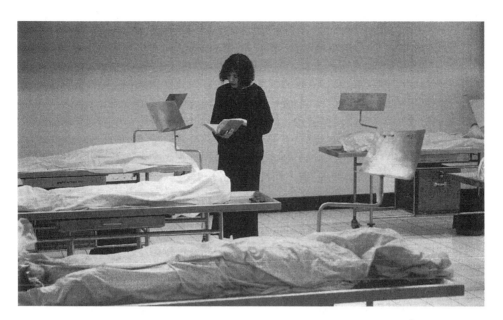

FIGURE 4.2. Araya Rasdjarmrearnsook, *Reading for Male and Female Corpses* (*An Inao Hai Rang Tai Pha Khlum,* 1998). Courtesy of Araya Rasdjarmrearnsook.

Relating to the dead solely through her voice and by how she positions herself spatially, the artist's performances are akin to rituals, without however reaching the kind of conclusion that would be expected in a funeral rite. Thus *Reading for Male and Female Corpses* (*An Inao Hai Rang Tai Pha Khlum,* 1998) is characterized by the fact that almost nothing *happens* during the five to six minutes of the video. *Reading* presents the artist's slow movement through the clinical space of a large room in the morgue (fig. 4.2). She reads a text of classical love poetry in a subdued voice, and her mode of reading and trajectory of movement remain constant throughout. The uniform, repetitive movement and use of voice throughout the performance suggest the refusal of ritual or psychic closure. However, Araya's work still achieves something more, besides showing an ongoing relation to loss that could be called melancholia. Even in these early works the contrast between the scenes of literalized loss and the texts of classical poetry being recited—often passages of flirtation—allows sentiments other than grief to enter the morgue.

In subsequent work, particularly that catalogued in *Why Is It Poetry Rather Than Awareness?* (*Thamai Thueng Mi Rot Kawi Thaen Khwam Ru Than?*,

2002), this split between registers is intensified, as Araya's reading to the dead turns into song and her movement among the dead becomes less tightly controlled. Her actions are now marked by greater intimacy as she incorporates an element of play into her performances and begins to dress the corpses, to sing to them, and to draw around them. As she brings color, textiles, and flowers into the mise-en-scène, her use of auditory effects also diversifies. She now sings Thai oldies (such as the 1960s songs of Suntharaporn in "Thai Medley"), reads from her own erotic writing, or simply improvises conversation with the dead. Finally, she addresses the issues of death and contingency on a metalevel in her series for the 2005 Venice Biennale. What emerge as recurrent phenomena of the entire oeuvre are that the artist's interactions with the dead become the canvas for a much wider affective range than solely that of grief and that the plots she suggests in her performances invoke a multiplicity of interpersonal relations. Throughout Araya's work the sphere of death—which, especially in a Theravadin Buddhist context, may be thought to exemplify the futility of erotic attachment—paradoxically becomes a space that allows for the staging of a variety of modes of attachment.

Conversations among Women

That Araya's sketches of nonnormative attachment are centrally concerned with women and femininity is evident in the amount and quality of the attention that the videos pay to the female dead. Although Araya performs with men, women, and mixed groups, all pieces that focus on individuals, depict bodies in detail, or are constructed around the identity of the dead concentrate on women and female bodies. As we see Araya perform with and for old women, their bodies small and decorated with *lan thom* (white frangipani, symbolizing death) and covered in cloths with bright prints, for women who died young, and whose beauty, as the artist says, compels her to perform for and with them, or as the camera takes in the minute details of female bodies in what the artist calls *femalescapes*, Araya's art exhibits a continuous, unparalleled concentration on women and on ordinary female bodies.[20]

In addition many of the artist's performances re-create all-female semi-public spheres common in Thailand. In interviews she states that the most natural addressees for conversations about love, attachment, and sexuality are other women and that her videos reflect this wherever possible.[21] The

FIGURE 4.3. Araya Rasdjarmrearnsook, *Conversation of Two Women* (1998). Courtesy of Araya Rasdjarmrearnsook.

morgue thus comes to function as a sphere of shared sorrow, confidences, and pleasures in which the artist is free to hold "conversations" with the dead on topics that might not ordinarily find serious consideration in public discussion.[22] Here the artist can present "that which is left out as life proceeds, is forgotten, not paid attention to, that which one is ashamed to speak of."[23] She thus holds "conversations" with the dead that bring into view subjects ranging from betrayal, rivalry, and love suicide to multiple attachments and same-sex desire. It is through "making contact" with the dead in this way that Araya critiques constraints in forms of relating to the living.

Conversation of Two Women (1998; fig. 4.3), frequently cited by the artist herself, best illustrates how the performances in the morgue enable what Lauren Berlant has called "minor intimacies." Berlant writes, "Desires for intimacy that bypass the couple or the life narrative it generates have no alternative plots let alone few laws, and stable spaces of culture in which to clarify and to cultivate them. What happens to the energy of attachment when it has no designated places? To the glances, gestures, encounters, collaborations, or fantasies that have no canon?"[24]

In *Conversation* Araya reads to the corpse of a young woman, probing the potential of death to represent a space for as yet impossible intimacies. Filmed at a descending angle, the image of the young woman is slightly blurred. Only the upper half of her body is visible; she is lying in a drawer in the morgue that has been pulled out. Her head is propped up on a pillow, and she is dressed in a colorful blouse. There is blood on the pillow next to her head. The young woman is one of the dead whose beauty and biography—of love suicide—compelled the artist to perform with and for her. To the left of the drawer a white sheet of text indicates the performer's presence at the young woman's side.

The English caption of *Conversation of Two Women* in the catalogue reads, "In the second room, a conversation between two women; one is alive, one is dead. The sound is a conversation during a love scene between a man and his lover, their parting and the beginning of a new love."[25] As Araya recites a passage from the *Inao*, a classical Thai literary text that she references as authored by a woman, she reads the speech of the male lover to the dead woman.[26] Directly addressing the young woman as a lover, the artist may be perceived to reenact the scene of attachment and desire in a gesture of consolation or cruelly to underline the loss of life and of love that has occurred.[27] But however one understands the video, it is clear that the "movement of desire" of this reading circulates among at least four persons: the artist, the dead woman, the male lover from the *Inao*, and the woman he speaks to.[28] At least one of the movements of desire that occurs in the performance is between two women: the performer and the dead woman. When the performer directly addresses the dead woman as a lover, speaking traditional terms of endearment from classical Thai poetry, the video makes the desire between women its issue. The exact nature of this desire is left open, though. It is not lesbian desire per se that is depicted here; rather this scene can be read as a longing for the open-ended movement of desire that this particular object of address enables. The affective relation that becomes possible in the address of the classical text to the dead woman centrally includes homoerotic desire, yet it can be said to incorporate other forms of desire as well.

This scene from *Conversation* illustrates how the performance of a particular form of continued attachment to a lost object can be correlated with affective relations or forms of desire that are either nonnormative or not easily classified. In her video work Araya thus creates a concise artistic language for intimacies that otherwise have no designation—although her videos also draw on seemingly normative forms of attachment, as is the case with the invocation of the encounter between the two lovers in the *Inao* that is recited in *Conversation*.

The invocation of minor intimacies in this work relies especially on the diversification of address that the performance with the corpse of the young woman makes possible. The multiple significations that the passage from the *Inao* takes on are further complicated by the camera perspective and by the installation mode in which *Conversation* is presented. In Sayan Daengklom's estimation, the static camera work of this video replicates the structures of the coffin as well as strictures placed on femininity.[29] I would argue that the video's stillness also functions to hold the viewer in place and to set her in a particular relation to the action on screen. In this installation the viewer is invited to occupy a single chair facing the screen. Both this spatial positioning and the static camera perspective compel the viewer to become a part of the mise-en-scène, addressing her as another counterpart in the scene of desire rather than merely an onlooker.

Commensality

In *The Senses Still*, Nadia Seremetakis describes the capacity of objects to store sensory histories. According to Seremetakis, "commensality" occurs when we enter into an exchange with objects, "a corporate communication between the body and things, the person and the world," to recover sensory histories.[30] As "bodies or traces of memory," the dead in Araya's videos represent such commensal objects, with which the artist is able to reproduce states of desire.[31] Rather than recover a history per se, however, the artist's video work on death is geared toward the performance of an unrealized ideal.

In order to sketch out her feminist anatomy of desire, Araya brings into play a commensality that is particular to Thai ways of transacting with the dead. She does this not to instantiate traditional proceedings and pedagogies around death and transience; in her performances and in the writing that accompanies her art, she invokes death ritual to mine it for other sensory and affective potentials. To understand how her work defamiliarizes conventional transactions with the dead, a look at such practices in Thailand is instructive. Araya both improvises on customary modes of tending to the dead in the Thai context and invents new ones.

Because of the centrality of voice and the ostensibly ritual action of Araya's art, Veena Das's and Seremetakis's writings on lamentation provide useful frames of reference. These authors' theories of gendered mourning and lamentation note especially the important roles that women occupy with regard to voice in death rituals. Das and Seremetakis examine traditions of lamentation in India and Inner Mani, Greece, which are marked by antiphonic elements and gendered divisions of labor. Under ordinary conditions of mourning, both authors ascribe extensive transformative qualities to women's public proclamations of loss. It is female lamentation that converts the death that has occurred into a "good death" and brings a reparative effect to bear on the worlds of the dead and the living.[32] For Das the expression of pain and the recognition of this pain by another further makes mourning a "conduit" between the private and the public and constitutes mourning's redemptive element.[33] Although Araya's actions in the videos do not represent mourning per se, she likewise uses the frame of ministering to the dead to transport affects that have to do with longing from privacy into publicity. Not concerned with social reconciliation, her work instead reinvents modes of lamentation and deploys traditions of ministering to the dead to effect ruptures in conventional ways of gendered relating.

A look at forms of mourning in Thailand reveals that women once occupied the roles of active lamenters. As in many traditions, desire or attachment were explicitly voiced parts of lamentation in the performances of Mon "crying women" (*nang rong hai*), who were employed in dominant funerary traditions in Thailand.[34] In contemporary urban Thai practice, however, traditions of voice that are not orthodox Buddhist have been all but abandoned. Conventions of female ritual such as that of the Mon crying women or of female dancers performing in front of the open coffin have become rare. Instead Theravadin Buddhist death ritual is concentrated almost entirely in the hands of men, while women perform the "silent" tasks of preparing the corpse, providing the food for the funeral, and taking care of all of the more intimate details around death. Women thus no longer have a formal part in ritual and funerary verbal exchange.[35] As in the cases described by Das and Seremetakis, a "good death" in the Thai contemporary urban context is also an acknowledged death, one that is witnessed by many mourners. In ceremonies that last several days, mourners come together nightly at the temple to listen to the recitation and sermons of the monks.

Accompanying official ritual is a kind of commensality between the dead and the living. These material and affective exchanges can be seen in the many services that one renders the dead during the funeral and until long after. The mourners take responsibility for the well-being of the dead, ensuring their felicitous passage to another state of being by offering food, keeping them company through the night, communicating with them, and adding to the crematory fire symbolic objects that the deceased might need. Depending on age, the circumstances of the death, and the status of the family, the dead are often kept for a number of days, months, or even years before cremation. Although orthodox Buddhist teaching decrees the swift relinquishing of attachment upon death, Thai practices of exchange with the dead are firmly anchored in everyday life and can last across lifetimes. In this respect mourning remains open-ended, and the attachment to the lost object is continuous. Araya improvises on Thai conventions of continuing intimacy with the dead, and we can further understand her performances as inventing new traditions of female voice and ritual role. In this context the artist mines especially classical Thai literature's extensive lexicon of desiring and of enduring attachment in the wake of loss. Araya's art can thus be said to avail itself of Buddhist form while deviating from strictly religious chartings of the relations of death and desire.

Araya's art can further be situated in relation to specifically Thai modes of eroticizing contingency, prominently represented in a popular visual culture that exploits the erotic possibilities of the deferral of detachment from the dead. From the traditional realm of Buddhist visual practices to the neofolklore of a reviving Thai cinema, female death is a ubiquitous trope in specialized periodicals, electronic media, and other visual culture. Stories and images of female death are therefore familiar to Thai audiences but would be expected to follow predetermined scripts as well as to convey a relatively fixed set of meanings, especially where gender norms, sexuality, and desire are concerned. By contrast Araya's videos undertake a thorough, feminist reworking of these erotics of femininity and loss.

What Is the Fragrance of the Video?

But what is the nature of the desires and affects brought into view by these performances? And what mood is conveyed? Or as the artist herself asks, referring to a series of videos in which she reads passages of love poetry and nature admiration from the epic *Inao* to bodies in various arrangements, "The fragrance of the flowers spread throughout the park in the poetry. The odor of the bodies spread throughout the room I was working in. What is the fragrance of the video?"[36]

Araya's description expresses the splits of diegetic and extradiegetic elements, of visual, auditory, and olfactory registers, of gravity and play, and of loss and abundance that mark her work on death as a whole. The question "What is the fragrance of the video?" addresses the affective quality that is achieved by combining scenes of consistent loss with performances of continued attachment. It also alludes to the kinesthetic experience of video viewing that engages senses beyond the visual.

In *Reading for Male and Female Corpses* metal gurneys are arranged along the sides of the long neon-lit, white-tiled hospital room (fig. 4.2). On the gurneys lie corpses covered with white sheets that move in a light breeze. The artist, dressed in black, comes in bent over a book, with her back to the camera. She walks slowly through the room between the corpses. After a few steps she begins reading a passage from the *Inao*. It is by reciting a scene of flirtation that Araya begins the performance:

> I will now tell of the illustrious Raden Montri,
> Residing in the city of Manya with the three women who are his
>   beloved.
> He looks admiringly at the figure of Jintara from up close
> And holds the beautiful woman in his lap.
> He caresses her back while lifting her chin.
> She glances at him coquettishly and pushes him away
> (in the way that women do).
>
> He then takes the hand of Mayarasami,
> "Come and sit with me, young one, and scratch my back."
> He pretends to lean on her voluptuous breasts,
> She twists away shielding them with her arms.
> He invites them to play a card game, with smiles, joking, and
>   laughter.

All play masterly hands, despite coy manners.
He offers the three women areca nut,
They prostrate themselves while fanning
And exchange affectionate words without missing a turn.[37]

The artist moves slowly through the room, pausing at individual gurneys while she reads the passage about the prince, Inao, and his three lovers flirting before preparing to go on a pleasure trip. The viewer hears the performer read in an even voice but, in the standard mode of reciting Thai poetry, with a melody. In the recitation, which lasts throughout most of the five or six minutes of the video, it is the mood evoked by the classical text that is even more important than the exact wording of the passage.

During the recitation the artist sometimes turns to the camera, moves toward it, then moves away again and, finally, slowly leaves the room, her voice fading. The camera remains on the two rows of gurneys for a long time before the video loops back to its beginning.

On the one hand, Araya's recitation of the scene of flirtation in the bleak setting of the morgue may be taken as an expression of sorrow over the loss of objects of desire or of conditions for attachment. At the same time, it is through the video's concentration of this poetry in a setting that exemplifies the futility of attachment that the morgue becomes an ideal space for desire and desiring: the female voice reciting this poetry to the numerous women and men in the morgue can thus be perceived as invoking the ideas of attachment to people not within reach, to women as well as to men, and to many people at once as much as to ordinary, nonglamorous bodies, or to love objects deemed undesirable.

A familiar context in which mourning was drawn into relation with desiring and erotic possibility was the AIDS crisis. In the context of art, politics, and experiences around AIDS, especially in the United States, what was mourned along with the individual and collective deaths was the loss of a particular gay male sexual culture.[38] As Douglas Crimp writes, the survivors grieved for "the ideal of perverse sexual pleasure itself rather than one stemming from its sublimation[.] Alongside the dismal toll of death, what many of us have lost is a culture of sexual possibility: back rooms, tea rooms, bookstores, movie houses, and baths; the trucks, the pier, the ramble, the dunes. Sex was everywhere for us, and everything we wanted to venture: golden showers and water sports, cocksucking and rimming, fucking and fist fucking." In the context of the AIDS epidemic "mourning our dead" thus coincided with "mourning our ideal," as Crimp writes.[39] His description of how a relation to death intersects with the notion of a sexual ideal concerns a different context but provides a useful contrast for determining how elements of loss and desire come together in Araya's video work.

In Araya's videos the loss sustained has no specific cause, nor do the scenarios of attaching and desiring belong to a sexual culture or delineate practices that can be easily identified. Yet the relation between death and sexuality is likewise used to protest social strictures in the domain of sexuality. Although it bears overtones also of future hope, Crimp's account presents a clear chronology: *I want something; it is no longer possible.*[40] By contrast the relation to loss that is performed in Araya's videos is not only one of mourning or retrospection; her work sketches out a more diffuse sexual ideal, one that has yet to be realized. While Crimp speaks in an explicitly sexual register, Araya lays claim to the register of death to signal the sexual. Lamenting the lack of sex publics—of frameworks in which women can express and act on sexual desires—her work relies on the starkness of the morgue and the dead bodies to push into view the issue of women's desires as well as to compel into national and international visibility the work of a Thai female artist in the first place.[41]

There is another instructive difference that arises from the artist's addressing sexuality in the register of death. Locating desire in the as yet unknown sphere of death rather than concretely in backrooms, baths, or piers, Araya's work extends the dimensions and idioms of fantasy as such: the artist's "lament of desire" not only projects scenes, affects, and practices of an aspirational "culture of sexual possibility" but, more fundamentally, draws our attention to the possibility of expanding the very terms in which we conceive of desirability, attachment, and the desiring subject.

Flirting

It is precisely by performing flirtation in a seemingly incongruous setting that Araya is able to reconfigure what and how one might imagine desiring. Adam Phillips describes flirtation as "the (consciously or unconsciously) calculated production of uncertainty" and contingency as the "recognition of one's life turning on a series of accidents in time, of events beyond one's power." He draws flirtation into relation with contingency when he writes, "Flirtation does not make a virtue of instability, but a pleasure. It eroticizes the contingency of our lives by turning doubt—or ambiguity—into suspense."[42] Even though he is not primarily referring to contingency in its harsh sense of actual death, his definitions are useful for an understanding of how Araya's work creates scenes of contingency and makes the morgue the setting for fantasies of desire and attachment. As she passes from body to body and from group to group of corpses throughout her videos, it becomes clear that her performances do not represent rites for individual lost (love) objects, in which case death ritual would tend to be personalized, commemorative, and come to some kind of completion. The mass of the dead and the repetition of the scenes instead suggest that the dead in these videos stand in for still something else.

If the loss in Araya's performances is impersonal, it would seem that her activities in the videos are not primarily those of a mourner but rather those of a witness to the deaths of strangers. In some exhibitions Araya explicitly roots her work in autobiography by juxtaposing her videos with photographs of family members and family funerals.[43] Yet even where she marks her work as personal, in the diegeses of the actual videos it is never only mourning that is performed. Rather her performances are always situated on the seam between personal memory infused with sorrow and the use of the domain of death for stagings of attachment, play, and indeterminacy. In the action that occurs in her videos it is ultimately the impersonal quality of the relation between the artist and the dead that weighs more strongly and that represents an ideal setting for staging the unpredictability and variety of attachment.

Thus throughout her videos the dead represent inanimate objects that at the same time still signify as human. It is in this capacity that they become fundamental in creating scenes in which all of Araya's actions and her address to the dead acquire an ambiguous quality. This accounts for much of the core effectiveness of Araya's videos. Through her interactions with the dead she is able to perform other inequalities—between lovers, between students and teachers, and between women and men—as well as the propensity of such dynamics to reverse.

As Araya creates a generalized state of contingency in its two partially competing meanings of "open to chance" and "subject to accident and loss," she exploits the ambiguous status of the dead as well as the asymmetry of the relation between the living and the dead. If the artist's reading to the dead is a "movement of desire" and an "impossible attempt to reverse a course of events," as she says, then it is these intentional confusions and

disjunctures—between the dead and the living and between the love poetry recited and the condition of those to whom it is addressed—that allow
for a freedom of signification not otherwise available.[44]

Female Subjectivity

Another critical component of this work is the artist's performance of female subjectivity: these scenarios of desire hinge, in large part, on the way
that she positions herself as a performer in these scenes. As Araya drama-
tizes the condition of contingency, the lines between the dead and the
living are blurred, and the performer is seen almost to merge with the dead.
This becomes evident most literally in *A Walk* (2002), where the artist
moves through rows of corpses similar to those she read to in *Reading for
Male and Female Corpses*, except that this time she does not read.[45] As her
silent walk is shown in slow motion, the figure of the artist becomes a blur
and she appears as a "wandering *winyan* [spirit/soul] among the gurneys,"
as she says.[46] *A Walk* thus visually exemplifies the merging with the dead
that Araya performs throughout her work.

In *This Is Our Creation* the artist engages the dead in a similar fashion
(fig. 4.1). The importance of the identity of the dead recedes. We no longer
know whether her conversation partners are men or women, old or young,
or what their faces look like, and the artist's performances are no longer
based on their biographies. In *This Is Our Creation* Araya enters the frame in
a white dress and proceeds to lie down carefully among six slightly raised
trays that hold bodies covered in white. After approximately one minute she
begins to hum softly, before announcing, "This is our creation," a phrase she
will repeat toward the end of the video. Throughout her performance Araya
seems to speak solitarily, dreamily, her voice sometimes dropping to almost
a whisper. At intervals she sings, "Twinkle, Twinkle, Little Star." *This Is Our
Creation* re-creates a scenario of intimate and playful nighttime conversation, in which the artist literally aligns herself with the dead when she
lies down in a row of corpses and states, in the first-person plural, "This is
our creation." This video is complemented by two others in which Araya
foregrounds the subject of her own contingency. In *The Class* and *Death
Seminar*, which cast the dead in the role of students and take the form of
classroom conversation, Araya presents the viewer with metaconversations
on death and contingency.[47] For the first time she speaks in English, and
her exchanges with the dead take the form of explicit conversation.[48] In the

FIGURE 4.4. Araya Rasdjarmrearnsook, *I'm Living* (2002). Courtesy of Araya Rasdjarmrearnsook.

question-and-answer format of academic discourse, she repeatedly returns to the issue of her contingent status as a living person.

As much as the artist aligns herself with the dead and performs her own contingency, however, she also performs her survival—her difference from the dead—each time she leaves a video and enters the frame of the next. The conventions of play become especially important in this context. *I'm Living* is a video in which the artist plays dress-up with the body of a young woman (fig. 4.4).

Here the corpse of a young woman lies on a white sheet on the ground. The camera provides a static image of the body from above. Her body is wet, and a negligee-like garment is draped over it. The lower part of her face below the nose is covered with a lace cloth. Her head is turned to her right and her wet hair spread out around her head. The artist, in a white dress, comes in with a stack of clothes. She dresses the young woman's corpse first in pants and a shirt, then in a dress, then puts a second dress on top of the first. The artist continues carefully to drape clothing onto the woman's body. She holds up some of the colorful and flower-print dresses against her own body and then continues her work, variously kneeling to the left and right of the body.

In producing video works with subjects who cannot consent, the artist enters a particular zone of risk and polysemy. While I cannot evaluate the ethical import of the artist's engagement with the dead, it is nevertheless instructive to consider the issue of consent in this context.[49] Because the dead were once living human beings and continue to signify as human, the question of consent remains pertinent. Carolyn Anderson and Thomas Benson use the case of Frederick Wiseman's documentary *The Titicut Follies*, a film about a "hospital for the criminally insane," to probe the limits of consent in artistic production. The problems regarding the consent of the subjects filmed in *The Titicut Follies* include the fact that "the incarcerated subjects could not provide 'informed' consent in any usual sense of that word"; at the time that consent was given, the exact shape that the artistic end product would take was as yet unclear; and at the time of acquiring consent it was impossible to gauge the effects that exhibition of the film would have (that is, whether it would benefit the subjects involved).[50] This complex case makes clear the precariousness of the consent of subjects whose agency or ability to be informed might be compromised in some way. It further points to the fact that the conditions for consent are likely to vary throughout the process of filmmaking and exhibition. Taking the dead as its subjects, Araya's video work pushes the issue of consent into a terrain of further precarity and temporal complexity: the artist is working with subjects who still signify as human but can no longer consent to their involvement in this artwork. Even if they had given consent while still alive, the question of the validity of this consent after death would remain.

The artist's engagement with subjects whose status as subjects is unclear and whose consent she cannot obtain thus calls into question the parameters of agency and the problematics of power even further. With the production of these videos Araya enters a particular terrain of unknowability—one about which it is also not possible to attempt to obtain further information or feedback. Each time the artist enters the morgue, the room is thus full of questions that cannot be answered. Is this a violation of the dead? Is this an entry into culpability on the part of the artist? Or does this performance constitute Buddhist-inflected merit-making for the dead? Do these performances affect the artist herself in a harmful manner? Could all of the above be the case?

In the exhibition of the finished artwork these questions translate into a performance of radical risk and produce a field of polysemy for the performer's actions with the dead. I am most interested in how the artist's engagement with subjects whose status as subjects is unclear and whose consent she cannot obtain allows her to explore the mobility of desiring positions in a highly experimental way. This becomes clear in *I'm Living*, in which the dynamics of play highlight the notion of such mobility. Placing countless outfits on the woman's body, the artist captions the video, "Paper doll lives in an exercise book, rooms drawn with lines. She is dressing."[51] Perhaps more than any other video, *I'm Living* exemplifies the taking on of multiple subject positions that play allows for: *I am dressing her / I am being dressed by her; I want her to do something to me / She wants to do something to me; I'm living / I'm dead; I'm in control of the fantasy / I'm not.*

The film scholar Linda Williams has stressed the mobility of women's desiring positions in horror film and sadomasochistic fantasy. To argue this point she brings Jean Laplanche and Jean-Bertrand Pontalis's reworking of the concept of originary fantasy to bear on the analysis of gender in film.[52] Laplanche and Pontalis's theory is notable for the fact that it positions the subject of desire impersonally *within* the scene of fantasy. Even more important, it states that the subject's position in this scene is not fixed but extraordinarily variable. Williams summarizes Laplanche and Pontalis's contention as follows: "Fantasy is not so much a narrative that enacts the quest for an object of desire as it is a setting for desire, a place where conscious and unconscious, self and other, part and whole meet. Fantasy is the place where 'desubjectified' subjectivities oscillate between self and other occupying no fixed place in the scenario."[53] In particular Williams uses this theory to make masochistic and other positions of seeming disempowerment available to women's pleasure.

Araya's work exemplifies the mobility of fantasy that Williams argues for in very ideal terms. The objects/subjects who become Araya's counterparts in the scene of desire represent strong cases of nonagency and impersonality. The field of signification that the artist creates further allows for the performance of radical instability with regard to the subjectivity of the living woman in the videos, and the enacting of fluctuation in female subjectivity becomes a central component of the ideal envisioned by the artist.[54] The erotics that Araya's videos sketch out can thus be understood as centrally based on what Kaja Silverman has called a "dispersed subjectivity" rather than on the unified, coherent subjectivity assumed to be at the basis of attachment in normative couplehood.[55] The female subject that emerges from these exchanges with the dead at once confidently proclaims the desire for attachments that are nonnormative and shows herself as disintegrating in the process. Viewers might thus read Araya's performances as the expression of a sovereign female subject's insistence on her desires. There is a word in Thai that would well describe such a position, *ahangkan*, a term that denotes assertive selfhood, also that of an artist.

However, the dissolution of the female subject that is also highlighted in the performance is weighted equally strongly. Araya's work therefore models a desiring subject that is not primarily based on the notion of sovereign subjectivity but is also based on a female self oscillating between disintegration and survival, between will and subjection to the conditions of loss and contingency. To an extent this performance of dissolution also mirrors the conditions of production of Araya's art: the making of the videos is excruciating, and the work in the morgue leaves the artist reeling between the impact that this work has on her and the desire and need to continue it.[56] Araya reveals these extradiegetic aspects of her performances in captions to stills from her videos as well as in accompanying texts in her catalogues. Because the question of the transgression of the boundaries of others always stands in their background and because the artist consistently performs the transgression of bounds of the self, these videos provide a highly polysemic context for probing the limits of agency, power, and desire.

AS ARAYA'S PERFORMANCES TURN the morgue into a place in which fantasy, play, melancholy, and intimacy come together, the discrepancies of register, tone, and signification that so strongly mark her work also let it become a concentrated study of contingency and its potential to hold open a space for intimacies beyond the normative scheme of male-female couplehood. As contingency is literalized in the morgue in its two partially competing implications of "open to chance" and "subject to accident and loss," the artist is able to express something fundamental about desire itself—about its accidental nature and its nondirectability as well as about its boundedness.

At the same time, however, she undertakes with these sustained dramatizations of loss, chance, and attachment an exploration of those modes of intimacy that at the turn of the twenty-first century became central to public contentions over rights, citizenship, and national-cultural identity in the

Thai public sphere, such as overt expressions of female sexuality, multiple attachments, and same-sex relations. By continuously suggesting attachment within scenes of death, Araya thus exploits the negativity of death to counter the social negativity of attachments that a vocal conservatism currently deems undesirable or impossible or aims to proscribe or marginalize. She thus uses the feminist performance of contingency, or the "emptiness of [an] art narrated by dejection and defeat," to consistently give voice to a mode of attachment that chooses its counterparts freely and variably.[57] In performing this ideal Araya's work remains in the registers of literary language and avant-garde visual representation and avoids exposing body parts that would make the videos explicitly pornographic. It is thus not through the transgression of form that her art becomes political. The challenge of Araya's work lies less in risking images that might incur censorship—a constant, substantial threat in the current political climate—than in the consistency with which it portrays ordinary female bodies and brings women's sexuality into public view.

In part Araya addresses her audience through the performance of feminine self-revelation.[58] In her actions for and with the dead in the morgue, she performs as someone who can have—or at least knows about—the specific attachments that she invokes in her videos. As Sayan Daengklom writes, "What makes up the risk in Araya's work is thus in all probability not its transgression of artistic convention. . . . But it risks 'self-revelation' in that it contains a high proportion of [the artist's] self. It risks linking feeling and memory to those elements that are the reason and origin of the work."[59]

Araya's artistic strategy proved successful in provoking a discussion in Thailand, but not in ways that one might expect. Instead of outright opposition or surprise, her work was met with derision, especially from male artist colleagues and teachers who accused her of making art that revolves only around *suan tua* (personal or private) issues instead of taking on socially relevant topics. Araya seized this opportunity to satirize her colleagues and to teach them and her readers about privacy, publicity, and women's sexuality in Thailand in a weekly column in *Matichon Sud Sapda* (Matichon Weekly Magazine) in 2003–4.[60] Her colleagues' criticisms may also have prompted her subsequently to perform a "9-day pregnancy" while in her late forties, an event that likewise sparked controversy. It is thus not only in content but also in contexts of reception as well as in the artist's pedagogic reincorporation of reception that the videos become part of a larger artistic, intellectual, and political project about female embodiment and sexual choice.

As art that centrally foregrounds images, idioms, and affects of loss on the one hand, and women's sexual desire on the other hand, Araya's work further picks up on conventional visual uses of female death and its pleasurable witnessing. Her videos defamiliarize the conventions of Buddhist melancholia to such an extent, however, that they cease to function as a vehicle for conservative modes of recovering Thai femininity. The artist's work thereby intervenes in a dominant convention that lets trajectories of women's desire seem largely inevitable. By situating fantasy in realist settings and refusing the tonality of the spectacular and predictable that marks this convention, Araya instead invests the domains of femininity and loss with open-ended possibilities for plots and trajectories of being, desiring, and relating.

Lending feminist meaning to a convention with a partially antifeminist history, Araya's work manipulates Buddhist melancholia to voice a complaint about the status quo of women's desires. The videos' dominant visual register of hygiene disbars cultural-nationalist elements from the sphere of death. The use of poetic language and Buddhist form, on the other hand, brings counterfactual possibility into the scenes of temporal incongruity presented in these pieces. Rather than reiterate Buddhist pedagogy, the videos draw on a popular Buddhist ontological framework that suggests that the boundary between the living and the dead is permeable.

I have delineated a situation in which sexuality since the late 1990s has come to occupy a precarious social and political center in Thailand. The sexual policy of this period inhabits a deplorable *avant* rather than merely evincing the "lagging behind" of an illiberal state. The avant of Thai sexual politics is constituted by its almost complete independence of prohibitionary legislation. Thai state sexual politics thereby distinguishes itself as temporally "advanced" when compared to measures adopted by other modern nation-states. In contradistinction to sexual politics that rely on criminalization or restriction through legal means, contemporary Thai policy anticipates an internalization of norms on the part of the population, relies on collective monitoring, and is promulgated almost entirely on a discursive level—a uniquely contemporary form of regulation.

The state's recasting of local and transnational rhetorics of negativity regarding gendered and sexual personhood during the past two decades proved difficult for activist, intellectual, and artistic intervention. Largely responsible for this difficulty is the extent to which political and artistic nationalist discourses lay claim to Buddhism and other domains of cultural heritage such as folklore. Buddhist tropes, stories, and images pervade the highly diverse cinematic texts and video work examined in *Ghostly Desires*.

However, rather than advocate a doctrinal notion of detachment or solve problems of social injustice in the manner of engaged Buddhism, these Buddhist citations have performed different kinds of work throughout these texts. These visual materials' borrowings from Theravadin and other Buddhist traditions have expanded the frameworks in which we can think about minoritized sexual personhood in a social-political context. In addition they have broadened the frameworks of fantasy.

In investigating Buddhism as a framework for argument and fantasy, I have opened up new perspectives on minoritized personhood and its place within the social, religious, and political orders in a period marked by the collapsing of temporal divisions into an enduring (neoliberal) present. The Buddhist framing of each story's problematics has provided a differentiated account of modes of arbitration and notions of agency regarding cases of women's desires for a variety of sexual and social pleasures and for reparative historical impact (in *Nang Nak, Mae Nak, The Eye,* and Araya Rasdjarmrearnsook's video work) and gay men's positions in social and ontological contexts (in *Tropical Malady*). Each problematic was broken down into several constituent parts, indicating a dispersal of agency among structural factors, sovereign individual will, collective strengths, and complex psychological forces. This notion of agency correlates with and in some cases can be mobilized to counter the dispersed, insidious, and ongoing forms of sexual regulation developed by state agencies since the late 1990s. By viewing agency from such a perspective, the films and videos under review direct attention to an expanded view of the political.

Through my review of Buddhist elements in contemporary cinema I have also examined how a particular history of legal, social, and ontological negativity shapes understandings of sexual personhood and psychological interiority in contemporary Thailand. I presented cases in which death functions as a register of sexuality, sex is not explicit, and political violence is addressed allegorically.

In contrast this coda investigates a film and a political context in which violence becomes concrete and sex explicit. Thunska Pansitthivorakul's documentary film *This Area Is Under Quarantine* (*Boriwen Ni Yu Phai Tai Kan Kak Kan,* 2008) uses explicit sexuality as a register of political complaint to present details of the 2004 Tak Bai massacre and to draw attention to systematic administrative and military violence against Muslims in Thailand's South. Whereas I have thus far examined all-Buddhist contexts, *Quarantine* makes interreligious intimacies in a situation of purportedly religious-based conflict—the "Buddhist" occupation of the majority-Muslim Thai South—its issue.

While Buddhism provided frameworks for fantasy and argument throughout the films and videos discussed in previous chapters, it occupies a very different position in Thunska's documentary. Rather than function in the service of conceptual expansion, Buddhism in *Quarantine* is synonymous with a dominant cultural and military formation; rather than enable expansion, it is responsible for a certain kind of foreclosure in this context. What my investigation of *Quarantine* thereby makes possible is consideration of yet another positioning of Buddhism vis-à-vis sexuality and liberalism in Thailand.

Quarantine: The Southern Exception

Thunska's banned film *This Area Is Under Quarantine* juxtaposes soft-porn sex scenes between a young Muslim Thai man and a young Buddhist Thai man with footage from Malaysian television of the Tak Bai massacre in which at least seventy-eight Muslim men were killed by the Thai Army in the province of Narathiwat in southern Thailand in October 2004.[1] While this juxtaposition may at first seem jarring, I argue that *Quarantine* ultimately succeeds in bringing the violent homoerotic abjection of the Narathiwat roundup and the homoeroticism of the intimate scenes between the two men into a productive relation. What is more, although Thunska's film tests the limits of what can currently be presented in visual media in Thailand on both counts, the film does more than make a case for freedom of speech. While *Quarantine* at first casts doubt on the viability of Buddhist-Muslim coexistence in Thailand, it ultimately devises a novel way of mobilizing bodies and the accidental features of a hybrid documentary as the basis for reimagining interethnic coexistence.

Against the background of the southern Thai conflict in which a perpetual state of emergency has become the norm since 2004, I delineate how a subset of contemporary Thai films furnishes an urgent alternative perspective on the quotidian and affective dimensions of southern citizenship. I further argue that this filmic archive reframes arenas of Buddhist-Muslim coexistence beyond conventional understandings of state and insurgent violence and beyond liberal frameworks that center solely on calls for due process.

The conflict in the Muslim-majority provinces of Yala, Pattani, and Narathiwat saw severe escalation in the 2000s.[2] With the Thai state's imposition of martial law in 2004 and an emergency decree in 2005 began the continuing state of exception in these provinces.[3] The situation of a population displaced legally and administratively within its own territory had persisted for decades—an occupation in all but name. From 2004 until now it has claimed approximately six thousand lives, the majority of which are Muslim.[4] Under the continuing state of exception the state has been able to commit human rights violations, such as the Tak Bai massacre, with impunity.

This analysis of Buddhist-Muslim coexistence in Thailand seeks to further complicate discussions of the relation of religion to gender and sexual freedoms. In particular I am concerned with a prominent strain of contemporary critiques of liberalism that trace the anti-Islam bias of contemporary European and U.S. public discourses to biases inherent in liberal thought. Authors such as Saba Mahmood, Jasbir Puar, and Judith Butler have tracked how, under the assumption of Islam's sexual illiberalism, the figure of the Muslim has become liberalism's paradigmatic other. This body of literature shows liberalism's ideals of universality and civic equality to be rooted in largely unacknowledged logics of exclusion that rely on class, racial, and ethnic difference.[5] Laying claim to the exclusive inheritance of liberal values, European and U.S. public discourses have in the past decade or more systematically set Islam in opposition to gender and sexual freedoms.

In *Frames of War*, Butler examines how discourses of sexual freedom have been co-opted into supporting the exclusion and destruction of Muslim populations. Basing her critique on arguments about temporality, Butler shows how liberal argumentation defines Muslims as intolerant of homosexuality and thereby as situated outside of the time of progressive modernity and the norms of the liberal human. The U.S. Army's framing of the 2004 torture of Muslim men at Abu Ghraib as an intervention into the tortured men's alleged homophobia represents only one of the more extreme instances of this phenomenon. This alignment of a purported championing of sexual freedoms with anti-Islamic rhetoric and violence has also let sexual rights agendas appear in a different light, and recent analyses of mainstream gay rights movements have highlighted the anti-Islamic content of their agendas.[6] In the context of these critiques, the hitherto seemingly self-evident critical potential of queer politics and representation has been shown to be severely compromised.

Taking into account these critiques of liberal deployments of the notion of sexual freedom in contexts in which ethnic or racial difference is invoked, how might we expect these logics to play out in a majority-Buddhist society and in a modernity that is not understood only as secular? Tamara Loos stresses that Thai modernity was never solely conceptualized as secular but was also always defined as a Buddhist modernity—and in opposition to Thailand's Muslim South.[7] What might this imply for Buddhist-Muslim intimacies and for the models of coexistence that contemporary films on this topic suggest?

Many of the independent documentary films about the South do not attribute a lack of sexual or political modernity to Muslims in Thailand. They further highlight quotidian features of what at least some of the filmmakers want to salvage as an essentially Southeast Asian Islam that is open to gender and sexual variance.[8] In this context rights discourses are then also not set in opposition to notions of justice and coexistence that are adapted from religious models. However, *Quarantine* occupies a still more complicated critical position. What ultimately constitutes this film's critical potential is the way the live elements of documentary filmmaking interact with and challenge the discourse on Muslim illiberalism.

The Filmic Archive

In contrast to the political science discourses that dominate the study of the southern Thai conflict, the extant filmic materials present an archive of vernacular notions of interethnic relations and allow for an account of the everyday manifestations of Buddhist-Muslim coexistence under extreme duress.[9] While *Buddhist* does not remain entirely unmarked in contemporary films about the South, it still represents the default, dominant position and is closely aligned with the Bangkok center's military politics in the South.

Since the 2000s much of the reflection on coexistence in Thai films about the southern conflict has been conducted in terms of negotiating interreligious intimacies. Thus Nonzee Nimibutr's *OK Baytong* (2004) envisions coexistence through the extension of kinship via marriage and conversion. Thunska's *Quarantine*, in contrast, uses same-sex romantic trajectories and sex scenes to discuss a failed Thai multiculturalism as well as to demonstrate continued melancholy attachment to its possibilities.

To an extent *Quarantine* is reminiscent of the video *Chic Point* (2003) by the Palestinian Israeli artist Sharif Waked.[10] In this work Waked juxtaposes a procession of Israeli and Palestinian models in "checkpoint fashion" with archival images of Palestinian men who are routinely humiliated at Israeli checkpoints by having to bare their upper bodies (to show that they are not carrying explosives). Alma Mikulinsky has interpreted this video as effectively impugning the viewer as complicit in the occupation, but also as a work that reinfuses a stalled situation with a modicum of mobility, at least in fantasy.[11]

Quarantine likewise aims to reanimate a different kind of relationality between Buddhists and Muslims, but its effectiveness hinges on a type of storytelling, on how the two actors play themselves, and on the film's mode of production as a hybrid documentary.[12] *Quarantine* is a densely constructed film composed of archival materials, interviews, and sequences that are staged. It is also a controversial film, banned from the Bangkok World Film Festival in 2009 and dismissed by others as failing to reach a certain standard of filmmaking. At the same time, Thunska's work as a whole represents an important alternative perspective in a landscape of queer Thai cinema in which even independent queer films invoke ideals of familial nationalism or, conversely, directors work in registers so symbolic that their films are frequently not understood as oppositional.

This Area Is Under Quarantine

Thunska's film addresses the heavily militarized Muslim-majority provinces of southern Thailand as well as the visual presentation of male same-sex desire as things that are "under quarantine." The film begins with scenes of the Muslim man Adeck lounging in a hotel room, underwritten by Yokee Playboy's "Phlae Pen" (Scar), a pop song about love and wounding. A monologue by Adeck about his past love life is followed by a more explicit conversation about Pe's, the Buddhist man's, past. Both conversations are characterized by the melancholy with which the men cleave to memories of past loves. A conversation between the filmmaker and both of the men about homosexuality and Islam and about the South under the Thaksin Shinawatra government, which was in power at the time of filming, is then followed by footage of the 2004 Tak Bai massacre. These scenes could not be viewed in Thailand at the time of the incident; the footage is taken from Malaysian television. It is inserted twice, the first time partially with its original sound and partially without sound. The second time the images, in which the army rounds up Muslim men, are accompanied by "Phlae Pen," the same pop song that underwrote semi-erotic shots of Adeck at the film's beginning. Finally, an erotic photo shoot and a sex scene between Adeck and Pe end the film.

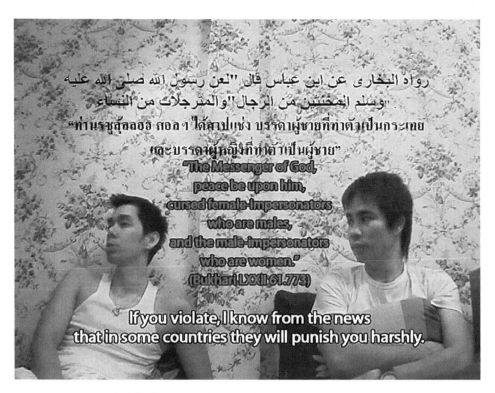

FIGURE C.1. Adeck (left) counters the charged questions put to him. Thunska Pansitthi-vorakul, *This Area Is Under Quarantine* (*Boriwen Ni Yu Phai Tai Kan Kak Kan*, 2008).

During the conversation about homosexuality and Islam the filmmaker repeatedly poses questions biased toward affirming Islam's supposed hostility to homosexuality ("Doesn't Islam forbid homosexuality?"). In his responses Adeck's evasiveness and hesitation signal his strong ambivalence to this positioning of Islam. Yet he seems to make the perhaps pedagogically motivated decision to answer these charged questions (fig. C.1). He thereby outlines a corrective to anti-Islamic prejudice. The way Adeck plays himself in the interview stands out in that he claims a position in the nation for himself as a southern Muslim and as a gay man within a Muslim community. In this scene he exceeds what seems to have been scripted for him in the film. This represents a first intervention into the conventional positioning of Islam vis-à-vis sexual freedoms in liberal frameworks as initially invoked by the filmmaker.

The second factor that contributes to the film's critical potential is its deployment of male bodies. Thunska's films routinely use the exposure of male bodies in tandem with the radical critique of various political contexts. In all recent films, such as *Reincarnate* (*Jutti*, 2010), the director juxtaposes explicit images of male bodies and sex scenes with cases of repressive state measures that do not at first seem related to sexuality. In this the filmmaker is not alone. Under the various states of exception currently in force across Thai geographic regions, and despite restrictions on visual representation, oppositional politics and aesthetics have increasingly taken recourse to (sexualized) bodies as critical media that remain when other political modes have been curtailed.[13] Previous chapters detailed how bodies became imbued with cultural meaning under a post-1997 refurbished nationalism. Thus for the state disciplinary programs of social ordering and cultural monitoring, bodies became a last national good—a kind of heritage to be cultivated for optimal social discipline and economic performance—and sexuality became an increasingly central component of citizenship.

Conversely bodies also became invested with new contestatory power. Under the state of exception in the South, bodies also represent the only evidence for state crimes. As Tyrell Haberkorn writes about cases of forcible disappearance of Muslims in the South, "Without a body, a murder trial cannot take place under Thai evidentiary rules."[14] Thus bodies represent targets of regulation and bear the burden of evidence for state crimes but also index alternative political worlds that artists and activists currently envision.[15]

In *Quarantine* the exposure of men's bodies becomes a central motif in relation to Buddhist-Muslim coexistence in Thailand's southernmost provinces. Like Waked's archival images of Palestinian men who are humiliated by having to bare their upper bodies at Israeli checkpoints, Thunska's film directs vital attention to the bodies of the hundreds of men who during the Tak Bai incident were stripped of their shirts and forced to lie face down in the dirt. The naked upper bodies of men have come to bear close associations with state violence in Thailand and became iconic especially of political massacres in Bangkok in the 1970s.[16] To an extent these events of the 1970s have entered national historiography. *Quarantine* repeatedly returns to the bared upper bodies of the men being rounded up by the army in Tak Bai and juxtaposes these images with those of the bodies of Adeck and Pe in the hotel room. The film thereby deploys the motif so centrally that it writes the killings of Muslim men into a national history that has traditionally excluded the losses and grievances of southern Muslims.

Quarantine's use of music further underlines the juxtaposition of male bodies across incongruous scenes of violence and intimacy. When the same pop song about the cruelty of love underwrites mildly erotic shots of a lightly clad Adeck lounging in the hotel room and the footage from Tak Bai in the film's middle part, this alignment draws anti-Muslim violence and the visual depiction of same-sex intimacies into a different kind of relation than simply stating that both are cases in which freedom of expression is curtailed.

Interreligious Intimacies

The deployment of the song about an unfinished course of attachment and the explicit sex scenes that follow it also represent the culmination of a narrative trajectory. Throughout, *Quarantine* has addressed the Thai state's anti-Islam bias with a particular way of mourning the failures of coexistence. The men's accounts of failed romantic trajectories both stand in for the story of a failed Thai multiculturalism and demonstrate continued melancholy attachment to the prospect of coexistence. The film's final scenes represent a reenactment of prior relationships and lingering attachments in the men's biographies.

Embedded in the political archive of coexistential failure—of anti-Muslim violence by the state—the intimacy between the two men also bears the burden of collective significance. While Adeck's and Pe's relationships from the past are being restaged, however, the trajectories of attachment take on new, live elements as the erotic photo shoot turns into a sex scene between the two actors. Through the photo shoot and sex scene Adeck and Pe reenact trajectories of attachment with new outcomes as well as physically stage a different relation of Buddhist and Muslim bodies to each other.

In "Acting to Play Oneself," Thomas Waugh claims that performance is an essential element of documentary film.[17] He distinguishes between representational elements in the genre that disavow the fact of performance and presentational elements that make visible the performative basis of documentary filmmaking. In Waugh's opinion presentational elements allow filmmakers to adhere more closely to the participatory ideals of politically engaged documentary filmmaking and to foreground the truth of the social actors' lives and perspectives. *Quarantine* is a hybrid documentary that contains both elements. I argue that it is especially the confusions

FIGURE C.2. The live, performative parts of the hybrid documentary ultimately represent its most critical elements. Thunska Pansitthivorakul, *This Area Is Under Quarantine* (*Boriwen Ni Yu Phai Tai Kan Kak Kan*, 2008).

between the film's presentational and representational elements, and between what has been scripted and what may exceed the film's scripting, that enable *Quarantine*'s critical potential.

Quarantine becomes most interesting when the events in the film seem to overtake the scripting and the men's intimacy exceeds the framing of what the filmmaker appears to have intended (fig. c.2). Throughout the film the men's exposure of their bodies and the action in the hotel room has seemed somewhat coerced. However, at the film's end, when the men are directed to engage in erotic play, they turn this play into a sex act. Their initial hesitation to perform sexually transforms into a reluctance to stop, and they exhibit a measure of defiance toward the filmmaker. It is thus not only on account of the film's juxtaposition of bodies in intimacy and violence but also due to the men's performance of unscripted desires that what we see on screen is able to counter the social negativity of same-sex desire and to intervene into anti-Muslim prejudice.

While other Thai documentaries about the South, such as *Citizen Juling* (*Polamuang Juling*, 2008), highlight the contemporaneity of Buddhism and Islam with regard to issues of gender, sexuality, or human rights, *Quarantine* reaches this point through a more contentious, live working through of such notions. It is due to the discursive agency performed by Adeck as well as the unpredictable turn that the film takes with the live sex act that *Quarantine* gains critical traction. At the film's end it is the interethnic queer sex scene that seems affectively to exceed the film's script that reopens the question of coexistence. But rather than orient itself to themes of love and family, the scene highlights casual pleasure. The incorporation of the accidental into the final artwork makes possible the staging of a seemingly live intervention into the conventions of anti-Muslim sentiment. In *Quarantine* the presentation of same-sex sexuality does not merely reinforce globally pervasive Islamophobic divides between Islam's purported illiberalism and a supposedly liberal modernity. Instead, under the current political conditions in Thailand, queer sexual representation and advocacy for the Muslim South are still able to enter into progressive alliance.

While a religious discourse and a discourse of human rights (and press freedom) furnish the background of *Quarantine*, casual intimacy becomes the film's primary trope of coexistential interaction. The insistence on coexistential ordinariness thus takes the form of an insistence on the ability of Muslim and Buddhist bodies to incite mutual pleasure rather than the reiteration of conventional models of coexistential intimacy such as marriage that other films focus on.[18] Aligning a Muslim subject's performance of himself with scenes of casual intimacy, *Quarantine*'s queer coexistential vision actualizes freedom of expression in a radical way and bypasses notions of ethnic reconciliation and multicultural nationalism espoused by some Bangkok governments.

However, it is not the film's gesture of revealing the truth by showing the footage from Tak Bai or its presentation of explicit sexual imagery per se that makes up *Quarantine*'s most effective claim to criticality. Rather than primarily represent a gesture against censorship, the film's explicit scenes set bodies in new relations to each other. It is thus intimacy's (in part accidental) place and function in the dynamics of a hybrid documentary narrative that furnishes the film's critical potential. In this way the film's pacing and its ability—or luck—in capturing liveness animates liberal, radical, and religious forms of argumentation to keep the question of coexistence open to further exploration. *Quarantine* has thus countered the anachronism of illiberalism that is imputed to Muslim communities by at first inhabiting this liberal charge and then working through it toward a radical figuration of contemporaneity.

Freedom of (Sexual) Expression

The independent cinema of Thunska Pansitthivorakul, Apichatpong Weerasethakul, and Pimpaka Towira as well as the video art of Araya Rasdjarmrearnsook infuse Buddhist-informed notions of negativity with queer and feminist meanings to produce entirely different representations of sexually and ethnically minoritized persons. Where modes of arbitration are blocked in the political domain, these materials envision resolutionary models on the level of the imaginary and enact them in struggles against limits placed on representation through film censorship.

The contemporary neoliberal moment requires new analytic lenses through which to gauge the transformative potential of media and modes of expression. As I indicated earlier, the configuration of the political present in Thailand, regrettably, seems ideally configured for such analysis. In particular I have outlined the novel organization of prohibition and permission in the domain of state sexual politics. The logics governing the exhibition of visual media and freedom of expression diverge from those of sexual regulation in that they seem to be more directly affected by legal intervention rather than "merely" by political rhetoric. However, the case of freedom of expression in Thailand similarly serves to complicate conventional, liberal notions of freedom.

In the introduction I critiqued analyses of the Thai political present that assess political freedom on the basis of state compliance with or deviation from liberal frameworks. Analyses that specifically focus on freedom of speech likewise evince a relatively circumscribed understanding of the domains of expression and freedom.[19] In designating Thailand solely an illiberal political sphere, they fail to recognize how the possibilities as well as the limits of expression extend across liberal and illiberal domains. In addition to passing over the question of how liberal public spheres become the sites of disavowed forms of repression, the legalistically oriented scholarship to date on freedom of expression has largely ignored the extensive public sphere of cultural production that produces elaborate codes of political critique. With regard to this archive, scholars have failed to consider the signification of more symbolic registers of political expression, nonspeech, how bodies are deployed, the variance of freedom of speech across different platforms, venues, and genres, and the controlled or sustained release of speech—as well as the question of how expression is at times enhanced by incidents of prohibition.

To be sure, the censorship and constraints that state institutions in Thailand currently place on verbal, visual, and even bodily expression are highly detrimental to the political culture. While protest against the increasingly unpredictable trends of the deployment of such legislation remains vital, it is nevertheless imperative that we extend notions of political expression beyond institutionalist understandings of media freedom and frameworks of state permission or prohibition.

In the context of Thai cultural production and political discourse, it is thus crucial to pay attention also to the forms of expression that fly, or hover, below the radar of state intervention, to the constant mutation of censorship's contours, and to the forms of expression that activists and artists have developed to say things without expressing them verbally or to present ideas by stating their obverse.

The analysis in this book included both films that became subject to censorship, such as *Quarantine* and *Syndromes and a Century*, and those that were spared state intervention, such as *Tropical Malady*. It is difficult to say which of these films bears the most critical potential. Rather my discussion highlights that what may count as radical in contemporary Thai cultural production occupies a broad spectrum. In this context *radical* does not merely index the vehemence of critique or degree of explicitness but also points to a complex set of compositional and generic elements as well as contexts of reception.

Thus while *Quarantine* includes as a seemingly radical feature the revelation of classified materials and the presentation of explicit sex, its most critical attribute may be the fact that it envisions interethnic relationality and that it does so through the incorporation of a series of accidents of documentary filmmaking. *Quarantine*'s banning moreover did not remove the film from circulation but merely altered its venues of exhibition. The censorship of Apichatpong's *Syndromes* also set in motion an alternate mode of publicity. After four (and later a total of six) scenes were censored, the director blackened out these scenes rather than cutting them from the film. The ultimate effect of the censorship was that the scenes in question were more widely publicized and saw higher circulation in clips on the Internet than they would have without state intervention. On the other hand, *Tropical Malady*, a film suffused with (homo)eroticism as well as criticism of national politics, was not censored—yet it would not be difficult to argue that it bears more radical potential than either *Quarantine* or *Syndromes*.[20]

Thai independent cinema not only complicates notions of what may count as radical; it also points us toward the savvy engagement with a neoliberalism that places appreciable limits on the domain of sexuality by promulgating prohibition almost entirely by rhetorical means and simultaneously imposing unpredictable constraints on freedom of expression. Independent cinema undertakes interventions into this context on three fronts: activism against censorship, the constant cinematic probing of the limits of filmic representation, and the development of cinematic codes that will not be censored yet are recognized as political at least by some audiences. In the archive under review the last objective was achieved in large part through the mobilization of Buddhist-inflected notions of negativity. Inasmuch as this cinema inhabits negativity as a register of the sexual, it always already undertakes a circumvention of constraints placed on expression. The analysis moreover showed how inhabiting this domain allowed several films to develop other nuanced modes of political expression as they, for instance, revise notions of women's agency. In this context Buddhist melancholia brought out perspectives on individual sovereignty in which agency is compromised, shared, and by necessity collective. *Tropical Malady* mined the domain of negativity further when it conceived of an expanded mode of addressing minoritarian grievances by combining a highly symbolic form of intercession with the critique of quotidian politics in the national arena.

Contemporary Thai independent cinema and video art thus constitutes an archive that performs systematic, politically informed interventions into the seemingly uninterruptible teleologies of a postdemocratic, neoliberal present. Engaging registers and conventions of negativity, this cinema and art put forth notions of freedom that move beyond strict concerns with freedom of speech in the sense of verbal expression or image presentation. As they invent ways of expression that rely on body, metaphor, and the recoding of cultural heritage, independent cinema and video art thereby provide rare, postliberal and nonnationalist perspectives on a desirable future-present.

1. I use a modified version of the Royal Thai Institute mode of transliteration, except in cases in which the filmmakers have a preferred style of transliteration. For an English-language readership, I list English film titles first, except in cases where the Thai title becomes significant for the analysis.

2. Throughout this study I use the term *attachment* in the broad sense of affective binding or libidinal investment to encompass both Buddhist-informed and other understandings of the term.

3. In his synopsis Apichatpong writes that, as the boat cruises on the borderline between Laos and Thailand, "the border links the worlds of the dead and of the living" (Pinyo, *Sat Wikan*, 288). See also Quandt, *Apichatpong Weerasethakul*, 239.

4. In this study the concept of Buddhist melancholia primarily serves to outline counternormative ways of inhabiting negativity and temporality. While my analysis does not primarily seek to intervene into Freudian concepts of mourning and melancholia, a few productive parallels and questions arise in relation to Freud's seminal text, "Mourning and Melancholia." If that work describes a trajectory of enduring attachment and subsequent progressive detachment for mourning and designates this trajectory as normative, it represents a parallel to normative formulations of attachment and detachment in Buddhist orthodox thought. In contrast to the trajectory that it outlines for mourning, "Mourning and Melancholia" is conventionally understood to delineate melancholia as an aberrance of mourning—a mourning without end, devoid of a logical, productive, or healthy economy. In coining the term *Buddhist melancholia*, I seek to provide a counterpart to normative Buddhist-informed understandings of the necessity of detachment and to make the excesses, counterintuitive economies, and temporal nonlinearity of a Buddhist version of melancholia available to queer and feminist interpretation. In this my analysis contributes to previous queer

reformulations of melancholia. In this context chapters 3 and 4 are in dialogue especially with Judith Butler's and Douglas Crimp's work on melancholia. Studying melancholia in a context informed by a Buddhist cultural imaginary yields many parallels to psychoanalytic formulations of melancholia, and I make use of some terminology that is cognate with the psychoanalytic concepts. Yet while it does not yield an absolute notion of difference, Buddhist melancholia nevertheless diverges from its psychoanalytic counterpart in several productive ways. The specificity of Buddhist melancholia can be traced to the central position that the concept of impermanence occupies in Buddhist thought as well as in its nondoctrinal citation outside of the domain of religion strictly speaking. I elaborate on this specificity in the section on anachronism that explains Buddhist melancholia's rooting in and relation to negativity.

5. *Kathoey* can roughly be translated as "transgender" or "transidentitarian."

6. See Jackson's insightful essay "Male Homosexuality and Transgenderism in the Thai Buddhist Tradition."

7. See Jackson, "Male Homosexuality and Transgenderism in the Thai Buddhist Tradition."

8. However, see two early interpretations that strive to draw connections between Buddhist thought and gender roles: Kirsch, "Text and Context"; Keyes, "Mother or Mistress but Never a Monk."

9. In *Subject Siam*, Loos describes how Siamese subjects were historically constituted as Buddhist subjects in the legal and administrative domains and in opposition to the Muslim subjects of Thailand's three southern Muslim-majority provinces. See especially the chapter "Colonial Law and Buddhist Modernity in the Malay Muslim South."

10. Barlow, "Femininity," 389.

11. The rationales of the sufficiency policy are detailed on the website of a foundation within the Crown Property Bureau that is appointed with the study of the sufficiency economy: Sufficiency Research Center, Youth Stability Foundation, "Khwam pen ma" (Background), accessed May 30, 2015, http://www.sufficiencyeconomy.org. See also the Institute for Sufficiency Economy, which shares a website with the Agrinature Foundation, accessed May 30, 2015, http://www.agrinature.or.th.

12. For an account of how sexuality becomes an element of citizenship in an "intimate public sphere," see Berlant, *The Queen of America Goes to Washington City*, 1–24.

13. Lim, *Translating Time*, 15.

14. Following John Stuart Mill, Singh defines *political liberalism* as an ideology "in which individuals are posited as *citizen-subjects*, formally equal within a civic order whose political institutions are designed to balance and preserve individual liberty and equality" ("Liberalism," 140, 141). Singh stresses liberalism's imbrication not only with market "freedom" but also with a history of slavery and with the notion of private property. With scholars such as Tani Barlow and Ann Laura Stoler, I understand liberalism and other facets of modernity as global heritage rather than solely as European inventions. See, for instance, Stoler, "A Colonial Reading of Foucault."

15. See Brown, "Wounded Attachments"; Berlant, "The Subject of True Feeling."

16. Berlant writes of the United States in the 1990s, "In the twenty years between *Roe* and *Planned Parenthood vs. Casey*, the general scene of public citizenship in the United States has become suffused with a practice of making pain count politically" ("The Subject of True Feeling," 70).

17. Quandt, *Apichatpong Weerasethakul*, 240–41.

18. Quandt, *Apichatpong Weerasethakul*, 241.

19. For the notion of a nostalgia that is progressively revisionary (rather than reactionary), see also Seremetakis's concept of *nostalghia*, which "evokes the transformative impact of the past as unreconciled historical experience" ("The Memory of the Senses," 4).

20. For an overview of terminology in Thai, see Jackson, "Queer Bangkok after the Millennium," 3–6. See also Sinnott, "The Language of Rights, Deviance, and Pleasure." By contrast the Thai coinage *lakkhaphet sueksa* (literally, "gender stealer" studies) never really took off.

21. This does not mean that the Buddhist borrowings of these visual texts are antidoctrinal. However, the instantiation of religious truths is not their primary aim.

22. Mahmood, *Politics of Piety*. Other works that persuasively critique liberal sexual politics include Puar, *Terrorist Assemblages*; Butler, "Sexual Politics, Torture, and Secular Time"; Haritaworn and Petzen, "Invented Traditions, New Intimate Publics."

23. Reynolds, "Dhamma in Dispute." For a prominent thinker who brings Buddhism to bear on the social (though not necessarily as an "engaged Buddhist"), see the work of Buddhadasa (Swearer, *Me and Mine*).

24. Berlant and Edelman, *Sex, or the Unbearable*, 2, vii–viii. See also Halberstam, *The Queer Art of Failure*; Love, *Feeling Backward*.

25. Edelman, "Ever After," 471–72. See also Brinkema's study of cinema and affect, *The Forms of the Affects*, which proposes a similar formalism of negative affect and seeks to revitalize the full negativity, for instance, of mourning.

26. Collins, *Nirvana*, 35. "The second of the Three Characteristics, impermanence, refers to the inevitable cessation of all Conditioning Factors. Whatever is conditioned is characterized by arising decay, and change in what is present, whereas the Unconditioned is not so characterized. Nirvana is permanent, constant, eternal, not subject to change. It is in this sense that nirvana is endless: not that it is characterized by unending temporal duration, but that being timeless, there are no ends in it" (34).

27. Collins, *Nirvana*, 37.

28. Loss (along with mourning, death, and haunting) is persuasively mobilized as a figure of critique by, for instance, Gordon, *Ghostly Matters*; Eng and Kazanjian, *Loss*; Edelman, *No Future*.

29. Lim, *Translating Time*, 12.

30. Lim, *Translating Time*, 12.

31. Lim, *Translating Time*, 12, 82. See especially 69–95, 14–16.

32. "Yet even in a postcolonial era, contemporaneity and anachronism continue to structure ideological rhetoric, wherever we hear the temporal cast of claims to legitimacy: politically, in the terms progressive or conservative, in thinkers who are 'ahead

of' or 'behind' the times, and with regard to style, the ideas of being 'hip' or 'current' as opposed to that which is 'dated' or 'passé'" (Lim, *Translating Time*, 83).

33. Lim, *Translating Time*, 16.

34. See, for instance, the foundational texts by Chakrabarty, "The Time of History and the Times of Gods" and "The Two Histories of Capital."

35. Harootunian, "Remembering the Historical Present," 471, 472.

36. See Freeman, *Time Binds*; Dinshaw, *How Soon Is Now?*

37. Rohy, "Ahistorical," 70. "As its canniest practitioners acknowledge, historicism is always to some degree ahistorical—or rather, anachronistic" (69).

38. Rohy, "Ahistorical," 73, 74.

39. Barlow, *The Question of Women in Chinese Feminism*. Povinelli's work on the overlap of autological and genealogical conceptions of subjectivity in "The Intimate Event and Genealogical Society" further supports the notion of contemporaneity.

40. Morris, "Three Sexes and Four Sexualities," 15.

41. On the question of emergence, see Hall, "Japan's Progressive Sex."

42. Morris maintains that homosexuality had largely not been visible to the state and therefore "remained beyond legislative reach" before the Ratchaphat incident ("Educating Desire," 58). This is true in the strict sense of legislation that directly criminalizes homosexuality. However, the classification of homosexuality and transgender embodiment as mental disorders in psychiatry, for instance, also had legal ramifications when it prevented kathoeys' access to documents such as passports or restricted their work opportunities.

43. "Discursive" here refers primarily to discourses consciously created by the state to impact the population on the level of policy. Butler's rereading of the relations of juridical and productive or discursively effected power in Foucault's *History of Sexuality* is pertinent here. Butler suggests that productive power does not replace juridical power, as Foucault argues, but that the two kinds of power continue mutually to influence each other ("Sexual Inversions," 65).

44. Morris's formula of "three genders and four sexualities" most succinctly summarizes the idea of multiple, overlapping conceptions of gender and sexuality. She argues that an older system of three genders (masculine, feminine, kathoey) coexists with a system of four sexualities (defined on the basis of sexual object choice). See Morris, "Three Sexes and Four Sexualities."

45. "Tang Kot Lek Kha Rachakan Rak Ruam Phet" (Establishing Iron Rule Regarding Homosexual Civil Servants), *Thai Rath*, June 4, 2004.

46. For a detailed analysis of the case, see especially Morris, "Educating Desire." Although Morris acknowledges some continuity, her main emphasis is on homosexuality's shift from public nonsignification to signification in the Thailand of the late 1990s. See also Sinnott, *Toms and Dees*.

47. In "Sex in the Inner City," Loos analyzes an instance of same-sex prohibition for women under Rama IV but notes that it affected only palace women.

48. Jackson, "Tolerant but Unaccepting." See also Chalidaporn, "Wathanatham Klied Tut Ke Thom Di."

49. This was not a court ruling; rather activists invoked the 1997 constitution in their efforts to overturn the ban.

50. Morris, "Educating Desire."

51. While academic inquiry has neglected the analysis of disciplinary campaigns, the measures were discussed critically in Thai print media. See Tomorn, "Khwam Pen Mae Lae Mia Khong Krasuang Wathanatham"; Nithi Aeowsriwong, "Wathanatham Rue Amnat" (Culture or Power?), *Matichon*, June 14, 2004. The scholarly literature on homosexuality in Thailand has privileged research on the geopolitics of male same-sex desire. See Jackson, "An Explosion of Thai Identities." Sinnott was the first to study female homosexuality and transidentitarian positions in Thailand. See *Toms and Dees* and "Gay vs. 'Kathoey.'"

52. While the social order campaign makes use of existing zoning laws and relies on the Entertainment Venues Act from 1966 (variously amended in the 2000s), cultural monitoring frequently takes recourse to Thai obscenity law (Section 287, Penal Code). Following Berlant's definition ("The Subject of True Feeling," 55), I use "citizenship" in this context to denote legal status as well as imaginary identifications with the state or national community.

53. The age of consent in Thailand is fifteen for both sexes. In the context of sex work the age of consent is eighteen.

54. This classification in some cases made it impossible for kathoeys to obtain passports and travel abroad or secure government positions and other kinds of work. A court decision in 2011 represented an effort to put an end to the practice of declaring kathoeys to be mentally ill. In addition several attempts were made to limit the transmission of images of kathoeys, gays, and lesbians on television. An example is the Bureau of Public Relations' ban on the appearance of homosexuals on television in 1998, which was also successfully challenged by activists.

55. For other cases, see Paisarn Likhitpreechakul, "It's Time for Thailand to End State Homophobia," *Nation*, November 20, 2010.

56. Thai Ministry of Culture, Culture Monitoring Center, "Kan Jad Tang Samnak Fao Rawang Thang Wathanatham," 8, 3. The paper states that the rationale for cultural monitoring is derived from rapid change due to globalization, an associated flooding with information and stimuli from the outside, and the decline and loss of Thai culture. (New) media, especially visual, are most frequently invoked as sources of cultural decline. A 2011 Ministry publication, *Khu Mue Fao Rawang Thang Wathanatham Samrap Dek Lae Yaowachon*, alerts readers to the dangers of "communication without limits" under globalization (96–97) and introduces the notion of cultural deviance (98–99). The appendix lists ten different types of media that include electronic and digital media (133).

57. Ladda Tangsuphachai, interview by author, September 5, 2005. See also Erika Fry, "Here Comes the Culture Brigade," *Bangkok Post*, March 18, 2007.

58. The website of what is now called the Culture Surveillance Bureau provides a comprehensive, 224-page report: Ladda Tangsuphachai, "Nueng Thotsawat Kan Fao Rawang Thang Wathanatham" (The First Decade of Cultural Monitoring), Culture Monitoring Center, Ministry of Culture, 2010, accessed November 10, 2015, http://www.m-culture.go.th/surveillance/index.php/องค์ความรู้-3/e-book/item/1-ทศวรรษการเฝ้าระวังทางวัฒนธรรม.

59. Pracha, *Jad Rabiap Sangkhom 2*, 19.

60. In "Pasuk Pongphaichit on Thailand," Pasuk describes the new forms of "care" as part of Thaksin's attempt to produce a more "managerial" state. These new forms are reminiscent of models of state nurture of productive populations found elsewhere in Asia. As Ong notes for Singapore and Malaysia, such a "postdevelopmental strategy of pastoral care seeks to produce citizens attractive to capital" (*Flexible Citizenship*, 202).

61. Peleggi examines aspects of Thai cultural policy in *Thailand and The Politics of Ruins and the Business of Nostalgia*. For an account of Thai cultural nationalism, see also Morris, "Returning the Body without Haunting."

62. Connors, "Ministering Culture." On the historical emergence of the concept of minorities and majorities in Thailand, see also Anderson, "Majorities and Minorities," in *The Spectre of Comparisons*; Kasian, "Questions of Minorities"; and Streckfuss, "The Mixed Colonial Legacy in Siam." These essays are concerned with the inception of a notion of *ethnic* minorities. While such a notion emerged only late, this does not mean that concepts of difference and minoritization were absent from the Siamese context.

63. "Clean-up" campaigns in Pattaya in 2014–15 represent an example of continued targeting of sex workers and venues that drew the attention even of the international press. See "A Thai Morality Drive Comes to Pattaya: Police Seek to Carry Out Junta's Mission by Targeting Transgender Sex Workers," *Wall Street Journal*, October 10, 2014.

64. For a critique of secular opposition to religiosity and an analysis of shared secular-religious affect, see Pellegrini, "Feeling Secular."

65. Of particular relevance in this context are the essays by Brown, "Wounded Attachments," and Berlant, "The Subject of True Feeling." See also the following by Brown: "Rights and Losses"; "Rights and Identity in Late Modernity"; "Suffering the Paradoxes of Rights."

66. For a description of recent logics of state impunity, see Haberkorn, "Thailand's State of Impunity" and "When Torture Is a Duty."

67. Anjana Suvarnananda speaks about efforts to introduce protection for sexual minorities into the 2007 constitution in Poore, "Thai LGBT Activists Fight for Constitutional Protection."

68. Brown, "Wounded Attachments," 391, 406, 407, my italics.

69. Berlant explains, "The central concern of this essay is to address the place of painful feeling in the making of political worlds. In particular, I mean to challenge a powerful popular belief in the positive workings of something I call national sentimentality, a rhetoric of promise that a nation can be built across fields of social difference through channels of affective identification and empathy" ("The Subject of True Feeling," 53).

70. Berlant, "The Subject of True Feeling," 57, 76.

71. Jackson reviews these developments in religious discourses on homosexuality in "Male Homosexuality and Transgenderism in the Thai Buddhist Tradition." See also the Northern Thai origin myth, *Pathamamulamuli, or The Origin of the World in the*

Lan Na Tradition, which some scholars interpret as according basic equality to a third gender. See also Morris, "Three Sexes and Four Sexualities" in this context.

72. In such interpretations the state of being a kathoey results from (heterosexual) misconduct in a previous life. As the karmic outcome of a past life, it is involuntary and represents a state that is presumed to include a high degree of suffering. As a result this strain of modern Thai Buddhist thought stresses that the state of being a kathoey is not sinful in itself and is to be accorded compassion rather than censure. See Jackson, "Male Homosexuality and Transgenderism in the Thai Buddhist Tradition."

73. Loos's work, on the other hand, provides a nuanced critique of the conception of freedom in Thai law. See "Issaraphap."

74. On liberalism's position within Thai authoritarian political tendencies, see Connors, "Notes towards an Understanding of Thai Liberalism."

75. Engel and Engel, *Tort, Custom, and Karma.*

76. While local writers' uses of polemical comparison to counter acute political crises, such as the 2014 coup d'état, serve a different purpose, invocations in transnational academic work of superior Western liberal standards remain surprising. An example of this mode of argumentation can be found in Jory, "The Rise and Fall of Empires and the Case for Liberal Imperialism."

77. Thus when the activist group Munnithi Phuea Sitthi Lae Khwam Pen Tham Thang Phet (Foundation for Sexual Rights and Justice) demonstrated on Sexual Diversity Day in 2010 with dozens of rainbow-colored umbrellas, this symbol did not stand for inclusion into privilege, as it might in other contexts. Lacking the history and associations that the gay rainbow might bear in the United States or Europe, and given the group's primary activist focus on depathologization, the rainbow umbrellas might well be understood as radical in the Thai context at the time.

78. In a later essay, "Neoliberalism and the End of Liberal Democracy," Brown contends that the existence of a liberal order, however compromised, represents a minimum condition for future, more radically progressive politics. Her claim is that the current neoliberal order in the U.S. makes such politics virtually impossible.

79. Therdsak details the development of thought about male homosexuality in the discipline of psychology from 1965 to 1999 in Thailand in "Jak 'Kathoey' Thueng 'Ke.'"

80. Brown, "Wounded Attachments," 390. Anjaree's politics thus bear a resemblance to what Hall describes for queer politics in Japan: "the significant transformation that such a rights model undergoes within a Japanese context" ("Area Studies at the Bedroom Door," 211).

81. In another action-research project on lesbian lives, Anjaree sought to publicize the many privations that lesbians faced. Rather than establish lesbians as only "subjects of pain," however, the group aimed to dismantle especially the entrenched notion that lesbians were psychologically and sexually abnormal. In addition to policy work, the project included conferences, an eighteen-month research project on the adversities faced by lesbians, the production of educational materials, and training of media and mental health personnel. See Anjaree Group, "A Proposal for an Action Research."

82. See Faure, *The Red Thread*; Cabezón, *Buddhism, Sexuality, and Gender*. Rotman's work, in contrast, draws sexual and Buddhist affect into relation when it brings the notion of sexual arousal through visual affection to bear on the mechanics of the generation of *prasāda*, a kind of faith. See "The Erotics of Practice." Studies of Thai Buddhism and homosexuality include Kulawee, "Naeo Khit Lae Jariyasat Thi Kiau Kap Phet Nai Phuthasasana Therawat"; Jackson, "Male Homosexuality and Transgenderism in the Thai Buddhist Tradition."

83. McDaniel has done considerable work to expand Buddhist studies' field of inquiry to include nonorthodox and nondoctrinal elements. See *The Lovelorn Ghost and the Magical Monk*. See also Pattana, "Beyond Syncretism."

84. Tambiah (*World Conqueror and World Renouncer*) and Keyes (*Thailand*) describe Buddhism's imbrication with the modern Thai nation-state. See also Gray, "Thailand."

85. Wilson, *Charming Cadavers*.

86. In Pali, *kamma-vipāka* refers to *kamma* and its results. *Wibak* (from *vipāka*) in Thai, however, also bears the connotation of adversity.

87. See Chai, "Ke-Lesbian Wibakkam Khong Khrai" and "Phrang Chomphu Khatha." Several other articles of Chai's are collected at the website Sadue Kaiwan: Khon Nok and in his book, *Kae Plueak Phet Phut*. As remarkable as this alternative Buddhist public is, it also vitally depends on the relative obscurity of the author of these texts: that Chai is able to do this work at the current moment depends on his refraining from working in visual media such as television as well as on his occupying a comparatively low position within the *sangha*.

88. Kasian, "Toppling Thaksin," 12.

89. These historians include Thongchai Winichakul, Kasian Tejapira, Tamara Loos, and Hong Lysa. See Hong, "Invisible Semicolony." In the field of Chinese history, Barlow likewise asserts "that China historiography might profitably consider the colonial origins of modernity when investigating the relation of Chinese semicolonialism broadly construed and the Chinese Revolution" ("One Single Catastrophe," 79). She considers this position in further detail in *Formations of Colonial Modernity in Eastern Asia*.

90. See Reynolds, "Thai Identity in the Age of Globalization."

91. In "Radicalism after Communism in Thailand and Indonesia," Anderson describes the oppositional history of these decades as a largely bourgeois history.

92. For an analysis of very recent political trends, see Baker and Pasuk, "Thailand in Trouble." See Brown, "American Nightmare," for a description of the convergence of neoliberal and neoconservative trends in the United States, many features of which are also evident in contemporary Thai politics.

93. On this point, see also Sanders, "The Rainbow Lobby."

94. Its roots may lie in earlier structural changes, but most writers locate the visible beginning of new Thai cinema in the late 1990s. See Chalida, "Coming of Age of New Thai Cinema."

95. May Adadol, "*Nang Nak*."

96. See Harrison, "Amazing Thai Film."

97. See May Adadol, "Dialectics of Independence," 13.

98. Lim, *Translating Time*, 190–244.

99. May Adadol, "Dialectics of Independence," 13.

100. May Adadol undertakes, for instance, the investigation of the logics of censorship, bourgeois publics and heritage cinema, and teen cinema. See May Adadol and MacDonald, "The Value of an Impoverished Aesthetic" and "Blissfully Whose?," and the following by May Adadol: "Disreputable Behaviour"; "Un-Thai *Sakon*"; "Animism and the Performative Realist Cinema of Apichatpong Weerasethakul."

101. May Adadol, "Dialectics of Independence," 1–14.

102. As conditions for the emergence of such a movement, May Adadol names "the greater accessibility of technology; a growing group of talented and politically frustrated filmmakers (and their teams) unable or unwilling to occupy the gravitational center of the monopolistic film industry; and a crisis of political-cultural legitimacy of a magnitude engendering a massive effort of denial" ("The Thai Short Film and Video Festival and the Question of Independence," 180).

103. In this chapter Ma investigates Chinese art cinema by developing an approach that refuses to rely only on contextualization either within a Western cinematic history or within national film histories (*Melancholy Drift*, 78).

104. Ma, *Melancholy Drift*, 91. Ma traces a trajectory regarding the notion of the author that includes "the auteur's death, reanimation, and transmutation in tandem with the development of art cinema in the post-classical, transnational period" (91).

105. Ma, *Melancholy Drift*, 94.

106. See, for instance, Aim Sinpeng, "The Cyber Coup," *Cultural Anthropology Online*, September 23, 2014, accessed November 1, 2015, http://www.culanth.org/fieldsights/568-the-cyber-coup.

107. The iLaw Freedom site follows cases related to freedom of expression, including cases related to cinema. See, for instance, the discussion of the court case regarding Tanwarin Sukkhapisit's film *Insects in the Backyard*: "Insects in the Backyard: Khadi [Case] #140," accessed December 1, 2015, http://freedom.ilaw.or.th/th/case/140#progress_of_case.

108. Apichatpong, *Saeng Sattawat*. Later the censors demanded that the director delete two additional scenes that showed statues of royalty that made it possible to identify the film's setting as Thailand. When in 2008 Apichatpong finally decided to show *Syndromes* in Thailand, he blackened out the offending scenes rather than deleting them.

109. Anderson, "The Strange Story of a Strange Beast." Also notable is that under Thaksin Shinawatra, censorship focused more on sexuality, while military governments after 2006 have concentrated more on the censoring of political content, especially that related to lèse majesté. See Ubonrat, "New Media for Civil Society and Political Censorship in Thailand."

110. May Adadol, "Disreputable Behaviour."

111. Thus Owens and Dissanayake claim, "Narrative structures are elucidated in contemporary Thai films in ways which reflect the meditative realities of Theravada Buddhism, the 'magical realism' of an animist culture in which magic and the spirit

world still exist as a strong counterpoint to modernization and technologic advances and the cultural displacement of economic empowerment, population change, and powerful commercial influences not only from the West, but also from other Asian urban centers across the region" ("Projecting Thailand," 156). This is not to say that interrelations between the inherent properties of cinema and Buddhist notions should not be considered. See Cho, "Buddhism."

112. For a more literal Buddhist reading of Apichatpong's work, see Rayns, "Towards the Wondrous Void."

113. The total research period during this time amounts to at least three years. The bulk of these data could unfortunately not be included in the text.

114. Sangwat Sewana, the "sex forum," was initiated by the Program for Appropriate Technology in Health, Thailand. See, for instance, "Sangwat Sewana Khrang Thi 5: Wairun, Sek, Lae Faechan" (The 5th Sex Forum: Youth, Sex, and Fashion), Teenpath: Sexual Education Community, August 26, 2006, accessed May 30, 2015, http://www.teenpath.net/data/event/30005/SexForum05.asp.

115. Harootunian, "Remembering the Historical Present," 473n33.

1. NANG NAK—GHOST WIFE

1. Nonzee, *Nang Nak*, 202–3. The poem is in *klon plao*, a Thai version of blank verse, but nevertheless makes use of the metrics of two traditional poetic forms: *klon* and *khlong*.

2. Berlant describes sexual anachronism as the way in which people cling to older forms and norms of intimacy despite the fact that "contemporary economic and intimate practices have surpassed some historic forms and no longer organize or describe the world of power, knowledge, and desire in which people are managing life" ("The Compulsion to Repeat Femininity," 235).

3. Jackson and Cook contrast "women's personal silence" with cultural representations of female sexuality as powerful but do not explore this discrepancy further (*Genders and Sexualities in Modern Thailand*, 17–18). Morris diagnoses "the odd silencing of female sexual expression in both popular and scholarly discourse about Thailand" in "Three Sexes and Four Sexualities" (23). For an analysis based on literary texts, see Harrison, "The Disruption of Female Desire and the Thai Literary Tradition of Eroticism, Religion and Aesthetics" and "'A Hundred Loves, a Thousand Lovers.'"

4. Harootunian, "Remembering the Historical Present," 475, 474, 473–74.

5. In older filmic versions it is frequently the very fact of the ghost's relentless devotion and the persistence with which she pursues her desire that is rendered as comical.

6. For a history of written accounts and stage and film adaptations of the legend since 1899, see Anake, *Poed Tamnan*. The Thai Film Foundation's website lists twenty-three films about Mae Nak made between 1950 and 1999. See Phayon, "Mae Nak Phrakhanong Phak Nai Thi Du Laeo Khon Luk Thi Sud Khrap."

7. See May Adadol, "*Nang Nak*," 186.

8. Nonzee Nimibutr, interview by author, Bangkok, September 12, 2005.

9. Stewart, *Crimes of Writing*, 90, 74. With Stewart, I use *distress* in the sense of "to afflict" as well as "to make old, to antique" (67).

10. Stewart, *Crimes of Writing*, 68. Ivy interprets Stewart's concept of distress further in her study of modes of cultural recovery in Japan: "The disappearance of the object—whether newly imagined as the folk, the community, authentic voice, or tradition itself—is necessary for its ghostly reappearance in an authoritatively rendered text. The object does not exist outside its own disappearance. If its coming-to-be is never simply punctual, a sheer event, neither is its death. There is always a temporal structure of deferral, of loss and recovery, across which the fantasy of folklore, or ethnography stretches. . . . It is only in the difference between those moments that the object of the fantasy can be said to exist. Susan Stewart has spoken of those genres that fantastically detemporalize the difference between loss and recovery as 'distressed'" (*Discourses of the Vanishing*, 67–68). Anake locates the first written version of the story in 1899 (*Poed Tamnan*, 23). The legend continues to bear traces of orality in its many performed versions and film adaptations as well as in popular talk and in the psychodevotional practices that are discussed at the end of this chapter.

11. The sartorial detail of films like *Nang Nak* and, shortly thereafter, *Suriyothai* (Chatrichalerm Yukol, 2001) found great acclaim especially with middle-class audiences. In his book about the making of *Nang Nak*, Nonzee dedicates more than twenty pages to the description of costume and to his understanding of dress and comportment in late nineteenth-century Siam (*Nang Nak*, 45–55, 93–104).

12. The voice-over relates the following story: "The legend of Nang Nak is a true story recounted through generations. It is said that Nang Nak of Bang Phra Khanong was a woman who loved her husband and was exceedingly loyal to him in life. Even in death her loyalty did not wane, and her soul lingered as she waited for her husband's return to continue their lives together."

13. May Adadol, "*Nang Nak*," 180–81.

14. May Adadol stresses that in the crucial period of economic crisis after 1997, *Nang Nak*'s success actualized a fantasy of economic parity on the level of the symbolic ("*Nang Nak*," 189).

15. Nonzee, *Nang Nak*, see especially 85–131.

16. In *The Lovelorn Ghost and the Magical Monk*, McDaniel uses the history of To to argue for the collapsing of distinctions between elite, popular, and esoteric orientations as well as between canonical and noncanonical traditions in Thai Buddhism.

17. Nonzee, *Nang Nak*, 88.

18. The 1997 economic crisis gave new direction to Thai nationalist impulses "after a century in which the values of arch-nationalism have been structured into the very organization of schools, the military, and official public culture" (Morris, "A Room with a Voice," 385). See also Morris, "Returning the Body without Haunting," 30–31. The programs of social ordering and cultural monitoring call to mind features of earlier instantiations of Thai nationalism's attention to form and representation where gender is concerned. Interventions into gender behavior and appearance had long been the norm in a state that based its programs for progress significantly on the performance

of gendered modernity and understood the selective adoption of Western models as crucial. Inasmuch as social ordering aims to streamline gender identity, it is thus reminiscent of programs dating back at least to the nationalist modernizing project of the sixth reign (1910–25). At that time the inscription of Western-style sexual difference on bodies and practices represented a core strategy of the nationalist program. It aimed to effect transformation not through legislation but through modes of representation. According to Fishel, "Romances of the Sixth Reign," the adoption of Western-style sexual difference included the domains of feminine and masculine behavior, patterns of socializing, notions and practices of respectability, and the institution of private and public spheres modeled on the West. Social ordering policies further recall the *Rathaniyom* cultural mandates (1939–46) of the Phibun Songkhram period. In extensive sumptuary laws these mandates instructed the population to wear "civilized" gender-specific Western clothing and to demonstrate gender-specific behavior. (The most frequently cited among the decrees is one that instructed men to kiss their wives before leaving the house in the morning. See Morris, "Three Sexes and Four Sexualities," 33; Connors, "Goodbye to the Security State".) As we saw, the current programs replicate this attention to form but invert the historical attention to Western models: the rhetoric of contemporary sexual politics contains anti-Western, anticolonial elements.

19. See, for instance, the United Nations Development Program's report, Baker, *Thailand Human Development Report.*

20. Connors describes the National Culture Commission as having modified its ideology from the late 1970s to the 1990s to make diversity profitable and amenable to a reformed Thai nationalism that is, however, more closely linked to capitalism than before (*Democracy and National Identity in Thailand*, 236–39).

21. Amporn, "Suriyothai," 298.

22. Connors, "Goodbye to the Security State," 442. The Tenth National Plan likewise focuses strongly on sufficiency.

23. These new standards for Thai sexualities became clear especially in public relations materials published by the Ministry of the Interior. See Pracha, *Jad Rabiap Sangkhom* 2.

24. Thus 2003 saw a controversy around Minister of Culture Uraiwan Thienthong's attempt to ban tank tops and shorts from Thai New Year's celebrations. See "Sexy Clothes Banned for Songkran: Thai Culture Ministry. Double Moral Songkran This Year?," *Nation*, March 29, 2003; "Breast Cloths an Even Bigger Worry," *Nation*, April 11, 2003.

25. For weeks the press discussed topics such as Thai teenagers' pubic hair styling, which the minister of the interior's teams had observed during drug testing in bar raids. See "Ji Fong Ran Tat Phom Lang Chi Anajan Lamoed Phet Dek Sao" (Pubic Hair Styling Salons Accused of Obscenity, Sexual Harassment of Girls), *Khao Sod*, June 2, 2003.

26. In "Pasuk Pongphaichit on Thailand" Pasuk presciently summarizes the detrimental effects of social ordering as the "clos[ing] down . . . of the political space opened up over the prior quarter-century" and alerts us to the fact that the new forms

of "care" represented also the quest for an increased, comprehensive management of society. "Behind these campaigns is an idea of the state's duty and ability to discipline what Habermas would call the life-world."

27. Pracha, *6 Duean Nai Kan Jad Rabiap Sangkhom Khong* M.T.2. This book and other publications were printed for public relations purposes and distributed to journalists and members of the public. In the early 2000s press coverage of social ordering was extensive.

28. Pracha, *6 Duean Nai Kan Jad Rabiap Sangkhom Khong* M.T.2, 53–56.

29. For an account of how Thai femininity is linked to markets, and especially to commodity distribution and consumption, see Wilson, *The Intimate Economies of Bangkok* and "Women in the City of Consumption."

30. Amporn, "Suriyothai," 296–308.

31. The scholarly literature ascribes a relatively high status to women in Thailand historically, as well as to women in Southeast Asia in general. See Pasuk and Baker, *Thailand's Boom and Bust*; Jeffrey, *Sex and Borders*; Mills, "Attack of the Widow Ghosts." Cultural representations of female sexuality as powerful and even dangerous are frequently cited, yet academic writing about sexuality in Thailand frequently speaks of a "silence" or "silencing" of female sexual expression. This view of the special restrictiveness of Thai society with regard to female sexual expression is also reproduced in Thai popular discourses. At the same time, both locally and transnationally, Thailand has become synonymous with the promise of freedom and variation in the domain of sexuality. See Morris, "Three Sexes and Four Sexualities," 15. See also Sinnott, *Toms and Dees*. Such fantasies coincide to some extent with delineations of femininity in Thai-language materials, as for instance in local tourism promotion and popular culture.

32. Phapphan, "Aen Jim Phok Ling." In addition the different state agencies themselves developed highly divergent ideological agendas with regard to sexuality. Thus while Ministry of Culture officials spent many Valentine's Days policing teenagers' activities, the Ministry of Public Health handed out condoms. In 2005 the Ministry of Culture objected to a "hugging marathon" on Valentine's Day and intervened in a promotional event for a breast-firming cream (*Thai Rath*, February 26, 27, 2005; *Nation*, February 26, 2005). On the other hand, in 2004 a massage parlor owner, Chuwit Kamolvisit, "the king of commercial sex," ran for Bangkok governor, detailing his own sex life in interviews during the campaign; in 2003 the Ministry of Health started public breast-enhancing exercises for women and announced that it was going to develop a program for the breasts of kathoeys; and public campaigns for contraception and safe sex have a long history in Thailand. See "Thailand Plans 'Bust-Boosting' Dance Classes," BBC World News, January 2, 2003.

33. The title of this section is from Bronfen, *Over Her Dead Body*.

34. Examples of ghost films from the 2000s include *The Snake Lady* (*Mae Bia*, 2001), *Body Jumper* (*Pop Whid Sayong*, 2001), *Bangkok Haunted* (*Phi Sam Baht*, 2001), *Demonic Beauty* (*Krasue*, 2002), *Tigress of King River* (*Sap Suea Thi Lamnam Kasat*, 2002), *The Eye* (*Khon Hen Phi*, 2002), *Three* (*Arom Athan Akhat*, 2002), *Omen* (*Sanghon*, 2003), *The Mother* (*Hien*, 2003), *Lhon* (2003), *Buppha Ratree* (2003), *The Shadow*

Lovers (*Khru Kae*, 2004), *Art of the Devil* (*Khon Len Khong*, 2004), *Shutter* (2004), *Alone* (*Faed*, 2007), and *Art of the Devil 3* (*Long Khong 2*, 2008). The liver-eating ghost, entrails-eating ghost, and a ghost that lives in a banana tree are examples of female ghosts whose haunting is frequently sexualized. Phaya Anuman's compendium of types of ghosts, *Mueang Sawan Lae Phi Sang Thewada*, provides more information.

35. A good example is *Body Jumper* (*Pop Whid Sayong*; Haeman Chatemee, 2001), in which the ghost's body changes from that of an attractive liver-consuming teenager to the body or corpse of an old female liver-consuming ghost.

36. See Lim, "Spectral Times," 316; Zeitlin, *Historian of the Strange*.

37. Many female ghosts are thought to attack men by sexually exhausting them to death or contaminating their bodies. Mills describes an incident in the northeast of the country in 1990 ("Attack of the Widow Ghosts," 244–73). The motif of sexual exhaustion also plays a role in the films *Lhon* (2003) and *Bangkok Haunted* (2001).

38. See Brenner, "Gender and the Domestication of Desire," on the role of desire within the complexly distributed roles of women and men in the economic and symbolic domains in Java.

39. Seltzer, *Serial Killers*, 1–2.

40. "But just as it was the dawn of a new public culture, it was at the same time, *inseparably*, the dawn of the new public cadaver. Politics of the public sphere in its full-fledged form was from this time, its first sovereign moment, a politics of the corpse" (Klima, *The Funeral Casino*, 66).

41. Klima, *The Funeral Casino*, 227–28.

42. In the immediate aftermath of the December 2004 tsunami, mostly uncensored images of corpses filled the pages of Thai newspapers, tour groups from Bangkok traveled to look at the dead in the South, the celebrity pathologist Dr. Pornthip Rochanasunan became a daily presence in the media, and even an image of a ghost thought to be intervening in the handling of the forensic operations appeared in the newspaper *Thai Rath*. See "Hue Ha Phap Winyan 'Phi' Suenami Phlo Khieng 'Pornthip'" (Commotion over Picture of Tsunami "Ghost" Soul Appearing Next to "Pornthip"), *Matichon*, February 6, 2005; "Mo Tho 3 Chae Borisat Ekachon Hen Kae Dai Jad Thua Phi Du Khwam Phinat Suenami: Yod La Sud Sia Chiwit Chiet 5 Phan" (Ministry of the Interior 3 Condemns Businesses Organizing Tsunami Disaster Ghost Tours: At Last Count, Almost 5,000 Dead), *Matichon*, January 3, 2005.

43. In "Phap Sop Lae Phap Nud" Chalidaporn criticizes the censoring of live female bodies and the simultaneous presentation of dead female bodies in daily photographic representation.

44. Knee, "Thailand Haunted," 142.

45. Gordon, *Ghostly Matters*, 22, 24.

46. In her analysis of Stanley Kwan's *Rouge* (Hong Kong, 1987) and Antonio Perez's *Haplos* (Philippines, 1982), Lim cautions that even in cases in which haunting effects historical critique, this intervention is achieved over a troubling distressing of femininity, "compensating for the breach of homogeneous time by idealizing patriarchal gender roles" (*Translating Time*, 181).

47. According to Collins, the "Three Characteristics" are constituted by "suffering, or unsatisfactoriness (*dukkha*), impermanence (*aniccatā*), and not-self (*anattā*)" (*Nirvana*, 33). The terms in parentheses are the Pali designations.

48. May Adadol, "*Nang Nak*," 184.

49. Anderson writes, "What has come to take the place of the mediaeval conception of simultaneity-along-time is, to borrow again from Benjamin, an idea of 'homogeneous, empty time,' in which simultaneity is, as it were, transverse, cross-time, marked not by prefiguring and fulfillment, but by temporal coincidence, and measured by clock and calendar" (*Imagined Communities*, 24).

50. May Adadol, "*Nang Nak*," 184. May Adadol analyzes the trajectory and difference in outcome of Nak's and Mak's struggles and treatment but does not examine their soteriological implications.

51. May Adadol, "*Nang Nak*," 187.

52. Wilson, *Charming Cadavers*, 70–71.

53. Somtow Sucharitkul's opera *Mae Naak* (2003) renders the spectacular malleability of Nak's body in a particularly pleasurable way when it lets Nak's hand stretch once around the whole stage.

54. How a woman is supposed to tend to her husband is codified in literary texts such as *Suphasit Son Ying* by the nineteenth-century poet Sunthorn Phu. See Plueang, *Prawat Wanakhadi Thai*, 315.

55. The story begins on the day of the famous total eclipse of the sun at Wako on August 18, 2411 (1868 CE), marking the occurrences in the film as events of historical import. On this day King Rama IV (Mongkut), inscribed in nationalist historiography as Siam's first great modernizer, had correctly predicted a total eclipse of the sun by means of Western astronomical calculations and set his scientific mastery scene in grand style for both Siamese and foreign observers. Thongchai (*Siam Mapped*) reads this public spectacle of Siamese rationalist triumph as marking Siam's shift from traditional concepts of space to Western concepts of bounded territory. This new understanding of space was subsequently to constitute the basis for the formation of a racialized elite Thai nationalism. See also May Adadol, "*Nang Nak*," 183.

56. Stewart, *Crimes of Writing*, 74.

57. Wilson, *Charming Cadavers*, 2–3, 86.

58. Collins's analysis in "The Body in Theravada Buddhist Monasticism" of how the monastic practitioner's psychological deconstruction of the body is integrated with the social construction of this same body omits feminist considerations but offers a valuable perspective on how text, body, and psyche combine in the context of Buddhist efforts at sexual discipline. In particular Collins stresses the essential role that the mind, or what we can think of as fantasy, plays in monastic practices.

59. Wilson, *Charming Cadavers*, 179.

60. Access to or familiarity with images of female death is not restricted to monks in Thailand. Such images are widely known and available to laypeople.

61. Stewart, *Crimes of Writing*, 91.

62. Connors, *Democracy and National Identity in Thailand*, 238.

63. Stewart, *Crimes of Writing*, 91.

64. The story of the courtesan Vāsavadattā and the perfume merchant Upagupta is told in the *Divyāvadāna* and the *Aśokāvadāna* and in Kṣemendra's *Avadānakalpalatā*. I refer here to Strong's translation of the story in the *Aśokāvadāna*, *The Legend of King Aśoka*, 179–84. Wilson cites the story of Upagupta as an "elaborate spectacle" of Buddhist aversion therapy (*Charming Cadavers*, 86).

65. See Berlant, "The Compulsion to Repeat Femininity," 2008.

66. Rohy, "Ahistorical," 73, 74.

67. Strong, *Legend of King Aśoka*, 180.

68. Strong, *Legend of King Aśoka*, 181.

69. Strong, *Legend of King Aśoka*, 181.

70. Rohy, "Ahistorical," 74.

71. Strong, *Legend of King Aśoka*, 179, 180.

72. However, it is only with the cessation of the flashbacks that Nak begins to relent. Her acquiescence to the exorcism and her relinquishing of her familial ideal are also indicated by the cessation of the pivotal camera movement and the ghost's bowing her head to the abbot.

73. Nak says that she has too little *wasana* (luck or fortune that results from past deeds) in this life to be able to stay and take care of Mak any longer. Mak says that they have acquired too little *bun* (Sanskrit, *puṇya*, merit) in this life to be able to stay together longer.

74. Mak seems physically (he frequently looks pale and exhausted) and emotionally damaged after his return from war. Thus not only Nak but also her husband begins to embody "impermanence."

75. May Adadol relates that, in a question-and-answer session, the director interpreted Mak's credulity (his naïve belief in the ghostly reality that Nak suggests to him) as symbolizing an essential Thai male conjugal loyalty ("*Nang Nak*," 190–91).

76. Ideal cohabitation is also threatened by the constant necessity for Nak to go out and take care of ghostly business, especially that of eliminating opponents.

77. At certain times during the year groups of men also come to the shrine to request from Mae Nak exemption from military duty.

78. These observations are based on conversations with women patrons of the shrine of Mae Nak between August 14, 2005, and December 19, 2006.

79. Freud outlines a trajectory for mourning and initially underlines the desirability of ultimate detachment from a lost object in "Mourning and Melancholia." More contemporary models of practical psychology also view the mourning process as one that follows certain stages and ultimately has to come to an end. See Kübler-Ross, *On Death and Dying*.

80. Berlant directs us away from an eventful notion of trauma toward "adversity," a conception of suffering that better encompasses "the subjective effects of structural inequalities" in duration ("The Subject of True Feeling," 79).

81. Collins, *Nirvana*, 34. In the field of cultural psychology, see Obeyesekere's "Depression, Buddhism, and the Work of Culture in Sri Lanka." See also Cassaniti, "Control in a World of Change" and *Living Buddhism*.

82. This conception differs from Caruth's account in "Trauma and Experience," in which cognition is evacuated from the traumatic event. Leys critiques the notion that cognition is evacuated from the traumatic event in "The Pathos of the Literal."

83. In *Silencing the Past*, Trouillot elaborates an understanding of agency that relies on the notion of distribution. In the context of Cambodia, see Thompson, "Performative Realities."

2. THE GHOST SEER

1. See Teo, *Hong Kong Cinema*; Knee, "Thailand in the Hong Kong Cinematic Imagination," 83.

2. Barlow, "Debates over Colonial Modernity in East Asia and Another Alternative." See also The Modern Girl around the World Research Group, *The Modern Girl around the World*.

3. Gopinath, *Impossible Desires*.

4. Terrence Rafferty, "Why Asian Ghost Stories Are the Best," *New York Times*, June 8, 2003.

5. Landsberg, *Prosthetic Memory*. Films that turn on this motif include the paradigmatic *The Thieving Hand* (1908), which Landsberg's analysis begins with, as well as *Heart Condition* (1990). Knee expounds on *The Eye*'s rich intertextual history with other films about ghost seeing in "The Pan-Asian Outlook of *The Eye*."

6. See Sobchack, "What My Fingers Knew."

7. See Williams, "Film Bodies."

8. Harvey analyzes *The Eye*'s story as allegorical of Chinese denigration in Thailand in "Fractured Visions."

9. Kasian, "Imagined Uncommunity," 76. See also Wasana, "From Yaowarat to Plab-plachai," and Chua, "The City and the City."

10. Michael Vatikiotis, "Sino Chic: Suddenly, It's Cool to Be Chinese," *Far Eastern Economic Review*, January 11, 1996, 22–25. See also James Hookway, "Now, It's Hip to Be Chinese," *Wall Street Journal*, March 16, 2004.

11. Kasian, "Imagined Uncommunity," 76, 86–88.

12. Or *khao suai muai ex*. Thanapol Limapichart drew my attention to the emergence of this phrase at this time.

13. Francis Nantasukhon, "Dajiahao: Sud Fan Khong Nang Sue Tham Mue" (Dajiahao: Highest Dream of a 'Zine), *Positioning Magazine*, February 21, 2005, accessed October 9, 2015, http://www.positioningmag.com/content/ต้าเจียห่าว-สุดฝันของหนังสือทำมือ.

14. "When I Meet Shanghai," *Dajiahao*, August 2005.

15. The symbol of Shanghai's Oriental Pearl TV tower is strewn across the page. In a Thai font that resembles Chinese characters, the magazine's name, *Dajiahao* (Hello Everyone!) appears in a bubble: Ja seems to be saying "Dajiahao!" to the new global Chinese world. The issue's title, "East Meets West," refers to the cosmopolitan history and culture of Shanghai and indicates that negotiations of Thai global Chineseness also occur in relation to Western globalization.

16. Barlow, "Debates over Colonial Modernity in East Asia and Another Alternative," 621.

17. See Saraswati's analysis of the relation between ideals of embodiment and global aspirations in "Cosmopolitan Whiteness."

18. Nantasukhon, "Dajiahao."

19. A 1992 article in *Sinlapawathanatham* evinces the same consciousness of the psychic complexities that accompany the Chinese cultural revival. Suni begins his essay about Chinese Thai female stars by demanding of the reader, "I want to ask you to look inside your consciousness. There is a chance that you will encounter a small feeling of difference that does not blend in well with [the notion of] Thai heritage. And then I want you to gauge how strong the effect of that feeling is: To what extent can you accept yourself?" ("Dara Sao Luk Jek," 160).

20. Since the early 1990s, TV series such as *Lod Lai Mangkon* (Under the Dragon's Scale) and *Mongkut Dok Som* (Bridal Crown) have recounted the vicissitudes of Chinese immigration into Thailand. For an analysis of *Lod Lai Mangkon*, see Kasian, "Imagined Uncommunity." In an essay in Thai, Kasian offers a personal account of his viewing experience of the series that indicates the extent to which the Chinese revival is accompanied by identification with the adversity that marked Chinese migration and acculturation to Thailand: "And after not even ten minutes of watching the series, I was crying. The episode in the story at that point was of a period of hardship. . . . The sorrowful face of Ah Liang, his anxious eyes, and his constant labored breathing made me think of the face and ways of my own father. . . . The more I saw, the more I felt that for *lookjin* like me, watching *Lod Lai Mangkon* was like looking at oneself in the mirror; it let me become aware of and understand myself better culturally" (*Lae Lod Lai Mangkon*, Peering Under the Dragon's Scale, 14, 15).

21. According to May Adadol, the first "shift away from caricaturing Chinese figures as the capitalist *jek* [chink]" in Thai cinema occurred in teen films of the 1980s. She links this cinematic reformulation of Chineseness to "the cultural break that occurred in the late 1980s during which it became possible, and desirable, to out oneself as *lookjin*" ("Un-Thai *Sakon*," 166n36).

22. See Knee, "The Pan-Asian Outlook of *The Eye*," 71.

23. Pao, "The Pan-Asian Co-production Sphere." On *The Eye* as a coproduction, see also Lim, *Translating Time*, 226–27.

24. For an incisive discussion of Hong Kong cinema in the context of the city-state's 1997 return to the mainland, see Lim, *Translating Time*, 182–89.

25. This is how Gordon (*Ghostly Matters*, 163–64) describes the remembering of the history of another that occurs in Toni Morrison's *Beloved*.

26. Corner, *The Art of Record*, 16. Nichols explains, "The logic organizing a documentary film supports an underlying argument, assertion, or claim about the historical world that gives this genre its sense of particularity" (*Introduction to Documentary*, 27).

27. Ma, *Melancholy Drift*, 40.

28. Kasian ("Imagined Uncommunity") and Reynolds (*Seditious Histories*, 259) locate the beginnings of the racialization of Chineseness in Thailand in the reign of King Vajiravudh (1910–25). Kasian describes as a key feature of Thai nationalism

the "imagining of an 'uncommunity' between the Thais and the Chinese in Siam in which a Chino-Siamese of Sino-Thai ethnocultural identity is discursively impossible" (78).

29. See Kasian, *Commodifying Marxism*, 189.

30. Kasian details the development of Thai anti-Sinicism and the racialization of Chineseness in Thailand in "Pigtail." For a discussion of Thainess and its others, see Reynolds, "Globalization and Cultural Nationalism in Thailand." See Streckfuss, "The Mixed Colonial Legacy in Siam," on how colonial contact prompted the generation of Siamese racial conceptions. Skinner's 1957 *Chinese Society in Thailand* continues to be referenced as a comprehensive study of the Chinese in Thailand. Since the 1980s scholars such as Nithi Aeowsriwong and Sujit Wongthes have also pushed for critical attention in the study of Thai history to Thai anti-Sinicism and Chinese contributions to Thai modernity. Much current writing in Thai on the subject appears in essays, magazine articles, and fictional and autobiographical forms.

31. Some restrictions were revoked only recently. Thus only in 1996 were election candidates allowed to make use of their Chinese ethnicity, for instance, to speak Teochew or to use their Chinese names in campaigning.

32. Bao, *Marital Acts*, 5. The writings of Vajiravudh (Rama VI) and Luang Wijit Wathakan are usually held responsible for the ideological preparation of anti-Chinese sentiment in Thailand. Vajiravudh called the Chinese racialized outsiders in "The Jews of the Orient" and "Awake Thailand!" Another period of policy expressly discriminatory of the Chinese followed under Field Marshall Phibun Songkhram's (1938–44, 1948–57) "militarist statism," in which the nation was imagined as "exclusively and monolithically Thai" and Chinese Thais were inscribed as others in the national imaginary. See Kasian, "Imagined Uncommunity," 76–78.

33. In *The Intimate Economies of Bangkok*, Wilson shows how Chinese identity is imbricated with the history of commercial forms, economic development, and cultural transformation in Thailand.

34. See Bao, *Marital Acts*, 31–52.

35. Fishel, "Romances of the Sixth Reign."

36. In the past, prostitutes in Thailand were called *I Kwang Tung* (roughly, "Cantonese woman"). The derogatory term *dok thong* for prostitutes may also derive from the name of a historical figure or from a word in Chinese. The sex trade in general has historically been tied to Chinese culture. Thus brothels have frequently been called *rong nam cha* (tea houses). And in many Thai literary works of the twentieth century the licentious villain, who sometimes tries to rape the female protagonist, is portrayed as ethnic Chinese. See also Wilson, "Women in the City of Consumption," 101. Dararat describes the migration of Chinese women into Thailand during the second half of the nineteenth century in "Kha Ying Jin Kham Chat Nai Prawatisat Sangkhom Thai." In *Marital Acts*, Bao claims that in more recent decades Chinese femininity in Thailand has been associated with propriety and with adherence to traditional feminine roles.

37. From approximately June 7 to 19, 2003, the media adopted the epithet *muay* for So and often combined it with *luang lok*, denigrating So as *muay luang lok*, or

"the deceptive Chinese girl." So was further discredited when the media produced information about her sexual behavior and connected her to a drug offense in Hong Kong. From behind bars, after she was sentenced in late June, she was made to apologize to the tuk-tuk driver and "to the whole Thai nation." Her apology commuted her sentence of three years to one and a half years. She was released by royal pardon and deported to Hong Kong after fourteen months in prison. See, for instance, "Tuk Tuk Phuea Chat Jaeng Jap Muai" (Patriotic Tuk Tuk Driver Brings About Chinese Woman's Arrest), *Khao Sod*, June 13, 2003; "Niyai Khong Muai Thi Taeng Mai Set Pro Don Jap Thet Sa Kon" ([Unfinished] Tale of the Chinese Woman Who Was Caught Lying), *Phu Jad Kan* (Manager), June 13, 2003.

38. In *The Melancholy of Race*, Cheng elaborates on incorporation, exclusion, entombment, interment, and suspension as dynamics related to melancholy (9–14).

39. Vatikiotis, "Sino Chic," 22.

40. "It is in these narratives that the diasporic paradigm is pushed to its limits, to the extent that any residual attachment to the center tends to fade" (Ang, "Can One Say No to Chineseness?," 236).

41. Rigg still speaks of Chinese social exclusion and of "wealth without power" in Southeast Asia, however. See "Exclusion and Embeddedness," 100.

42. Harvey, "Fractured Visions."

43. Tong and Chan, *Alternate Identities*.

44. Chan and Tong, "Rethinking Assimilation and Ethnicity," 22, 23.

45. With the motif of Man's possession by Ling's story the film establishes a theme of what Cheng has called "loss-but-not-loss." Cheng uses this phrase to describe the dynamic of exclusion and retention that occurs in racial melancholia. Identifying Chineseness as the lost-but-not-lost object of the story, the film thus moves it from entombment to disinterral (*The Melancholy of Race*, 9).

46. Halberstam, *Skin Shows*, 160.

47. Halberstam's and other queer readings follow upon a development in interpretations of Western horror that moved from an emphasis on the fixedness of gender roles (Laura Mulvey, Mary Anne Doane) to theorizations of the relative mobility of the female position in horror. See Clover, "The Eye of Horror"; Williams, "Film Bodies."

48. Thus Yue, for instance, builds on the work of Barbara Creed in "Preposterous Horror."

49. Barlow, "Femininity."

50. Possession has received exhaustive scholarly consideration, especially in the study of Southeast Asia. In this context, possession retains significant semantic elasticity: it appears at once as a site in which either social prohibition or permission manifests; drives, desires, and questions of prestige come to the fore; healing is effected; gender transgressions and limits are performed; and genealogies are claimed or contested. In the strictest sense, possession refers to the inhabiting of a medium's body and psyche by a spirit, deity, or historical figure. See Ho, "Transgender, Transgression, and Translation"; Spiro, *Burmese Supernaturalism*; and Morris, "A Room with a Voice."

51. In *The Commitment* (*Athan Kae Bon Phi*, Montri Kong-Im, 2003) haunting mediates relations of desire and friendship between a group of girls, their families, and a bereft lesbian ghost.

52. "Informing the Taiwan Trilogy's non-chronological modes of historical imagining is the association of asynchronous temporalities with feminine subjectivity" (Ma, *Melancholy Drift*, 47). Ma further explains, "In particular *A City of Sadness* and *Good Men, Good Women* work the tension between femininity as a signifier of powerlessness and as a source of discursive agency by articulating memory with a feminine voice" (44).

53. Abbas, *Hong Kong*, 6. See also Lu, "Hong Kong Diaspora Film and Transnational Television Drama," 300.

54. *The Eye 2* and *The Eye 10* more explicitly invoke commonalities between Thai and Hong Kong Buddhism.

55. Feeley, "Transnational Spectres and Regional Spectators," 41.

56. Cheng, *The Melancholy of Race*, 1.

57. Cheng's description of melancholy in terms related to haunting further illuminates the painful, intimate entanglement between minority and majority subjects: "Thus the melancholic ego as formed and fortified by a spectral drama, whereby the subject sustains itself through the ghostly emptiness of a lost other." In the social realm this spectral drama unfolds as a "peculiar and uneasy dynamic of retaining a denigrated but sustaining loss [that] resonates most acutely against the mechanisms of the racial imaginary" (*The Melancholy of Race*, 10).

58. Cheng writes, "Freudian melancholia is anything but mild!" (*The Melancholy of Race*, 8).

59. Knowledge might also stand for a collective social role, that is, for the kinds of occupations that Chinese pursue in contemporary Thailand. The figure of Ling represents one version of how minoritized persons are figured as simultaneously outstanding and marginal. On this configuration of minority personhood, see Berlant, *The Queen of America Goes to Washington City*, 103–4.

60. Cheng, *The Melancholy of Race*, 100.

61. See *Shutter* (Parkpoom Wongpoom and Banjong Pisanthanakun, 2004).

62. Lim, *Translating Time*, 12.

63. Iwabuchi, "Nostalgia for a (Different) Asian Modernity," 569.

64. *The Unbelievable* can be found at I-Cable, accessed December 1, 2015, http://ent.i-cable.com/program/unbelievable/index.php#.

65. Seltzer, *Serial Killers*, 1.

66. Iwabuchi, "Nostalgia for a (Different) Asian Modernity," 266–67.

67. Set off from the faster theme music that indicates haunting occurrences and turns in the plot, similar passages of quiet piano music also underscore many of the earlier scenes of loss and resolution in Thailand, such as the scene at Ling's grave.

68. On the triumph of survival, see Canetti, *Crowds and Power*. For a different take on the theme of traumatic witnessing and triumphant survival in the context of wound culture, see Seltzer, *Serial Killers*.

69. Buddhist teaching figures more explicitly in *The Eye 2*, where it is conveyed in sermons.

70. That such expertise is elevated to the level of a science in Thailand, in the Pangs' filmic depictions, becomes even clearer in *The Eye 10*, in which a group of friends seek out experiences of the occult according to a Thai manual that provides instruction on how to see ghosts and how to enter the sphere of death. On the question of this expertise, see also Klima, *The Funeral Casino*.

71. Lim, *Translating Time*, 161.

3. TROPICAL MALADY

1. Apichatpong and Stephens, *Tropical Malady: Commentary*. The hand-devouring scene and other invocations of animality in *Tropical Malady* are reminiscent of João Pedro Rodrigues's 2000 queer film *The Phantom* (*O Fantasma*).

2. May Adadol and MacDonald, "Blissfully Whose?"

3. Dennis Lim, "To Halve and to Hold," *Village Voice*, June 21, 2005, accessed May 30, 2015, http://www.villagevoice.com/2005-06-21/film/to-halve-and-to-hold/.

4. See especially Oradol, "The Very First Series of Thai Queer Cinemas."

5. See also Ünaldi, "Back in the Spotlight."

6. See Saran, "Haunting Body, Hideous Beauty."

7. An exception is the short film *(Sex) Toy Story* (2005) by Chantalak Raksayu. More recently, see the short films of Jirassaya Wongsutin (e.g., *That Day of the Month* [*Wan Nan Khong Duean*], 2014). The feature *Sayiu* (2003) presented a main character who is a lesbian but "converts" to heterosexuality at the end. In *Satree Lek* the coach of the volleyball team is a *tom* (masculine-presenting) lesbian. Lesbian characters are also central to a number of horror films, such as *Ab-normal Beauty* (Oxide Pang, 2004), *The Commitment* (*Athan Kae Bon Phi*, Montri Kong-Im, 2003), and Danny Pang's *Nothing to Lose* (*Nueng Buak Nueng Pen Soon*, 2002). Lesbians were more strongly represented in fiction and nonfiction writing. See the website Sapaan, "Sapaan: Klum Sang Sue Phuea Sanap Sanun Song Soem Sitthi Ying Rak Ying Lae Khwam Lak Lai Tang Phet" (Sapaan: Alternative Media for SOGI Rights), accessed November 15, 2015, http://www.sapaan.org.

8. Farmer, "Loves of Siam," 96, 97, 98.

9. Other short films by Michael Shaowanasai include *Le Cirque de L'homme* (2008), *Observation of the Monument* (2008), and *Long Night Short Film* (2008).

10. I follow the filmmakers' modes of transliteration when available.

11. Tanwarin subsequently directed *It Gets Better* (*Mai Dai Kho Hai Ma Rak*, 2012) and *Red Wine in the Dark Night* (*Khuen Nan*, 2015). She has also produced numerous short films (e.g., *I'm Fine*, 2008; *Look at Me!*, 2007). See also the shorts of the filmmakers Korn Kanogkekarin (e.g., *X*, 2010), Ratchapoom Boonbunchachoke (e.g., *Ma Vie Incomplète et Inachevée*, 2007), and Chama Lekpla (e.g., *Essence de Femme*, 2011), among many others.

12. See Jackson, "Male Homosexuality and Transgenderism in the Thai Buddhist Tradition."

13. *Blissfully Yours* contained heterosexual sex scenes that led to the temporary banning of the film and were subsequently cut from versions to be shown in Thailand.

14. See Quandt, "Exquisite Corpus," 231.

15. Apichatpong and Stephens, *Tropical Malady: Commentary*.

16. Berlant calls such forms of intimacy "minor intimacies" (*Intimacy*, 5).

17. This critique is particularly explicit in Eng's discussion of Ang Lee's film *The Wedding Banquet* (1993) in his chapter "The Structure of Kinship."

18. Nord, "Shape Shifter," 200.

19. Quandt, "Exquisite Corpus," 229.

20. Nord, "Shape Shifter"; Quandt, "Exquisite Corpus," 227.

21. Anchalee, "A Perceiver of Sense." Chalida seconds this view in "Sleepy Consciousness of Thai Documentary Film." The critic Kong Rithdee writes, "The docudramatic rendering of small-town life has, in fact, been a signature of every Apichatpong opus" ("Jungle Fever," 45).

22. Chalida, "Sleepy Consciousness of Thai Documentary Film."

23. Dumm, *A Politics of the Ordinary*, 19. See also Das, *Life and Words*.

24. Apichatpong and Stephens, *Tropical Malady: Commentary*.

25. This is, in essence, Morris's argument about the current status of homosexuality in Thai society in "Educating Desire."

26. See also Apichatpong and Stephens, *Tropical Malady: Commentary*.

27. Morris, "Educating Desire," 70.

28. As Morris writes, "Nostalgia for a moment in which homoerotic acts were not yet prohibited—because they did not signify publicly—cannot suffice for a time in which they are" ("Educating Desire," 73).

29. Dumm, *A Politics of the Ordinary*, 19.

30. Mbembe, "The Aesthetics of Vulgarity."

31. Morris, "Educating Desire," 69.

32. Anderson's survey in "Sat Pralat Arai Wa?" of the nonmetropolitan and nonbourgeois Thai reception of the film further confirms that the province is a site not only of the prevalence but also of the acceptance of queerness.

33. In her evaluation of state cultural monitoring, "Wathanatham Klied Tut Ke Thom Di," Chalidaporn attributes the survival of dissident sexual cultures not only to expanded political opportunities but also to the dispersed locales in which they operate.

34. Pracha, *Jad Rabiap Sangkhom 2*.

35. "When we inspected an all-male sauna establishment in metropolitan Bangkok's Klong Tan precinct in Wathana district, the interior revealed very clear characteristics of being 'rao'-'us.' Rao-We in this case means men and men. The team tried to ask about the patrons' reasons for coming to this venue and about their homosexual behavior." The author of this text, written in the voice of Pracha, uses *rak phet diau kan* (loving the same sex/gender) rather than *rak ruam phet*, which is generally used in colloquial language and media reporting but considered derogatory by some activists. *Ruam phet* also means to have sex, underwriting a notion that homosexuality is about constant sexual activity. See Pracha, *Jad Rabiap Sangkhom 2*, 138.

36. In this report the patrons' accounts are rendered in direct speech and gay slang and take the form of defiant complaint. See Pracha, *Jad Rabiap Sangkhom 2*, 139.

37. See Pracha, *Jad Rabiap Sangkhom 2*, 140.

38. In "Geographies of Contagion" Reddy describes a different collusion of local stigma and global ideologies when she investigates how transnational regimes of care reinforce traditional stigma for *hijras* in the context of AIDS work in Hyderabad, India.

39. Nord, "Shape Shifter."

40. These terms are used by Berlant in "The Subject of True Feeling" to describe and critique the frameworks in which minoritarian suffering is negotiated.

41. Quandt cites the director saying this about himself ("Exquisite Corpus," 227).

42. On male bottomhood, see Nguyen, *A View from the Bottom*.

43. Samreung calls Noi her *phi sao* (older sister), but this may also be a term used between friends, and, as Tong points out, they do not look like sisters.

44. Quandt notes this for the women in all of Apichatpong's films ("Exquisite Corpus," 230).

45. Barlow, "'Green Blade in the Act of Being Grazed,'" 147, 148.

46. Barlow, "'Green Blade in the Act of Being Grazed,'" 144, 148.

47. "The bodies of women produce surplus value but cannot reproduce biologically. Human reproduction is strictly regulated while women's productivity is increasingly sexualized" (Barlow, "'Green Blade in the Act of Being Grazed,'" 144–45). Examining the sexual possibilities of the female characters in *Scented Souls*, Barlow writes, "Caught between a brutal husband and a retarded son, the mother-in-law has only a daughter-in-law to love, and yet the erotic possibilities fade as the transitions are forestalled, one at a time: no procreative sexuality; no recreational sexuality; no second chances; no relation other than the strictly subordinated mother and daughter-in-law bound together, yet forbidden to create anything but capital together" (147).

48. "The new economy eccentrically predicates 'women in transition' while also mobilizing constraints on the emergence of women into social satisfaction, and it does so as willfully as it mobilizes surplus value" (Barlow, "'Green Blade in the Act of Being Grazed,'" 146).

49. Barlow, "'Green Blade in the Act of Being Grazed,'" 147.

50. 10,000 Baht is approximately $300.

51. Berlant defines "national fantasy" as follows: "Law dominates the field of citizenship, constructing technical definitions of the citizen's rights, duties, and obligations. But the National Symbolic also aims to link regulation to desire, harnessing affect to political life through the production of 'national fantasy.' By 'fantasy' I mean to designate how national culture becomes local—through the images, narratives, monuments, and sites that circulate through personal/collective consciousness" (*The Anatomy of National Fantasy*, 5). Scholars argued that until 1997 homosexuality in Thailand enjoyed an unusual measure of noninterference. Although notions of discipline played a vital role in the national imaginary of modernity, the field of homosexuality remained largely unregulated. The claim that would follow is that Thai national fantasy had not fundamentally included a notion of sexual normativity or deviance. In contrast the disciplinary campaigns of the 2000s turned precisely on the

notion that the regulation, on an everyday level, of the sexualities of broad sections of the population was essential to the national good.

52. Pracha, *Jad Rabiap Sangkhom 2*, 140.

53. "Krasuang Wathanatham Yi Tut-Ke-Thom-Di" (Ministry of Culture Freaked Out by Fags-Gays-Butches-Femmes), *Thai Post*, June 4, 2004, accessed February 1, 2008, http://www.kapook.com/hilight/main/216.html. An English translation, "Cultural Ministry Irate over Gay Civil Servants, Blaming TV Media as a Distributing Source," is available at Utopia, accessed November 10, 2015, http://www.utopia-asia.com/unews/article_2004_06_4_034037.htm.

54. Hall, "Japan's Progressive Sex."

55. Mills, "Attack of the Widow Ghosts."

56. Barlow, "'Green Blade in the Act of Being Grazed,'" 143.

57. Kong, "Jungle Fever," 47.

58. Kong, "Jungle Fever," 47. Kong's emphasis on the indigenous is in contradistinction to critics who likened *Tropical Malady*'s second half to *Apocalypse Now* and *Lost Highway*.

59. Quandt, "Exquisite Corpus," 227. Quandt identifies Apichatpong's deployment of Thai *film* genres when he writes, "Weerasethakul's films derive from the domestic horror films and melodramas he imbibed as a child in the Thai provinces" (228).

60. For a description of the heritage genre, see May Adadol, "Un-Thai *Sakon*."

61. Noi, *Long Phrai*. Sat Pralat (Strange Beast), the Thai title of the film, is taken from the title of the tenth chapter of this book. Noi Inthanon is a pen name of the writer Malai Chupinit (1906–63).

62. Apichatpong says, "The break in the middle of the film is a mirror in the center that reflects both ways" (quoted in Quandt, "Exquisite Corpus," 230).

63. Once again, the DVD's commentary soundtrack confirms this.

64. The assessments of the Thainess of Apichatpong's films also fail to take into account the fact that many are international collaborations that are produced and circulated globally.

65. A *pret* (Thai, from Sanskrit, *preta*) is a kind of spirit that, according to Buddhist cosmology, inhabits the *abayaphum* (*abhayabhumi*), or realm of suffering. A pret is a hungry kind of spirit that is thought to be very thin.

66. Barthes compares the "amorous catastrophe" to the catastrophic losses of the Holocaust: "*catastrophe*/catastrophe. Violent crisis during which the subject, experiencing the amorous situation as a definitive impasse, a trap from which he can never escape, sees himself doomed to total destruction" (*A Lover's Discourse*, 48–49).

67. According to the director, the two "disintegrate, like wind, and become spirit" (Apichatpong and Stephens, *Tropical Malady: Commentary*).

68. Kong, "Jungle Fever," 47. Adding to his Buddhist interpretation, Kong describes the answer to the conundrum of the meaning of Keng's journey as "emerg[ing] from a philosophy of letting go, of acceptance, of self-discovery, and of erasing one's own identity as well as from the wish for a return to the compassion and violence of nature that human beings can never prevail over" ("Chamlae Sat Pralat").

69. Kong, "Chamlae Sat Pralat." *Thuk* comes from Sanskrit, Pali, *dukkha*.

70. Butler, *Psychic Life of Power*, 135, 166. See Butler's "Melancholy Gender / Refused Identification" and Adam Phillips's commentary "Keeping It Moving" in Butler, *Psychic Life of Power*.

71. As much as the film situates homosexuality at the core of the human, it also retains a measure of its alterity with Tong's transformation into the *sat pralat*, the "strange beast" of the film's Thai title. The trope of animality, foreshadowed especially by the hand-devouring scene in the film's first half, rescues queerness from figuring merely as a question of (good) citizenship.

72. Hall, "Japan's Progressive Sex."

73. Nord reads the film's very structure, its bifurcation, as performing queerness: "So why not dispense with the rules of narrative cinema and try something completely different? To trace, through the suspension of conventional film grammar, the move that *queerness* performs when it questions gender roles and relations?" ("Shape Shifter," 200).

74. Lim's careful assay of the temporal and political valences of the queer occupation of *aswang* ("a supernatural creature of Philippine folklore") positions in contemporary Philippine transmedia represents a path-breaking contribution to this discussion (180). In her nuanced assessment of contemporary queer reappropriations of the viscera-sucking figure, Lim unmoors these Southeast Asian queer figures from limiting temporal trajectories that either bind them to a discourse of origins or situate them exclusively within the present. See "Queer Aswang Transmedia," 178–225. For a position that asserts the historical continuity of gender and sexual diversity in Southeast Asia, see Peletz, *Gender Pluralism*.

4. MAKING CONTACT

1. Araya Rasdjarmrearnsook's and Montien Boonma's work was exhibited in Venice from June 12 to November 6, 2005. The Thai exhibition was curated by Luckana Kunavichayanont, Sutee Kunavichayanont, and Panya Vijinthanasarn and commissioned by Apinan Poshyananda. See Universes in Universe, "51st Venice Biennale," 2005, accessed May 30, 2015, http://universes-in-universe.de/car/venezia/bien51/eng/tha/index.htm.

2. Araya Rasdjarmrearnsook, interview by author, Mae Rim District, Chiang Mai, Thailand, August 21–22, 2005.

3. Araya's work on death and desire is collected in three catalogues: *Thuk Haeng Prathana*, *Thamai Thueng Mi Rot Kawi Thaen Khwam Ru Than?*, and *Sinlapa Kap Thoi Khwam*.

4. Rofel, *Desiring China*.

5. Stills of the artist's work can be viewed at "Artist: Araya Rasdjarmrearnsook," Rama IX Art Museum, accessed August 19, 2013, http://www.rama9art.org/araya/index.html.

6. Despite its national and international acclaim, Araya's art has thus far failed to elicit a meaningful body of scholarly response. Notable exceptions are the writings of Sayan Daengklom. See his essay on Araya's 2002 exhibition at Bangkok's National

Gallery, "Waeo Krading Krung Kring Klin Kawi Wa 'Chan Chue Araya.'" See also Chamnongsri Hanjenlak, "Araya Rasdjarmrearnsook Khon Pen Khon Tai Sen Khan Thi Lop Luean" (Araya Rasdjarmrearnsook: The Living and the Dead—Vanishing Disparities), *Matichon Sud Sapda*, January 24–30, 2003; Pettifor, "Embracing Taboos." The artist herself provides conceptual framing and critical commentary on her own work in texts accompanying her videos as well as in her analytic writing. For a good overview and analysis, see Katrib, "Speechless."

7. Examples of earlier work that centered on Thai femininity, and specifically on topics such as sex work and women's rural-urban migration, include *Prostitute's Room* (1994), *Has Girl Lost Her Memory?* (1993), and *The Dance of Three Thai Girls* (1995).

8. *Great Times Message: Storytellers of the Town* and *In a Blur of Desire* were shown at 100 Tonson Gallery.

9. The title can also be translated as *Returning the Scent of Desire Altogether*. This book followed her collection of short stories, *Phu Ying Tawanok*.

10. As Araya states, "If loss could be openly revealed and accepted like any other human delight, then there would not be so many suppressed feelings" (Gimpel Fils, "Corinne Day").

11. Solo exhibitions showcasing her video installations and photographic work on death include a show at Gimpel Fils Gallery in London in 2006; a live performance with corpses in Turin in 2005; *Lament* at Tensta Konsthall, Stockholm (2003); *At Nightfall Candles Are Lighted* at Chulalongkorn University Art Gallery, Bangkok (2000); and *Lament of Desire* at ArtPace, San Antonio, Texas, and the Faculty of Fine Arts Gallery, Chiang Mai, Thailand (1998–99). After showing in Venice, Araya's videos were also included in the group exhibition *Politics of Fun*, at Haus der Kulturen der Welt in Berlin (2005). Other group exhibitions include *The Pantagruel Syndrome*, Castello di Rivoli, Turin (2005–6); the *54th Carnegie International*, Pittsburgh (2004–5); *Poetic Justice*, 8th International Istanbul Biennial (2003); *Parallel Time*, Hangzhou, China (2003); *Time after Time*, Yerba Buena Center for the Arts, San Francisco (2003).

12. Quoted by Araya, interview by author.

13. Araya, *Phom Pen Sinlapin*, 55. The grammatically conventional form in Thai would be *khwam pen thai phut*. The omission of *khwam pen*, which in this case would stand for "-ness" (Buddhist-Thainess), adds to the dismissive tone of the phrase.

14. What Barlow writes about the Chinese feminist Dai Jinhua applies also to Araya's art: "Her theoretical landscape cannot be reduced to the national melodrama" (*The Question of Women in Chinese Feminism*, 307). I take the concept of a "transaesthetic" from Dabashi, "Transcending the Boundaries of an Imaginative Geography."

15. Araya, *Phom Pen Sinlapin*, 62.

16. See Manas, "Poetic Conventions and Modern Thai Poetry," 39; Reynolds, "Sedition in Thai History."

17. See the collection *Isatri Irotik*, which includes Kham Paka's story "Khuen Wan Phut" (Wednesday Night).

18. Araya, "The Class, Death Seminar."

19. Araya, *Thuk Haeng Prathana*, 41.

20. See Araya, *Thuk Haeng Prathana*, 34–35, and *Thamai Thueng Mi Rot Kawi Thaen Khwam Ru Than?*, 12–13. Araya decorates bodies with lan thom and bright prints in *Thai Medley* (*Thamai Thueng Mi Rot Kawi Thaen Khwam Ru Than?*, 28–30). Some femalescapes can be viewed in Araya, *Thamai Thueng Mi Rot Kawi Thaen Khwam Ru Than?*, 24–27.

21. Araya, interview by author.

22. These are conversations in the sense that the artist recites to the dead—and sometimes her recitations include passages of conversation—however, she does not answer for the dead in these videos. Conversations held in a simulated question-and-answer format between the artist and the dead only begin with the videos *Death Seminar* (2005) and *The Class* (2005).

23. Referring to what can be expressed in literature, Araya writes, "That which is left out as life proceeds, forgotten, not paid attention to, that which one is ashamed to speak of, appears in scenes, passages, in the rows of letters, reflecting an absorbing image of life, without creating a gap in understanding, experience, age, belief and/or perspective" (*Thuk Haeng Prathana*, 41).

24. Berlant, *Intimacy*, 5.

25. Araya, *Thuk Haeng Prathana*, 34.

26. The *Inao* is believed to have been written by a woman, although the extant version from the second reign (of King Phraphuthaleutla Naphalai, 1809–24) is not.

27. These two possible readings were suggested by the artist in conversations as well as in a discussion of this video at Chiang Mai University's Faculty of Arts, August 22, 2005.

28. Araya, *Thuk Haeng Prathana*, 43.

29. Sayan, "Waeo Krading Kring Krung Khlung Klin Kawi Wa 'Chan Chue Araya.'"

30. Seremetakis, "The Memory of the Senses," 6, 10–11.

31. Sayan, "Waeo Krading Kring Krung Khlung Klin Kawi Wa 'Chan Chue Araya,'" 31.

32. Seremetakis, *The Last Word*, 101.

33. Das, "Language and Body," 70.

34. Santi, "Prawad Pithi Mon Rong Hai" and "Nang Rong Hai Ma Jak Nai? Kiao Arai Kap Mon Rong Hai?"

35. In contemporary ritual there is antiphony, or responsive verbal exchange, only in the listening and occasional answering of the mourners to the recitation and sermons of the monks. The standard text for recitation by monks at funerals comes from the *Abhidhammapitaka* of the Pali canon. Its recitation does not sound mournful, and the atmosphere of funerals is mostly calm and subdued. Only special forms of recitation carry the mood of sorrow, such as the *Phra Malai* and *Sangkhaha* forms of recitation.

36. This quote is taken from the text of a lecture that the artist gave in Amsterdam in October 2005.

37. Translation from Phraphuthaleutla, *Inao*, 230–31.

38. Araya also takes up the topic of AIDS in one of her videos, *Village Kids Singing* (2004), but does not relate it to sex.

39. Crimp, "Mourning and Militancy," 238.

40. In contrast the Japanese multimedia performance group Dumb Type uses the AIDS crisis to speculate on future sexualities. For a clip of Dumb Type's performance of *S/N*, see http://www.youtube.com/watch?v=2UbRQZ5LpN4, published April 5, 2012.

41. Berlant writes, "As with minor literatures, minor intimacies have been forced to develop aesthetics of the extreme to push these spaces into being by way of small and grand gestures" (*Intimacy*, 5). On sex publics, see Berlant and Warner, "Sex in Public." Araya's work parallels recent intellectual projects that strive to make abjection, HIV infection, and other kinds of social negativity available to critiques of liberal notions of sexual freedom and also to the forging of new kinds of social relations. See, for instance, Dean, *Unlimited Intimacy*; Bersani, "Gay Betrayals"; Bersani and Phillips, *Intimacies*; Berlant, "Neither Monstrous nor Pastoral, but Scary and Sweet."

42. Phillips, *On Flirtation*, xvii, 8, xxiii.

43. See, for instance, Araya, *Thamai Thueng Mi Rot Kawi Thaen Khwam Ru Than?*, 52–53.

44. Araya, *Thuk Haeng Prathana*, 43.

45. Araya, *Thamai Thueng Mi Rot Kawi Thaen Khwam Ru Than?*, 8–9.

46. Araya Rasdjarmrearnsook, interview by author, Chiang Mai, Thailand, September 2002.

47. *Death Seminar* was part of the Venice series but could ultimately not be shown at the Venice Biennale due to technical reasons.

48. Araya subtitled these videos *Teaching the Masters*, with the dead as the *ajarn yai*, the "masters" or "great teachers," as bodies are conventionally called in pathology in Thai. This suggests a further kind of reversal between the positions of the dead and the living.

49. The artist obtained formal, official consent from an ethics commission composed of doctors.

50. Anderson and Benson, "Direct Cinema and the Myth of Informed Consent," 59.

51. From the English catalogue text accompanying *I'm Living* (Araya, *Thamai Thueng Mi Rot Kawi Thaen Khwam Ru Than?*, 33).

52. Laplanche and Pontalis write, "Fantasy, however, is not the object of desire, but its setting. In fantasy the subject does not pursue the object or its sign: he appears caught up himself in the sequence of images. He forms no representation of the desired object, but is himself represented as participating in the scene although, in the earliest forms of fantasy, he cannot be assigned any fixed place in it (hence the danger, in treatment, of interpretations which claim to do so). As a result, the subject, although always present in the fantasy, may be so in a desubjectivized form, that is to say, in the very syntax of the sequence in question" ("Fantasy and the Origins of Sexuality," 26).

53. Williams, "Film Bodies," 10. In "Power, Pleasure, and Perversion" Williams argues for the mobility of gendered positions within sadomasochistic pornography to make especially masochism available to women's pleasure.

54. In this Araya's art is strongly reminiscent of the supposed inequalities that make up the erotic charge of Krista Beinstein's photography. See Beinstein, *Rituale der Begierde*.

55. Silverman, "Girl Love."

56. Araya, interview by author, August 21–22, 2005.

57. Araya, *Thamai Thueng Mi Rot Kawi Thaen Khwam Ru Than?*, 23.

58. I do not mean to imply that this is an externalization of the artist's thoughts and feelings. Rather I understand her to *perform*—and play with—a notion of self-revelation. See Araya, *Phom Pen Sinlapin*, 60.

59. Sayan, "Waeo Krading Kring Krung Khlung Klin Kawi Wa 'Chan Chue Araya,'" 31.

60. See, for instance, Araya Rasdjarmrearnsook, "Sangkhom Suantua" (Private Society), *Matichon Sud Sapda*, January 23–29, 2004, 67–68.

CODA

1. *Quarantine* was banned from showing in the World Film Festival in Bangkok in 2009.

2. McCargo argues for the southern Thai conflict's difference from other global cases in *Tearing Apart the Land*, 188.

3. See Haberkorn, "Dispossessing Law."

4. "South Unrest Death Toll Close to 6,000," *Bangkok Post*, January 3, 2014.

5. See especially Butler, "Sexual Politics, Torture, and Secular Time"; Mahmood, *Politics of Piety*; Puar, *Terrorist Assemblages*.

6. Haritaworn and Petzen, "Invented Traditions, New Intimate Publics."

7. Loos, *Subject Siam*.

8. See Kong et al., *Baby Arabia*, which recovers a female tradition of voice in Islam. For an account of Buddhist-Muslim contemporaneity, see Horstmann, "Ethnohistorical Perspectives on Buddhist-Muslim Relations and Coexistence in Southern Thailand," on the history of southern Thai Buddhist-Muslim coexistence and shared cosmologies.

9. This archive includes films such as Pimpaka Towira's *The Island Funeral* (*Mahasamut Lae Susan*, 2015), Ing K, Manit Sriwanichphum, and Kraisak Chunhavan's *Citizen Juling* (*Phonlamueang Juling*, 2008), and Panu Aree, Kaweenipon Ketprasit, and Kong Rithdee's *In Between* (2006), *The Convert* (*Muallaf*, 2008), and *Baby Arabia* (2010). Along with print materials such as short stories, poetry, and new Muslim lifestyle magazines (e.g., *Halal Life*), as well as materials such as spoken-word performances and Internet television scoops (e.g., *Shallow News in Depth* [*Jor Khao Tuen*]), the filmic archive provides a radically different outlook on coexistence.

10. See Hochberg, "'Check Me Out'" and "The (Soldier's) Gaze and the (Palestinian) Body."

11. Mikulinsky, "Chic Point."

12. Waugh, "Acting to Play Oneself."

13. See Haberkorn, "Dispossessing Law." In addition Article 112, the lèse-majesté law, creates a permanent exception because it puts a monarchy (and its allied networks) that is by definition constitutional above the law. In connection with other laws and policies Article 112 is responsible for a context in which citizens are a priori deprived of rights of expression and can at present instantly and arbitrarily be

deprived of liberty. Finally, the military-promulgated constitution of 2014 invalidates most vital civil rights.

14. See Haberkorn, *Revolution Interrupted*, 156.

15. On the critical political potential of bodies assembled in public, see also Butler, "Bodily Vulnerability, Coalitions, and Street Politics."

16. Sudarat, "Art for October," 32.

17. Waugh, "Acting to Play Oneself."

18. For comparison, see other Muslim diaspora films that strongly rely on the deployment of bodies and same-sex intimacies, such as Burhan Qurbani's *Shahada* (2010) and Remi Lange's *The Road to Love* (2001). See also Nguyen, *A View from the Bottom*, which models an incisive queer reading of the subversive potential of interracial intimacy in Jean-Jacques Annaud's *The Lover* (1992).

19. While Thaksin vitally relied on court cases and to a great extent focused also on sexual content, governments since 2006 have largely relied on the lèse-majesté law and the Computer Crime Act to target political dissent. See Brooten and Klangnarong, "People's Media and Reform Efforts in Thailand"; Ubonrat, "New Media for Civil Society and Political Censorship in Thailand."

20. The same can be said about the filmmaker's *Uncle Boonmee Who Can Recall His Past Lives* (2010).

Abbas, Ackbar. "Cosmopolitan De-scriptions: Shanghai and Hong Kong." *Public Culture* 12, no. 3 (2000): 769–86.

———. *Hong Kong: Culture and the Politics of Disappearance.* Minneapolis: University of Minnesota Press, 1997.

Amporn Jirattikorn. "Suriyothai: Hybridizing Thai National Identity through Film." *Inter-Asia Cultural Studies* 4, no. 2 (2003): 296–308.

Anake Nawigamune. *Poed Tamnan: Mae Nak Phra Khanong—Mae Nak Classical Ghost of Siam.* Bangkok: Nora, 2000.

Anchalee Chaiworaporn. "A Perceiver of Sense—Apichatpong Weerasethakul." Thai Cinema. Accessed May 30, 2015. http://www.thaicinema.org/Essays_07apichatpong.php.

Anderson, Ben. "Sat Pralat Arai Wa?" (What Goddamn "Strange Beast" Is This?). *Sinlapawatthanatham* 27, no. 9 (2006): 140–53.

Anderson, Benedict. *Imagined Communities: Reflections on the Origin and Spread of Nationalism.* London: Verso, 1983.

———. "Radicalism after Communism in Thailand and Indonesia." *New Left Review* 202 (November–December 1993): 3–14.

———. *The Spectre of Comparisons: Nationalism, Southeast Asia, and the World.* London: Verso, 1998.

———. "The Strange Story of a Strange Beast: Receptions in Thailand of Apichatpong Weerasethakul's *Sat Pralaat.*" In *Apichatpong Weerasethakul*, ed. James Quandt, 158–77. Vienna: SYNEMA, 2009.

Anderson, Carolyn, and Thomas Benson. "Direct Cinema and the Myth of Informed Consent: The Case of *Titicut Follies.*" In *Image Ethics: The Moral Rights of Subjects in Photographs, Film, and Television*, ed. Larry Gross, John Stuart Katz, and Jay Ruby, 58–90. New York: Oxford University Press, 1988.

Ang, Ien. "Can One Say No to Chineseness? Pushing the Limits of the Diasporic Paradigm." *boundary 2* 25, no. 3 (1998): 223–42.

Anjaree Group. "A Proposal for an Action Research: Disposing Policy Myths, Exposing Real Life Experiences of Lesbians in Thailand." 2001.

Apichatpong Weerasethakul, dir. *Saeng Sattawat* (Syndromes and a Century). DVD.
New York: Strand Releasing, 2007.

———, dir. *Sat Pralat* (Tropical Malady). DVD. Chiang Mai: Kick the Machine Films,
2004.

———, dir. *Tropical Malady*. DVD. New York: Strand Releasing, 2004.

Apichatpong Weerasethakul and Chuck Stephens. *Tropical Malady: Commentary by
Director and Film Critic Chuck Stephens*. DVD. New York: Strand Releasing, 2004.

Araya Rasdjarmrearnsook. "The Class, Death Seminar." Asymptote. Accessed May 30,
2015. http://www.asymptotejournal.com/article.php?cat=Visual&id=6&curr
_index=0.

———. *Khuen Sin Klin Kamarot* (The Night the Scent of Desire Ceased). Bangkok:
Sam Si, 1999.

———. *(Phom) Pen Silapin* ((I) Am an Artist). Bangkok: Matichon, 2005.

———. *Phu Ying Tawanok* (Oriental Woman). Bangkok: Si San, 1993.

———. *Sinlapa Kap Thoi Khwam* (Art and Words). Bangkok: Matichon, 2006.

———. *Thamai Thueng Mi Rot Kawi Thaen Khwam Ru Than?* (Why Is It Poetry
Rather Than Awareness?). Bangkok: Amarin, 2002.

———. *Thuk Haeng Prathana* (Lament of Desire). Bangkok: Amarin, 1999.

Askew, Marc. "Landscapes of Fear, Horizons of Trust: Villagers Dealing with Danger in
Thailand's Insurgent South." *Journal of Southeast Asian Studies* 40, no. 1 (2009): 59–86.

Baker, Chris. *Thailand Human Development Report 2007: Sufficiency Economy and
Human Development*. Bangkok: UNDP, 2007.

Baker, Chris, and Pasuk Pongpaichit. "Thailand in Trouble: Revolt of the Downtrod-
den or Conflict among Elites?" In *Bangkok May 2010: Perspectives on a Divided Thailand*, ed. Michael Montesano, Pavin Chachavalpongpun, Aekapol Chongvilaivan,
214–29. Singapore: Institute of Southeast Asian Studies, 2012.

Bao, Jiemin. *Marital Acts: Gender, Sexuality, and Identity among the Chinese Thai
Diaspora*. Honolulu: University of Hawai'i Press, 2005.

Barlow, Tani E. "Debates over Colonial Modernity in East Asia and Another Alternative." *Cultural Studies* 26, no. 5 (2012): 617–44.

———. "Femininity." In *The Palgrave Dictionary of Transnational History*, ed. Akira
Iriye and Pierre-Yves Saunier, 388–92. London: Palgrave Macmillan, 2009.

———, ed. *Formations of Colonial Modernity in Eastern Asia*. Durham, NC: Duke
University Press, 1997.

———. "'Green Blade in the Act of Being Grazed': Late Capital, Flexible Bodies, Critical Intelligibility." *differences: a journal of feminist cultural studies* 10, no. 3
(1998): 119–58.

———. "One Single Catastrophe." *Radical History Review* 79, no. 1 (2001): 77–80.

———. *The Question of Women in Chinese Feminism*. Next Wave: New Directions in
Women's Studies Series. Durham, NC: Duke University Press, 2004.

Barthes, Roland. *A Lover's Discourse*. New York: Hill and Wang, 1978.

Beinstein, Krista. *Rituale der Begierde* (Rituals of Desire). Tübingen: Konkursbuch Verlag, 1993.

Berlant, Lauren. *The Anatomy of National Fantasy: Hawthorne, Utopia, and Everyday Life*. Chicago: University of Chicago Press, 1991.

———. "The Compulsion to Repeat Femininity: *Landscape for a Good Woman* and *The Life and Loves of a She-Devil*." In *The Female Complaint: The Unfinished Business of Sentimentality in American Culture*, 233–63. Durham, NC: Duke University Press, 2008.

———. *Intimacy*. Chicago: University of Chicago Press, 2000.

———. "Neither Monstrous nor Pastoral, but Scary and Sweet: Some Thoughts on Sex and Emotional Performance in *Intimacies* and *What Do Gay Men Want?*" *Women & Performance: A Journal of Feminist Theory* 19, no. 2 (2009): 261–73.

———. *The Queen of America Goes to Washington City: Essays on Sex and Citizenship*. Durham, NC: Duke University Press, 1997.

———. "The Subject of True Feeling: Pain, Privacy, and Politics." In *Cultural Pluralism, Identity Politics, and the Law*, ed. Austin Sarat and Thomas R. Kearns, 49–84. Ann Arbor: University of Michigan Press, 1999.

Berlant, Lauren, and Lee Edelman. *Sex, or the Unbearable*. Durham, NC: Duke University Press, 2014.

Berlant, Lauren, and Michael Warner. "Sex in Public." *Critical Inquiry* 24, no. 2 (1998), 547–66.

Bersani, Leo. "Gay Betrayals." In *Is the Rectum a Grave? And Other Essays*, 36–44. Chicago: University of Chicago Press, 2010.

Bersani, Leo, and Adam Phillips. *Intimacies*. Chicago: University of Chicago Press, 2008.

Brenner, Suzanne April. "Gender and the Domestication of Desire." In *The Domestication of Desire*, 134–70. Princeton: Princeton University Press, 1998.

Brinkema, Eugenie. *The Forms of the Affects*. Durham, NC: Duke University Press, 2014.

Bronfen, Elisabeth. *Over Her Dead Body: Death, Femininity, and the Aesthetic*. New York: Routledge, 1992.

Brooten, Lisa, and Supinya Klangnarong. "People's Media and Reform Efforts in Thailand." *International Journal of Media and Cultural Politics* 5, nos. 1–2 (2009): 103–17.

Brown, Wendy. "American Nightmare: Neoliberalism, Neoconservatism, and De-democratization." *Political Theory* 34, no. 6 (2006): 690–714.

———. "Neoliberalism and the End of Liberal Democracy." *Theory & Event* 7, no. 1 (2003). Accessed May 30, 2015. http://muse.jhu.edu/journals/theory_and_event /v007/7.1brown.html.

———. "Rights and Identity in Late Modernity: Revisiting the 'Jewish Question.'" In *Identities, Politics, and Rights*, ed. Austin Sarat and Thomas R. Kearns, 85–130. Ann Arbor: University of Michigan Press, 1995.

———. "Rights and Losses." In *States of Injury: Power and Freedom in Late Modernity*, 96–134. Princeton: Princeton University Press, 1995.

———. "Suffering the Paradoxes of Rights." In *Left Legalism / Left Critique*, ed. Wendy Brown and Janet Halley, 420–34. Durham, NC: Duke University Press, 2002.

———. "Wounded Attachments." *Political Theory* 21, no. 3 (1993): 390–410.

Butler, Judith. "Bodily Vulnerability, Coalitions, and Street Politics." *Critical Studies* 37 (2014): 99–119.

———. *The Psychic Life of Power: Theories in Subjection*. Stanford, CA: Stanford University Press, 1997.

———. "Sexual Inversions." In *Feminist Interpretations of Michel Foucault*, ed. Susan J. Hekman, 59–75. University Park: Pennsylvania State University Press, 1996.

———. "Sexual Politics, Torture, and Secular Time." In *Frames of War: When Is Life Grievable?*, 101–35. London: Verso, 2009.

Cabezón, José Ignacio. *Buddhism, Sexuality, and Gender*. Albany: State University of New York Press, 1992.

Canetti, Elias. *Crowds and Power*. 1962. New York: Farrar, Straus and Giroux, 1984.

Caruth, Cathy. "Trauma and Experience: Introduction." In *Trauma: Explorations in Memory*, ed. Cathy Caruth, 3–12. Baltimore: Johns Hopkins University Press, 1995.

———. *Unclaimed Experience: Trauma, Narrative, and History*. Baltimore: Johns Hopkins University Press, 1996.

Cassaniti, Julia. "Control in a World of Change: Emotion and Morality in a Northern Thai Town." PhD diss., University of Chicago, 2009.

———. *Living Buddhism: Mind, Self, and Emotion in a Thai Community*. Ithaca, NY: Cornell University Press, 2015.

Chai Worathammo. *Kae Plueak Phet Phut* (Unpacking Buddhist Sex). Petchabun: Sapaan, 2010.

———. "Ke-Lesbian Wibakkam Khong Khrai" (Gays and Lesbians: Whose [Karmic] Adversity?). Sadue Kaiwan: Khon Nok (Nirvana Core: The Outsider), 2006. Accessed May 30, 2015. http://child1968.blogspot.com/2006/12/blog-post_2796.html.

———. "Phrang Chomphu Katha" (The [Buddhist] Tale of Private Pink). *Sekhiyatham* 55 (2003): 40–41.

Chakrabarty, Dipesh. "Minority Histories, Subaltern Pasts." *Postcolonial Studies* 1, no. 1 (1998): 15–29.

———. "The Time of History and the Times of Gods." In *The Politics of Culture in the Shadow of Capital*, ed. Lisa Lowe and David Lloyd, 35–59. Durham, NC: Duke University Press, 1997.

———. "The Two Histories of Capital." In *Provincializing Europe: Postcolonial Thought and Historical Difference*, 47–71. Princeton: Princeton University Press, 2000.

Chalida Uabumrungjit. "Coming of Age of New Thai Cinema." Thai Film Foundation, January 1, 2004. Accessed May 30, 2015. http://thaifilm.com/articleDetail_en.asp?id=35.

———. "Sleepy Consciousness of Thai Documentary Film." Documentary Box. Accessed May 30, 2015. http://www.yidff.jp/docbox/21/box21-2-e.html.

Chalidaporn Songsamphan. "Phap Sop Lae Phap Nud" (Death Imagery and Images of Nudity). *Nechan Sudsapda*, December 23–24, 2000.

————. "Wathanatham Klied Tut Ke Thom Di" (Culture Hates [of Hating] Fags, Gays, Butches, Femmes, Etc.). Sapaan, 2004. Accessed August 14, 2013. http://sapaan.org/index.php?option=com_content&task=view&id=70&Itemid=39.

Chan, Kwok B., and Tong Chee Kiong. "Rethinking Assimilation and Ethnicity: The Chinese in Thailand." In *The Chinese Diaspora: Selected Essays*, ed. Wang Ling-chi and Wan Gungwu, 2: 1–27. Singapore: Times Academic Press, 1998.

Cheng, Anne Anlin. *The Melancholy of Race*. Oxford: Oxford University Press, 2000.

Cho, Francisca. "Buddhism." In *The Routledge Companion to Religion and Film*, ed. John Lyden, 162–77. New York: Routledge, 2009.

Chua, Lawrence. "The City and the City: Race, Nationalism, and Architecture in Early Twentieth-Century Bangkok." *Journal of Urban History* 40, no. 5 (2014): 933–58.

Clover, Carol J. "The Eye of Horror." In *Viewing Positions: Ways of Seeing Film*, ed. Linda Williams, 184–230. New Brunswick, NJ: Rutgers University Press, 1995.

Coffee with Open. "Apichatpong Weerasethakul: Mueang Thai Ko Pen Baep Ni?" (Apichatpong Weerasethakul: This Is What Thailand's Like?). January 29, 2008. Accessed November 10, 2015. http://www.thaiontario.com/index.php?topic=3322.0;imode.

Collins, Steven. "The Body in Theravada Buddhist Monasticism." In *Religion and the Body*, ed. Sarah Coakley, 185–204. Cambridge: Cambridge University Press, 1997.

————. *Nirvana: Concept, Imagery, Narrative*. Cambridge: Cambridge University Press, 2010.

Connors, Michael Kelly. *Democracy and National Identity in Thailand*. New York: Routledge Curzon, 2003.

————. "Goodbye to the Security State: Thailand and Ideological Change." *Journal of Contemporary Asia* 33, no. 4 (2003): 431–48.

————. "Ministering Culture: Hegemony and the Politics of Culture and Identity in Thailand." *Critical Asian Studies* 37, no. 4 (2005): 532–51.

————. "Notes towards an Understanding of Thai Liberalism." In *Bangkok May 2010: Perspectives on a Divided Thailand*, ed. Michael Montesano, Pavin Chachavalpongpun, and Aekapol Chongvilaivan, 97–107. Singapore: Institute of Southeast Asian Studies, 2012.

Corner, John. *The Art of Record: A Critical Introduction to Documentary*. Manchester, UK: Manchester University Press, 1996.

Crimp, Douglas. "Mourning and Militancy." In *Out There: Marginalization and Contemporary Cultures*, ed. Russell Ferguson, 233–45. New York: Museum of Contemporary Art, MIT Press, 1990.

Dabashi, Hamid. "Transcending the Boundaries of an Imaginative Geography." In *Shirin Neshat: La Ultima Palabra / The Last Word*, 31–85. Milan: Charta, 2005.

Dararat Mettarikanon. "Kha Ying Jin Kham Chat Nai Prawatisat Sangkhom Thai" (The Transnational Trafficking in Chinese Women in Thai Social History). *Sinlapawatthanatham* 21, no. 4 (2000): 26–39.

Das, Veena. "Language and Body: Transactions in the Construction of Pain." In *Social Suffering*, ed. Veena Das, Arthur Kleinman, and Margaret Lock, 67–91. Berkeley: University of California Press, 1997.

———. *Life and Words: Violence and the Descent into the Ordinary*. Berkeley: University of California Press, 2007.

Dean, Tim. *Unlimited Intimacy: Reflections on the Subculture of Barebacking*. Chicago: University of Chicago Press, 2009.

Dechavuth Chanthakaro. *One Day Show*. Bangkok: Kai Marut, 2003.

Dinshaw, Carolyn. *How Soon Is Now? Medieval Texts, Amateur Readers, and the Queerness of Time*. Durham, NC: Duke University Press, 2012.

———. "Theorizing Queer Temporalities: A Roundtable Discussion." GLQ 13, no. 2 (2007): 177–95.

Dumm, Thomas L. *A Politics of the Ordinary*. New York: New York University Press, 1999.

Edelman, Lee. "Ever After: History, Negativity, and the Social." *South Atlantic Quarterly* 106, no. 3 (2007): 469–76.

———. *No Future: Queer Theory and the Death Drive*. Durham, NC: Duke University Press, 2004.

Eng, David L. "The Structure of Kinship: The Art of Waiting in *The Book of Salt* and *Happy Together*." In *The Feeling of Kinship: Queer Liberalism and the Racialization of Intimacy*, 58–92. Durham, NC: Duke University Press, 2010.

Eng, David L., and David Kazanjian, eds. *Loss*. Berkeley: University of California Press, 2003.

Engel, David M., and Jaruwan S. Engel. *Tort, Custom, and Karma: Globalization and Legal Consciousness in Thailand*. Stanford, CA: Stanford Law Books, 2010.

Farmer, Brett. "Loves of Siam: Contemporary Thai Cinema and Vernacular Queerness." In *Queer Bangkok: 21st Century Media, Markets, and Rights*, ed. Peter A. Jackson, 81–98. Hong Kong: Hong Kong University Press, 2011.

Faure, Bernard. *The Red Thread: Buddhist Approaches to Sexuality*. Princeton: Princeton University Press, 1998.

Feeley, Jennifer. "Transnational Spectres and Regional Spectators: Flexible Citizenship in New Chinese Horror Cinema." *Journal of Chinese Cinemas* 6, no. 1 (2012): 41–64.

Fishel, Thamora. "Romances of the Sixth Reign: Gender, Sexuality, and Siamese Nationalism." In *Genders and Sexualities in Modern Thailand*, ed. Peter A. Jackson and Nerida M. Cook, 154–67. Chiang Mai, Thailand: Silkworm Books, 1999.

Foucault, Michel. *The History of Sexuality, Vol. 1: An Introduction*. 1976. New York: Vintage, 1990.

Freeman, Elizabeth. *Time Binds: Queer Temporalities, Queer Histories*. Durham, NC: Duke University Press, 2010.

Freud, Sigmund. "Mourning and Melancholia." 1917. In *The Standard Edition of the Complete Psychological Works of Sigmund Freud*, ed. and trans. J. Strachey, 14: 243–58. London: Hogarth Press, 1961.

Gimpel Fils. "Corinne Day: 15 / Araya Rasdjarmrearnsook: The Class." Press release. 2006. Accessed May 30, 2015. http://www.gimpelfils.com/pages/exhibitions /exhibition.php?exhid=45&subsec=1.

Gopinath, Gayatri. *Impossible Desires: Queer Diasporas and South Asian Public Cultures.* Durham, NC: Duke University Press, 2005.

Gordon, Avery F. *Ghostly Matters: Haunting and the Sociological Imagination.* Minneapolis: University of Minnesota Press, 1997.

Gray, Christine. "Thailand: The Soteriological State in the 1970s." PhD diss., University of Chicago, 1986.

Haberkorn, Tyrell. "Dispossessing Law: Arbitrary Detention in Southern Thailand." In *Accumulating Insecurity: Violence and Dispossession in the Making of Everyday Life*, ed. Shelley Feldman, 122–37. Athens: University of Georgia Press, 2011.

———. *Revolution Interrupted: Farmers, Students, Law, and Violence in Northern Thailand.* Madison: University of Wisconsin Press, 2011.

———. "Thailand's State of Impunity." *Open Democracy*, June 3, 2008. Accessed May 30, 2015. http://www.opendemocracy.net/article/thailand-s-state-of -impunity.

———. "When Torture Is a Duty: The Murder of Imam Yapa Kaseng and the Challenge of Accountability in Thailand." *Asian Studies Review* 39, no. 1 (2015): 53–68.

Haeman Chatemee, dir. *Pop Whid Sayong* (Body Jumper). Bangkok: Sahamongkol, 2001.

Halberstam, Judith. *The Queer Art of Failure.* Durham, NC: Duke University Press, 2011.

———. *Skin Shows: Gothic Horror and the Technology of Monsters.* Durham, NC: Duke University Press, 1995.

Hall, Jonathan M. "Area Studies at the Bedroom Door: Queer Theory, Japan, and the Case of the Missing Fantasy." *Japanese Studies* 23, no. 2 (2003): 205–12.

———. "Japan's Progressive Sex: Male Homosexuality, National Competition, and the Cinema." In *Queer Asian Cinema: Shadows in the Shade*, ed. Andrew Grossman, 31–82. New York: Haworth Press, 2000.

Haritaworn, Jin, and Jennifer Petzen. "Invented Traditions, New Intimate Publics: Tracing the German 'Muslim Homophobia' Discourse." In *Islam in Its International Context: Comparative Perspectives*, ed. Chris Flood and Stephen Hutchings, 48–64. Cambridge: Cambridge Scholars Press, 2011.

Harootunian, Harry. "Remembering the Historical Present." *Critical Inquiry* 33, no. 3 (2007): 471–94.

Harrison, Rachel. "Amazing Thai Film: The Rise and Rise of Contemporary Thai Cinema on the International Screen." *Asian Affairs* 36, no. 3 (2005): 321–38.

———. "The Disruption of Female Desire and the Thai Literary Tradition of Eroticism, Religion and Aesthetics." *Tenggara* 41 (2000): 88–125.

———. "'A Hundred Loves, a Thousand Lovers': Portrayals of Sexuality in the Work of Thidaa Bunnaak." *Journal of Southeast Asian Studies* 33, no. 2 (2002): 451–70.

Harvey, Sophia. "Fractured Visions: Locating the Pan-Asian Gaze in *The Eye*." Paper presented at the Society for Cinema and Media Studies Conference, Vancouver, March 2006.

Ho, Tamara C. "Transgender, Transgression, and Translation: A Cartography of *Nat Kadaws*. Notes on Gender and Sexuality within the Spirit Cult of Burma." *Discourse* 31, no. 3 (2009): 273–317.

Hochberg, Gil Z. "'Check Me Out': Queer Encounters in Sharif Waked's *Chic Point: Fashion for Israeli Checkpoints*." GLQ 16, no. 4 (2010): 577–97.

———. "The (Soldier's) Gaze and the (Palestinian) Body: Power, Fantasy, and Desire in the Militarized Contact Zone." In *Visual Occupations: Violence and Visibility in a Conflict Zone,* 79–96. Durham, NC: Duke University Press, 2015.

Hong Lysa. "Invisible Semicolony: The Postcolonial Condition and Royal National History in Thailand." *Postcolonial Studies* 11, no. 3 (2008): 315–27.

Horstmann, Alexander. "Ethnohistorical Perspectives on Buddhist-Muslim Relations and Coexistence in Southern Thailand: From Shared Cosmos to the Emergence of Hatred?" *Sojourn* 19, no. 1 (2004): 76–99.

Isatri Irotik (Female Erotic). Bangkok: Open Publishing, 2002.

Ivy, Marilyn. *Discourses of the Vanishing: Modernity, Phantasm, Japan.* Chicago: University of Chicago Press, 1995.

Iwabuchi, Koichi. "Nostalgia for a (Different) Asian Modernity: Media Consumption of 'Asia' in Japan." *positions: asia critique* 10, no. 3 (2002): 547–73.

Jackson, Peter A. *Dear Uncle Go: Male Homosexuality in Thailand.* Bangkok: Bua Luang Books, 1995.

———. "An Explosion of Thai Identities: Global Queering and Re-imagining Queer Theory." *Culture, Health & Sexuality* 2, no. 4 (2000): 405–24.

———. "Male Homosexuality and Transgenderism in the Thai Buddhist Tradition." In *Queer Dharma: Voices of Gay Buddhists,* ed. Winston Leyland, 1: 55–89. San Francisco: Gay Sunshine, 1998.

———. "Queer Bangkok after the Millennium: Beyond Twentieth-Century Paradigms." In *Queer Bangkok: 21st Century Media, Markets, and Rights,* ed. Peter A. Jackson, 1–14. Hong Kong: Hong Kong University Press, 2011.

———. "Tolerant but Unaccepting: The Myth of a Thai 'Gay Paradise.'" In *Genders and Sexualities in Modern Thailand,* ed. Peter A. Jackson and Nerida M. Cook, 226–42. Chiang Mai, Thailand: Silkworm Books, 1999.

Jackson, Peter A., and Nerida M. Cook, eds. *Genders and Sexualities in Modern Thailand.* Chiang Mai, Thailand: Silkworm Books, 1999.

Jeffrey, Leslie Ann. *Sex and Borders: Gender, National Identity, and Prostitution Policy in Thailand.* Vancouver: UBC Press, 2002.

Jory, Patrick. "The Rise and Fall of Empires and the Case for Liberal Imperialism." *Kyoto Review of Southeast Asia,* February 2010. Accessed May 30, 2015. http:// kyotoreview.org/issue-8-9/review-article-the-rise-and-fall-of-empires-and-the-case -for-liberal-imperialism/.

Kapur, Ratna. *Erotic Justice: Law and the New Politics of Postcolonialism.* London: Glasshouse Press, 2005.

Kasian Tejapira. *Commodifying Marxism: The Formation of Modern Thai Radical Culture, 1927–1958.* Kyoto: Kyoto University Press, 2001.

———. "Imagined Uncommunity: The *Lookjin* Middle Class and Thai Official Nationalism." In *Essential Outsiders: Chinese and Jews in the Modern Transformation of Southeast Asia and Central Europe*, ed. Anthony Reid and Daniel Chirot, 75–98. Seattle: University of Washington Press, 1997.

———. *Lae Lod Lai Mangkon: Ruam Kho Khien Wa Duai Khwam Pen Jin Nai Sayam* (Peering under the Dragon's Scale: Selected Writings on Chineseness in Siam). Bangkok: Khob Fai, 1994.

———. "Pigtail: A Pre-history of Chineseness in Siam." *Sojourn* 7, no. 1 (1992): 95–122.

———. "Questions of Minorities." *Items—Social Science Research Council* 52, no. 4 (1998): 81–82.

———. "Toppling Thaksin." *New Left Review* 39 (May–June 2006): 5–37.

Katrib, Ruba. "Speechless." In *Araya Rasdjarmrearnsook*, 2–7. Exhibition catalogue. SculptureCenter, New York, 2015.

Keyes, Charles. "Mother or Mistress but Never a Monk: Buddhist Notions of Female Gender in Rural Thailand." *American Ethnologist* 11, no. 2 (1984): 223–41.

———. *Thailand: Buddhist Kingdom as Modern Nation-State*. Boulder, CO: Westview, 1987.

Kirsch, Thomas A. "Text and Context: Buddhist Sex Roles / Culture of Gender Revisited." *American Ethnologist* 12, no. 2 (1985): 302–20.

Klima, Alan. *The Funeral Casino: Meditation, Massacre, and Exchange with the Dead in Thailand*. Princeton: Princeton University Press, 2002.

Knee, Adam. "The Pan-Asian Outlook of *The Eye*." In *Horror to the Extreme: Changing Boundaries in Asian Cinema*, ed. Jinhee Choi and Mitsuyo Wada-Marciano, 69–84. Hong Kong: Hong Kong University Press, 2009.

———. "Thailand Haunted: The Power of the Past in the Contemporary Thai Horror Film." In *Horror International*, ed. Steven Jay Schneider and Tony Williams, 141–59. Detroit: Wayne State University Press, 2005.

———. "Thailand in the Hong Kong Cinematic Imagination." In *Hong Kong Film, Hollywood and the New Global Cinema: No Film Is an Island*, ed. Gina Marchetti and Tan See Kam, 77–90. London: Routledge, 2007.

Kong Rithdee. "Chamlae Sat Pralat" (Dissecting a Strange Animal [Tropical Malady]). Thai Film Foundation, 2004. Accessed August 14, 2013. http://www.thaifilm .com/thaiFilmDetail.asp?id=3.

———. "Jungle Fever." *Film Comment* 41, no. 3 (2005): 44–47.

———. "Scenes from a Marriage." Thai Film Foundation, October 11, 2007. Accessed May 30, 2015. http://www.thaifilm.com/articleDetail_en.asp?id=103.

Kong Rithdee, Panu Aree, and Kaweenipon Ketprasit, dirs. *Baby Arabia*. DVD. Bangkok: Walad Dorleen Film, 2010.

Kübler-Ross, Elisabeth. *On Death and Dying*. New York: Macmillan, 1969.

Kulawee Prapapornpipat. "Naeo Khit Lae Jariyasat Thi Kiau Kap Phet Nai Phuthasasana Therawat" (Thoughts and Ethics of Sexuality in Theravada Buddhism). Master's thesis, Thammasat University, 2002.

Landsberg, Alison. *Prosthetic Memory: The Transformation of American Remembrance in the Age of Mass Culture*. New York: Columbia University Press, 2004.

Laplanche, Jean, and Jean-Bertrand Pontalis. "Fantasy and the Origins of Sexuality: Retrospect, 1986." In *Formations of Fantasy*, ed. James Donald, Victor Burgin, and Cora Kaplan, 5–34. London: Routledge, 1989.

Leys, Ruth. "The Pathos of the Literal: Trauma and the Crisis of Representation." In *Trauma: A Genealogy*, 266–97. Chicago: University of Chicago Press, 2000.

Lim, Bliss Cua. "Queer Aswang Transmedia: Folklore as Camp." *Kritika Kultura* 24 (2015): 178–225.

———. "Spectral Times: The Ghost Film as Historical Allegory." *positions: asia critique* 9, no. 2 (2001): 287–329.

———. *Translating Time: Cinema, the Fantastic, and Temporal Critique*. John Hope Franklin Center Book Series. Durham, NC: Duke University Press, 2009.

Loos, Tamara. "Issaraphap: Limits of Individual Liberty in Thai Jurisprudence." *Crossroads: An Interdisciplinary Journal of Southeast Asian Studies* 12, no. 1 (1998): 35–75.

———. "Sex in the Inner City: The Fidelity between Sex and Politics in Siam." *Journal of Asian Studies* 64, no. 4 (2005): 881–909.

———. *Subject Siam: Family, Law, and Colonial Modernity in Thailand*. Ithaca: Cornell University Press, 2006.

Love, Heather. *Feeling Backward: Loss and the Politics of Queer History*. Cambridge: Harvard University Press, 2007.

Lu, Sheldon. "Hong Kong Diaspora Film and Transnational Television Drama: From Homecoming to Exile to Flexible Citizenship." In *Chinese-Language Film: Historiography, Poetics, Politics*, ed. Sheldon H. Lu and Emilie Yueh-Yu Yeh, 104–21. Honolulu: University of Hawai'i Press, 2005.

Ma, Jean Yun-chen. *Melancholy Drift: Marking Time in Chinese Cinema*. Hong Kong: Hong Kong University Press, 2010.

———. "Time without Measure, Sadness without Cure: Hou Hsiao-Hsien's Films of History." PhD diss., University of Chicago, 2003.

Mahmood, Saba. *Politics of Piety: The Islamic Revival and the Feminist Subject*. Princeton: Princeton University Press, 2005.

Manas Chitakasem. "Poetic Conventions and Modern Thai Poetry." In *Thai Constructions of Knowledge*, ed. Manas Chitakasem and Andrew Turton, 37–62. London: University of London, School of Oriental and African Studies, 1991.

May Adadol Ingawanij. "Animism and the Performative Realist Cinema of Apichatpong Weerasethakul." In *Screening Nature: Cinema beyond the Human*, ed. Anat Pick and Guinevere Narraway, 91–109. Oxford: Berghahn Books, 2013.

———. "Dialectics of Independence." In *Glimpses of Freedom: Independent Cinema in Southeast Asia*, ed. May Adadol Ingawanij and Benjamin McKay, 1–14. Ithaca: Southeast Asia Program, Cornell University, 2012.

———. "Disreputable Behaviour: The Hidden Politics of the Thai Film Act." *Vertigo* 8, no. 8 (2008): 30–31.

———. "Hyperbolic Heritage: Bourgeois Spectatorship and Contemporary Thai Cinema." PhD diss., University of London, 2006.

———. "*Nang Nak*: Thai Bourgeois Heritage Cinema." *Inter-Asia Cultural Studies* 8, no. 2 (2007): 180–93.

———. "The Thai Short Film and Video Festival and the Question of Independence." In *Glimpses of Freedom: Independent Cinema in Southeast Asia*, ed. May Adadol Ingawanij and Benjamin McKay, 165–81. Ithaca: Southeast Asia Program, Cornell University, 2012.

———. "Un-Thai *Sakon*: The Scandal of Teen Cinema." *Southeast Asia Research* 14, no. 2 (2006): 147–77.

May Adadol Ingawanij and Richard L. MacDonald. "Blissfully Whose? Jungle Pleasures, Ultra-Modernist Cinema and the Cosmopolitan Thai Auteur." *New Cinemas: Journal of Contemporary Film* 4, no. 1 (2006): 37–54.

May Adadol Ingawanij and Richard L. MacDonald. "The Value of an Impoverished Aesthetic: *The Iron Ladies* and Its Audiences." *Southeast Asia Research* 13, no. 1 (2005): 43–56.

Mbembe, Achille. "The Aesthetics of Vulgarity." In *On the Postcolony*, 102–41. Berkeley: University of California Press, 2001.

McCargo, Duncan. *Tearing Apart the Land: Islam and Legitimacy in Southern Thailand.* Ithaca: Cornell University Press, 2008.

McDaniel, Justin. *The Lovelorn Ghost and the Magical Monk: Practicing Buddhism in Modern Thailand.* New York: Columbia University Press, 2011.

McRoy, Jay. *Nightmare Japan: Contemporary Japanese Horror Cinema.* New York: Rodopi, 2008.

Mikulinsky, Alma. "Chic Point: Fashion for Israeli Checkpoints." *Critical Studies in Fashion & Beauty* 3, nos. 1–2 (2012): 219–25.

Mills, Mary Beth. "Attack of the Widow Ghosts: Gender, Death, and Modernity in Northeast Thailand." In *Bewitching Women, Pious Men: Gender and Body Politics in Southeast Asia*, ed. Aihwa Ong and Michael G. Peletz, 244–73. Berkeley: University of California Press, 1995.

The Modern Girl around the World Research Group, Tani E. Barlow, Madeleine Yue Dong, Uta G. Poiger, Priti Ramamurthy, Lynn M. Thomas, and Alys Eve Weinbaum, eds. *The Modern Girl around the World: Consumption, Modernity, and Globalization.* Durham, NC: Duke University Press, 2008.

Morris, Rosalind C. "Educating Desire: Thailand, Transnationalism, and Transgression. A Ban on Gay Teachers: Education and Prohibition in the 'Land of the Free.'" *Social Text* 52/53 15, nos. 3–4 (1997): 53–79.

———. "Returning the Body without Haunting: Mourning 'Nai Phi' and the End of Revolution in Thailand." In *Loss: The Politics of Mourning*, ed. David L. Eng and David Kazanjian, 29–58. Berkeley: University of California Press, 2003.

———. "A Room with a Voice: Mediation and Mediumship in Thailand's Information Age." In *Media Worlds: Anthropology on New Terrain*, ed. Faye D. Ginsburg et al., 383–98. Berkeley: University of California Press, 2002.

———. "Three Sexes and Four Sexualities: Redressing the Discourses in Gender and Sexuality in Contemporary Thailand." *positions* 2, no. 1 (1994): 15–43.

Nantiya Sukontapatipark. "The Relationship between Modern Medical Technology and Gender Identity in Thailand: Passing from 'Male Body' to 'Female Body.'" Master's thesis, Mahidol University, 2005.

Nguyen, Tan Hoang. *A View from the Bottom: Asian American Masculinity and Sexual Representation*. Durham, NC: Duke University Press, 2014.

Nichols, Bill. *Introduction to Documentary*. Bloomington: Indiana University Press, 2001.

Nithi Aeowsriwong. *Wa Duai Rueang Phet* (On Sexuality). Bangkok: Matichon, 2002.

Noi Inthanon. *Long Phrai: Suea Kueng Puthakan* (Roaming the Jungle: Tiger of Half a Buddhist Age). 1955. Ed. Khanitha (Chupinit) Na Bang Chang. Bangkok: Krathom, 1990.

Nonzee Nimibutr, dir. *Nang Nak*. DVD. Bangkok: Tai Entertainment, 1999.

———. *Nang Nak*. Bangkok: Phraeo Entertain, 1999.

Nord, Cristina. "Shape Shifter: Queer Cinema jenseits der Identitätspolitik" (Shape Shifter: Queer Cinema beyond Identity Politics). In *Das Achte Feld: Geschlechter, Leben und Begehren in der Kunst seit 1960* (The Eighth Square: Gender, Life, and Desire in the Arts since 1960), ed. Kaspar König, Frank Wagner, and Julia Friedrich, 195–200. Cologne: Museum Ludwig Köln, Hatje Cantz, 2006.

Obeyesekere, Gananath. "Depression, Buddhism, and the Work of Culture in Sri Lanka." 1985. In *Culture and Depression: Studies in the Anthropology and Cross-Cultural Psychiatry of Affect and Disorder*, ed. Arthur Kleinman and Byron Good, 134–52. Berkeley: University of California Press, 1996.

Ong, Aihwa. *Flexible Citizenship: The Cultural Logics of Transnationality*. Durham, NC: Duke University Press, 1999.

Oradol Kaewprasert. "The Very First Series of Thai Queer Cinemas—What Was Happening in the 1980s?" Paper presented at Sexualities, Genders and Rights in Asia, first International Conference of Asian Queer Studies, Bangkok, July 2005.

Owens, William, and Wimal Dissanayake. "Projecting Thailand: Thai Cinema and the Public Sphere." *Asian Cinema* 22, no. 2 (2012): 139–59.

Paisarn Likhitpreechakul. "Semen, Viagra and Pandaka: Ancient Endocrinology and Modern Day Discrimination." *Journal of the Oxford Centre for Buddhist Studies* 3 (2012): 91–127.

Pang, Danny, and Oxide Pang, dirs. *The Eye* (*Khon Hen Phi*). DVD. Bangkok: Sahamongkol Film and Phaphayon Hansa with Applause Pictures and Raintree Pictures, 2002.

Pang, Danny, and Oxide Pang, dirs. *The Eye 2*. DVD. Bangkok: Sahamongkol Film, Phaphayon Hansa, Mediacorp Raintree Pictures with Applause Pictures, 2004.

Pang, Danny, and Oxide Pang, dirs. *The Eye 10*. DVD. Bangkok: Sahamongkol Film International, Phapayon Hansa with Applause Pictures, 2005.

Pao, Jin Long. "The Pan-Asian Co-production Sphere: Interview with Director Peter Chan." *Harvard Asia Quarterly* 6, no. 3 (2002): 45–47.

Pasuk Pongphaichit. "Pasuk Pongphaichit on Thailand." *Kyoto Review of Southeast Asia* (2005). Accessed August 14, 2013. http://kyotoreview.org/issue-6/pasuk -pongphaichit-on-thailand/.

Pasuk Pongpaichit and Chris Baker. *Thailand's Boom and Bust*. Chiang Mai, Thailand: Silkworm, 1998.

Pathamamulamuli, or The Origin of the World in the Lan Na Tradition. Trans. Anatole-Roger Peltier. Chiang Mai, Thailand: Suriwong Book Centre Limited, 1991.

Pattana Kitiarsa. "Beyond Syncretism." In *Mediums, Monks, and Amulets: Thai Popular Buddhism Today*, 11–34. Seattle: University of Washington Press, 2012.

Peleggi, Maurizio. *The Politics of Ruins and the Business of Nostalgia*. Bangkok: White Lotus, 2002.

———. *Thailand: The Worldly Kingdom*. London: Reaktion Books, 2007.

Peletz, Michael. *Gender Pluralism: Southeast Asia since Early Modern Times*. New York: Routledge, 2009.

Pellegrini, Ann. "Feeling Secular." *Women & Performance: A Journal of Feminist Theory* 19, no. 2 (2009): 205–18.

Pettifor, Steven. "Embracing Taboos." *Asian Art News* 16, no. 4 (2006): 79–83.

Phapphan Raksrithong. "Aen Jim Phok Ling. Ik Kaempaen Khunatham" (If You're Going to Stick Your Cunt Out, Do Wear Underwear: Another Moral Campaign). Prachatai, 2007. Accessed January 27, 2008. http://blogazine.pub/blogs/hitandrun /post/17.

Phaya Anuman Rajadhon. *Mueang Sawan Lae Phi Sang Thewada* (Heaven, Spirits, and Deities). Bangkok: Rung Wathana, 1972.

Phayon. "Mae Nak Phrakhanong Phak Nai Thi Du Laeo Khon Luk Thi Sud Khrap" (Mae Nak Phrakhanong: Which Version Is the Most Hair-Raising?). Thai Film Foundation, 2007. Accessed May 30, 2015. http://www.thaifilm.com/forumDetail .asp?topicID=3715&page=1&keyword.

Phillips, Adam. "Keeping It Moving: Commentary on Judith Butler's 'Melancholy Gender / Refused Identification.'" In Judith Butler, *The Psychic Life of Power: Theories in Subjection*, 151–59. Stanford, CA: Stanford University Press, 1997.

———. *On Flirtation*. Cambridge, MA: Harvard University Press, 1994.

Phraphuthaleutla Naphalai. *Inao: Chabab Ho Samut Haeng Chat* (Inao: National Library Edition). Bangkok: Khlang Phitaya, 1963.

Pimpaka Towira, dir. *Mae Nak*. VHS. 1997.

Pinyo Trisuriyatamma. *Sat Wikan: Phap Rueang Saeng Khong Apichatpong Weerasethakul* (Unknown Forces: The Illuminated Art of Apichatpong Weerasethakul). Bangkok: Openbooks, 2007.

Pliu. *Phom Mai Chai Phu Chai Khrap* (I Am Not a Man). Bangkok: Dok Ya, 2002.

Plueang Na Nakhorn. *Prawat Wanakhadi Thai* (History of Thai Literature). Bangkok: Thai Wathanaphanit, 1998.

Poore, Grace. "Thai LGBT Activists Fight for Constitutional Protection." International Gay and Lesbian Human Rights Commission, November 7, 2007. Accessed May 30, 2015. http://www.iglhrc.org/content/thailand-lgbt-activists-fight-constitutional -protection.

Povinelli, Elizabeth A. "The Intimate Event and Genealogical Society." In *The Empire of Love: Toward a Theory of Intimacy, Genealogy, and Carnality*, 175–236. Durham, NC: Duke University Press, 2006.

Pracha Malinond. *2 Pi Thi Mahad Thai Khong Mo Tho 2* (The Deputy Minister's Two Years in the Ministry of the Interior). Ed. Acharaphan Jarasawat. Bangkok: Ministry of the Interior, 2005.

———. *6 Duean Nai Kan Jad Rabiap Sangkhom Khong M.T.2 (Tulakhom 2545–Minakhom 2546)* (Six Months of Social Ordering by the Ministry of the Interior 2 [October 2002–March 2003]). Ed. Acharaphan Jarasawat. Bangkok: Ministry of the Interior, 2003.

———. *Jad Rabiap Sangkhom 2* (Social Ordering 2). Ed. Acharaphan Jarasawat. Bangkok: Ministry of the Interior, 2003.

Puar, Jasbir. *Terrorist Assemblages: Homonationalism in Queer Times*. Durham, NC: Duke University Press, 2007.

Quandt, James, ed. *Apichatpong Weerasethakul*. Vienna: SYNEMA, 2009.

———. "Exquisite Corpus: The Films of Apichatpong Weerasethakul." *ARTFORUM*, May 2005, 226–31.

Rayns, Tony. "Towards the Wondrous Void." *Vertigo* 3, no. 4 (2007). Accessed November 9, 2015. https://www.closeupfilmcentre.com/vertigo_magazine/volume-3 -issue-4-winter-2007/blissfully-yours-towards-the-wondrous-void/.

Reddy, Gayatri. "Geographies of Contagion: *Hijras, Kothis*, and the Politics of Sexual Marginality in Hyderabad." *Anthropology & Medicine* 12, no. 3 (2005): 255–70.

Reynolds, Craig J. "Globalization and Cultural Nationalism in Thailand." In *Southeast Asian Identities: Culture and the Politics of Representation in Indonesia, Malaysia, Singapore, and Thailand*, ed. Joel S. Kahn, 115–45. New York: St. Martin's Press, 1998.

———. "Sedition in Thai History: A Nineteenth-Century Poem and Its Critics." In *Thai Constructions of Knowledge*, ed. Manas Chitakasem and Andrew Turton, 15–36. London: University of London, School of Oriental and African Studies, 1991.

———. *Seditious Histories: Contesting Thai and Southeast Asian Pasts*. Seattle: University of Washington Press, 2006.

———. "Thai Identity in the Age of Globalization." In *National Identity and Its Defenders: Thailand Today*, ed. Craig J. Reynolds, 308–38. Chiang Mai, Thailand: Silkworm Books, 2002.

Reynolds, Frank E. "Dhamma in Dispute: The Interactions of Religion and Law in Thailand." *Law & Society* 28, no. 3 (1994): 433–52.

Rigg, Jonathan. "Exclusion and Embeddedness: The Chinese in Thailand and Vietnam." In *The Chinese Diaspora: Space, Place, Mobility, and Identity*, ed. Lawrence J. C. Ma and Carolyn Cartier, 97–116. Oxford: Rowman and Littlefield, 2003.

Rofel, Lisa. *Desiring China: Experiments in Neoliberalism, Sexuality, and Public Culture*. Durham, NC: Duke University Press, 2007.

Rohy, Valerie. "Ahistorical." *GLQ: A Journal of Lesbian and Gay Studies* 12, no. 1 (2006): 61–83.

Rotman, Andy. "The Erotics of Practice: Objects and Agency in Buddhist Avadana Literature." *Journal of the American Academy of Religion* 71, no. 3 (2003): 555–78.

Sanders, Douglas. "The Rainbow Lobby: The Sexual Diversity Network and the Military-Installed Government in Thailand." In *Queer Bangkok: 21st Century Media, Markets, and Rights*, ed. Peter A. Jackson, 229–50. Hong Kong: Hong Kong University Press, 2011.

Sanitsuda Ekachai. *Keeping the Faith: Thai Buddhism at the Crossroads*. Bangkok: Post Books, 2001.

Santi Phakdikham. "Prawad Pithi Mon Rong Hai" (The History of the Ceremony of Mon Rong Hai—The Crying Mon) and "Nang Rong Hai Ma Jak Nai? Kiao Arai Kap Mon Rong Hai?" (Crying Women—Where Do They Come From and What Do They Have to Do with [the Song and Ceremony of] the Crying Mon?). *Sinlapawatthanatham* 23, no. 11 (2002): 158–63.

Saran Mahasupap. "Haunting Body, Hideous Beauty: Genre and the Representation of a Queer Gothic in the *Hor Taew Tak* Trilogy." In "Haunting and Globalization," ed. Chutima Prakatwutisarn and Arnika Fuhrmann, special issue, *Aksornsat: Journal of Letters* 45, no. 1 (2013): 187–213.

Saraswati, L. Ayu. "Cosmopolitan Whiteness: The Effects and Affects of Skin-Whitening Advertisements in a Transnational Women's Magazine in Indonesia." *Meridians: Feminism, Race, Transnationalism* 10, no. 2 (2010): 15–41.

Sayan Daengklom. "Waeo Krading Kring Krung Khlung Klin Kawi Wa 'Chan Chue Araya'" (A Faint Sound of Fragrant Poetry: "My Name Is Araya"). *Art Record* 10, no. 23 (2003): 26–31.

Seltzer, Mark. *Serial Killers: Death and Life in America's Wound Culture*. New York: Routledge, 1998.

Seremetakis, C. Nadia. *The Last Word: Women, Death, and Divination in Inner Mani*. Chicago: University of Chicago Press, 1991.

———. "The Memory of the Senses, Part I: Marks of the Transitory." In *The Senses Still: Perception and Memory as Material Culture in Modernity*, ed. C. Nadia Seremetakis, 1–18. Boulder, CO: Westview Press, 1994.

Silverman, Kaja. "Girl Love." *October* 104 (Spring 2003): 4–27.

Singh, Nikhil Pal. "Liberalism." In *Keywords for American Cultural Studies*, ed. Bruce Burgett and Glenn Hendler, 139–45. New York: New York University Press, 2007.

Sinnott, Megan. "Gay vs. 'Kathoey': Homosexual Identities in Thailand." *IIAS Newsletter*, no. 29 (November 2002): 7–8.

———. "The Language of Rights, Deviance, and Pleasure: Organizational Responses to Discourses of Same-Sex Sexuality and Transgenderism in Thailand." In *Queer Bangkok: 21st Century Media, Markets, and Rights*, ed. Peter A. Jackson, 205–28. Hong Kong: Hong Kong University Press, 2011.

———. *Toms and Dees: Transgender Identity and Female Same-Sex Relationships in Thailand*. Honolulu: University of Hawai'i Press, 2004.

Skinner, G. W. *Chinese Society in Thailand: An Analytical History*. Ithaca: Cornell University Press, 1957.

Sobchack, Vivian. "What My Fingers Knew: The Cinesthetic Subject, or Vision in the Flesh." In *Carnal Thoughts: Embodiment and Moving Image Culture*, 53–84. Berkeley: University of California Press, 2004.

Somtow Sucharitkul. *Mae Naak*. Bangkok: Bangkok Opera, 2003.

Spiro, Melford E. *Burmese Supernaturalism: A Study in the Explanation and Reduction of Suffering*. Upper Saddle River, NJ: Prentice-Hall, 1967.

Srisompob Jitpiromsri and Panyasak Sophonvasu. "Unpacking Thailand's Southern Conflict: The Poverty of Structural Explanations." *Critical Asian Studies* 38, no. 1 (2006): 95–117.

Stewart, Susan. *Crimes of Writing: Problems in the Containment of Representation*. New York: Oxford University Press, 1991.

Stoler, Ann Laura. "A Colonial Reading of Foucault: Bourgeois Bodies and Racial Selves." In *Carnal Knowledge and Imperial Power: Race and the Intimate in Colonial Rule*, 140–61. Berkeley: University of California Press, 2002.

Streckfuss, David. "The Mixed Colonial Legacy in Siam: Origins of Thai Racialist Thought, 1890–1910." In *Autonomous Histories, Particular Truths: Essays in Honor of John R. W. Smail*, ed. Laurie Sears, 123–53. Madison: University of Wisconsin Press, 1993.

Strong, John S. *The Legend of King Aśoka: A Study and Translation of the Aśokāvadāna*. Princeton: Princeton University Press, 1983.

Sudarat Musikawong. "Art for October: Thai Cold War State Violence in Trauma Art." *positions: asia critique* 18, no. 1 (2010): 19–50.

———. "Mediating Memories of the 1970s in Thai Cultural Production." PhD diss., University of California, Santa Cruz, 2006.

Sulaiporn Chonwilai. "Tua Ton Nai Rueang Lao: Kan To Rong Thang Attalak Khong Ying Rak Ying" (Narrating Selves: Negotiating Lesbian Identity). Master's thesis, Thammasat University, 2001.

Sulak Sivarak. "Rueang Phet Kap Khwam Chuea Sasana Amnat Rawang Ying Chai Phu Yai Dek Lae Jariyatham" (Sexuality and Religious Belief: Questions of Power and Ethics between Men and Women, Adults and Children). Samana Rueang Phathana Yauwachon Cheung Buak (Seminar on Positive Youth Development), March 19, 2008. Accessed May 30, 2015. http://www.teenpath.net/data/event /40003/Teen01/content-005.html.

Suni Thiwawej. "Dara Sao Luk Jek" (A Female Star of Chinese Descent). *Sinlapawatthanatham* 13, no. 4 (1992): 160–65.

Swearer, Donald K., ed. *Me and Mine: Selected Essays of Bhikkhu Buddhadasa*. Albany: State University of New York Press, 1989.

Tambiah, Stanley. *World Conqueror and World Renouncer: A Study of Buddhism and Polity in Thailand against a Historical Background*. Cambridge Studies in Social and Cultural Anthropology Series. Cambridge: Cambridge University Press, 1976.

Teo, Stephen. *Hong Kong Cinema: The Extra Dimensions*. London: BFI, 1997.

Thai Ministry of Culture, Culture Monitoring Center. "Kan Jad Tang Samnak Fao Rawang Thang Wathanatham" (The Establishment of the Culture Monitoring Center). Policy paper, n.d.

———. *Khu Mue Fao Rawang Thang Wathanatham Samrap Dek Lae Yaowachon* (Guidebook of Cultural Monitoring for Children and Youth). 2011.

Thai Ministry of the Interior. "Nayobai Kan Jad Rabiap Sangkhom Khong Krasuang Mahad Thai" (The Ministry of the Interior's Policy of Social Ordering). Policy paper, n.d.

Therdsak Romjampa. "Jak 'Kathoey' Thueng 'Ke': Prawatisat Chai Rak Ruam Phet Nai Sangkhom Thai" (From "Kathoey" to "Gay": A History of Homosexuality in Thailand). *Warasan Aksonsat* 32 (January–June 2003): 301–35.

———. "Wathakam Kiao Kap 'Gay' Nai Sangkhom Thai Phuthasakarat 2508–2542" (Discourses about "Gays" in Thai Society from 1965 to 1999). Master's thesis, Chulalongkorn University, 2002.

Thompson, Ashley. "Performative Realities: Nobody's Possession." In *At the Edge of the Forest: Essays on Cambodia, History, and Narrative in Honor of David Chandler*, ed. Anne Ruth Hansen and Judy Ledgerwood, 93–119. Ithaca, NY: Southeast Asia Program Publications, 2008.

Thongchai Winichakul. "Remembering/Silencing the Traumatic Past: The Ambivalent Memories of the October 1976 Massacre in Bangkok." In *Cultural Crisis and Social Memory: Modernity and Identity in Thailand and Laos*, ed. Shigeharu Tanabe et al., 243–83. Honolulu: University of Hawai'i Press, 2002.

———. *Siam Mapped: A History of the Geo-Body of a Nation*. Honolulu: University of Hawai'i Press, 1994.

Tomorn Sukpricha. "Khwam Pen Mae Lae Mia Khong Krasuang Wathanatham" (The Motherhood and Wifehood of the Ministry of Culture). In *Genderism*, 22–27. Bangkok: A Book, 2005.

Tong Chee Kiong and Chan Kwok Bun, eds. *Alternate Identities: The Chinese of Contemporary Thailand*. Singapore: Times Academic Press with Brill Academic, 2001.

Trouillot, Michel-Rolph. *Silencing the Past: Power and the Production of History*. Boston: Beacon, 1995.

Ubonrat Siriyuvasak. "New Media for Civil Society and Political Censorship in Thailand." Paper presented at the Conference on New Media and Civil Society, Bhatapur, Nepal, April 29–May 2, 2007.

Ünaldi, Serhat. "Back in the Spotlight: A Comparison of Recent Mainstream and Alternative Thai Queer Cinema." In *Queer Bangkok: 21st Century Media, Markets, and Rights*, ed. Peter A. Jackson, 59–80. Hong Kong: Hong Kong University Press, 2011.

Wasana Wongsurawat. "From Yaowarat to Plabplachai: The Thai State and Ethnic Chinese in Thailand during the Cold War." In *Dynamics of the Cold War in Asia: Ideology, Identity, and Culture*, ed. Tuang Vu and Wasana Wongsurawat, 165–85. New York: Palgrave Macmillan, 2009.

Waugh, Thomas. "Acting to Play Oneself: Performance in Documentary (1990)." In *The Right to Play Oneself: Looking Back on Documentary Film*, 71–92. Minneapolis: University of Minnesota Press, 2011.

Williams, Linda. "Film Bodies: Gender, Genre, and Excess." *Film Quarterly* 44, no. 4 (1991): 2–13.

———. "Power, Pleasure, and Perversion: Sadomasochistic Film Pornography." *Representations*, no. 27 (Summer 1989): 37–65.

Wilson, Ara. *The Intimate Economies of Bangkok: Tomboys, Tycoons, and Avon Ladies in the Global City*. Berkeley: University of California Press, 2004.

———. "Women in the City of Consumption: Markets and the Construction of Gender in Bangkok, Thailand." PhD diss., City University of New York, 1997.

Wilson, Liz. *Charming Cadavers: Horrific Figurations of the Feminine in Indian Buddhist Hagiographic Literature*. Chicago: University of Chicago Press, 1996.

Yue, Audrey. "Preposterous Horror: On *Rouge, A Chinese Ghost Story* and Nostalgia." In *The Horror Reader*, ed. Ken Gelder, 364–73. New York: Routledge, 2000.

Zeitlin, Judith. *Historian of the Strange: Pu Songling and the Chinese Classical Tale*. Stanford, CA: Stanford University Press, 1993.